The Book of Silver

KU-591-885

Eva M. Link

The Book of Silver

Translated by Francisca Garvie

Barrie & Jenkins

London

WATFORD PUBLIC LIBRARY

21. JUN 1974

H50 243 773 3

© 1973   First published in Great Britain
by Barrie & Jenkins, Ltd.,
24 Highbury Crescent, London N 5 IRX

© 1968 by Verlag Ullstein GmbH, Frankfurt/M - Berlin - Wien
English translation © 1973 by Pall Mall Press Ltd, London

All rights reserved

SBN 214 65129 0

Printed in Germany by Poeschel & Schulz-Schomburgk, Eschwege

R73 17369
739.23

Contents

Preface

The precious metals silver and gold have usually appeared together since earliest times, both being used as currency and for ornament. Old songs and legends often mention them in the same breath, and in ancient mythology gold represented the sun god Sol, silver the moon goddess Luna. This view became so deep-rooted that even today we speak of the "golden sun" and the "silver moon". In the distant past, the rarity of gold and silver and the expense of the rudimentary techniques of mining made articles of gold and silver rare and precious, available only to the élite which made the metals even more desirable. Gold and silver also became the basis of the currency system, and they retained their standard of value even when used artistically. Even then people were collecting silver as a stable capital investment upon which they could rely when necessary.

Although it was used for most precious metalwork, silver has generally been overshadowed by gold. Throughout history great artists have worked with both metals, often encrusting the works they created with precious stones and enamel and using various decorative techniques. With the exception of some periods when gold also became a basic material of metalwork, silver was most often used, and as an artist's material it gained particular importance. Silversmiths evolved particularly beautiful decorative techniques, and surviving silver works give us a vivid picture of the history of our culture. The key figure in the history of silver is the silversmith, who trained and developed his technical and artistic skills under the stern discipline of the guilds during periods when the art of silver flourished. He produced works which belong among the greatest masterpieces of the visual arts for both religious and secular patrons.

This book is devoted to silver in the hope that it will give the reader a deeper understanding of the magnificent art. Silver work throughout the ages reflects the artist's joy in working with a precious metal and at the same time mirrors changing artistic styles; it reflects the client's curiosity and desire for display and the relationship between representational images and decoration. Moreover, it shows the owner's pride in possessing an object of such material value as silver.

Introduction

Silver has been valued and worked as a precious metal since earliest times. We know of silver ornaments, silver objects of worship and daily use, coins and ingots from the cultures of early times and the arts of all races at all times. The form in which we find it is indissolubly bound up with its provenance and with the artistic and technical developments of the respective cultures. We can only understand and do justice to a work of art if we can appreciate these contingencies. This book deals with the history of European silver in relation to our own western culture.

We shall begin by examining silver as an artistic material. It is not only the finished silver work that fascinates the connoisseur and the amateur; it is no less fascinating to examine the process of creation and the technical and sociological conditions under which the work was executed. Above all, the history of silver work, as of any other art form, is part of the history of art as a whole. What we call style is the expression of a period, a particular race or an individual artist, so we cannot separate the formal structure, plastic concept and decoration of silver from the overall picture of stylistic developments. The gold and silver works that have come down to us from earlier times are only a fraction of what existed, as great losses were caused by melting down, particularly in the field of silver, and even the most precious pieces were sacrificed for their material value. This destruction in times of need has left great gaps in our knowledge and makes it impossible to convey a complete picture of the development of silver.

The history of princely silver cabinets shows how often such times of need occurred. No hoard was spared the fate of being partly or even completely denuded and melted down for currency on various occasions. The many wars that ravaged Europe made these rigorous measures necessary. The collection in the Prussian silver treasure for instance was almost entirely converted into coinage twice, once under Frederick the Great, and again during the wars of liberation against Napoleon. The silver treasures of London, Copenhagen and Stockholm, and those of Moscow and Leningrad are the best preserved. But even there most of the medieval pieces are missing as are many from the sixteenth and seventeenth centuries. The hoard of almost five thousand pieces from the silver cabinet of the princes and kings of Bavaria which has remained intact since the eighteenth century, is a rare and fortunate find. The 'municipal' silver which certain towns amassed was usually no less affected. In 1533 the Mayor of Lübeck, Jürgen Wullenwever, had all the church silver of Lübeck melted down; it consisted of hundreds of chalices, monstrances, figures and reliquary busts weighing in all twelve tons. In this way, the early silver of Lübeck was almost entirely destroyed, although each church was allowed to keep no more than two chalices.

Although, on the whole, church silver was safer: the precious reliquaries were less liable to be destroyed because of their holy nature. In addition, its rather conservative attitude made the church less keen to renew its existing resources for the sake of fashion than the secular collectors. But here too the changing times have meant infinite losses. Much of the French church silver found its way into the melting pot after secularization during the French Revolution and even brocade vestments were burned for the sake of the gold and silver thread.

Silver was not always considered the more important material for metalwork. The Byzantines preferred gold, and this applied even more to the Carolingians and Ottonians. Gold was used for the imperial insignia as a symbol of absolute power; to the medieval mind, it mirrored the omnipotence of God and reflected the divine light. But this consistent preference for pure gold had already been abandoned in the twelfth century and copper gilt became widely used. Most metalwork of this period combines silver, gold and copper. The artist/ craftsman who worked the different metals was the goldsmith, whose craft is named after the most precious of the metals he worked, even after the thirteenth century when he almost exclusively used silver. Today we usually speak of the "goldsmith, as in earlier times when the term was not only confined to the craftsman who worked in gold but included the silversmith who worked both gold and silver", (C. J. Jackson). This is justified in that there is no technical difference in the working of the two metals; they can both be forged, cast, embossed, chased, engraved and enamelled. Often the combined use of gold and silver enhanced the artistic effect. It was only from the eighteenth century onwards that the pure silver was valued for itself; up to that time most silver plate was gilt. The visual difference between gilt and solid gold is so slight that it is undetectable to the untrained eye, and as there is no stylistic difference, the choice between working in gold or silver was simply a matter of cost after the Middle Ages. For this reason we shall also consider a few works in gold where artistic reasons seem to require it, as in Carolingian and Ottonian times when gold work was a major art form.

Towards the end of the Middle Ages, in the early sixteenth century, what we know as applied art came into being. Pattern books of engraved designs, made possible by the invention of printing, were widely circulated and offered numerous inspirations, facilitating the task of the goldsmith. Impressions of silver reliefs, reproduced on lead, like the reproductions of the base of the bowls by Paul van Vianen, served as models. We even have evidence of the transmission of model designs in the thirteenth century. Besides this, great artists who were not necessarily goldsmiths themselves have at all times produced designs for gold work. Martin Schongauer, Albrecht Dürer (who was a trained goldsmith), Holbein, Giulio Romano, Jacques Callot (who had also learned the goldsmith's trade), Permoser, Ignaz Günther and Schinkel are but a few. This makes it impossible to distinguish between applied art and art as a whole; the former is part of the development of the latter. As in painting and architecture so too in gold and silver work, individual regions or countries flourished at certain times, became leading artistic centres that inspired or influenced others with new, lovely formal concepts, declined, and gave way to new ones. This applies until modern times, although silver no longer plays an important role in art. But silver plate made after modern designs still emanates the aura of exclusivity that has always radiated from this precious metal. So even today silver remains what it has always been—a precious material of exceptional beauty.

Antiquity

Greece. The Greek conception of man as an individual made contemporary life and thought into a standard model for Western culture. Man stood at the centre of the world, supreme as a free individual, embodying the measure of all things. It was this that gave him potential greatness and power. It also meant potential fall; but even in subjection man retained his human dignity. The vast scope and wealth of this new vision of man was reflected in the works of the Greek philosophers, poets, sculptors and painters. Among the visual arts, sculpture seemed the medium best qualified to realize this lofty and spiritual view of man. It is true that man was not the only subject of the sculptor's creative energies, but he incarnated the ideal and the deepest preoccupation of the time. On the basis of the freedom of mankind and the law of man as the measure of all things, Greek architecture, the consummate and beautiful products of the Greek potters and the various types of metalwork moulded their forms and proportions on this spiritual ideal of freedom and uprightness.

Undoubtedly Greece produced masterpieces in the art of metalwork, but silver and gold would not have always been available. We know of no gold or silver from the early Greek period, the geometric period, between the twelfth and seventh centuries B.C., but we have some small evidence that it existed at an earlier age. In the early second millenium B.C., Greek tribes had penetrated from the Balkans to central Greece and as far as the Peloponnese where they founded a rich and magnificent culture, strongly marked by the highly advanced art and culture of Minoan Crete. We call this the Mycenaean culture. But this culture, of which Homer sung in his Epics, is distinct from the true Greek culture. The beginnings of what we know as Greek culture came with the 'Doric migration', the renewed advance of north-western Greek tribes during the twelfth century, which led to the collapse of the Mycenaean world.

In the first three centuries B.C. the geometric style developed within strictly defined limits as an indigenous Greek art form, free from foreign influences. Our only information about this is based on ceramics, but presumably the style of decoration was also used on utensils made of other materials. Works of sculpture usually on a small-scale, which were executed in various materials, cannot be dated earlier than the ninth century B.C.

The eighth century brought a massive expansion of Greek culture, when lack of space forced the Greeks to colonize. From about 750 B.C. they founded numerous towns in southern Italy and Sicily, such as Syracuse, Naxos and Tarent, as well as around the Black Sea and in North Africa; flourishing new settlements even grew up on the coasts of Spain and southern France. This expansion came at a time when the geometric style had declined into weak formalism and was therefore receptive to strong new stimuli. Oriental works of art, in which there was a lively import trade, offered a pictorial repertory hitherto unknown in Greece. This alien art penetrated Greek civilization, which made it its own in a massive creative process, and raised it to monumental form.

The transformation of the basic canons of art took place around the turn of the eighth and seventh centuries B.C. and introduced the so-called archaic period. It coincided with the birth of gold and silver work, presumably inspired by the growing wealth of the Greeks and the increasing availability of precious metal from natural resources and by way of imports. Silver was imported from Spanish mines, for instance, from 650 B.C. Again the main artistic inspiration came from the East, particularly from the 'Phoenician' bowls. They had no handles and were decorated with concentric bands of engraved figurative patterns in low relief—a fusion of ancient Eastern and Egyptian motifs. An even more important source of inspiration, and one that is easier to retrace, was the *phiale mesomphalos*, from the same area, which the Greeks quickly adapted and which, in different forms, became the most widely used vessel for ritual libation sacrifices for centuries. Again it has no handles; it is a shallow, flat-bottomed bowl with a punched up boss in the centre – the *omphalos* (navel) which was used as a finger grip.

We know very little about silver and gold work in this early period. The few surviving pieces give no clear picture of styles and methods of production. As a whole, we can assume that it evolved along the same lines as the far better known ceramics and works in bronze, and it is probable that gold and silver work of a very similar style was also produced at Corinth, an important centre of bronze casting. What is certain is that silver plate was not yet common in private homes at that time. Gold and silver vessels were still almost exclusively devoted to ritual purposes or sacrificial offerings to divinities. We know this from written sources and surviving inventories of the treasures of the sanctuaries. The dedications were not always made by the Greeks themselves. When King Gyges of Lydia presented the first gold and silver to the Temple of Apollo at Delphi, in the first half of the seventh century, he created a precedent which the Greeks and other rulers soon followed. According to Herodotus, Alyattes II of Lydia commissioned an important dedication for Delphi in 580 from the Greek craftsman Glaukos of Chios; this was a silver krater with an iron base, which Pausanias saw and described, stressing the fact that the individual parts were not riveted but welded together. Croesus, son of Alyattes II, also presented gifts to Delphi. One of them is descriptive of his legendary wealth – an enormous silver krater with a capacity of no less than 15.6 litres, allegedly made by another Greek craftsman, Theodoros of Samos, whom we also know as master builder, jeweller and stone cutter. It was he who made the ring of Polycrates.

Although the constant increase in production in the Greek classical period from 480 to 330 B.C. brought lively development to gold and silver work, silver plate was not used domestically until the fifth century, despite the growing prosperity in the land. For the time being, the silversmiths confined themselves to ritual vessels and dedications, swelling the temple treasures with numerous petitional gifts, gifts of atonement or dedications to the divinity in thanks for victory in athletic contests. Some of these gifts were used as ritual vessels, the rest were stored away. Occasionally earlier works were melted down when money was needed.

Few pieces survive from this period, even in Greece itself, and our knowledge of classical gold and silver work is mainly based on finds outside Greece. All that survives owes its preservation to the fact that it was buried underground for thousands of years until it was found in recent times. As far as we know, no classical metalwork has survived above ground as it was lost through looting or melted down. The same applies to works from the late Roman Empire. The objects that found their way underground at the time were mainly buried with their owners. The Greeks themselves did not initiate the custom of burying the deceased with rich attributes as a sign of his wealth; it came from their barbarian neighbours, particularly the Thracian tribes in the Balkans and the Scythians north of the Black Sea in the region of the Dnieper and Kuban. Here the graves of the wealthy citizens and noblemen have yielded a series of pieces that were no doubt imported from Greece or executed by Greek silversmiths locally. Today they form our main concrete evidence of the metalwork of this period.

The formal repertory remained comparatively narrow until the mid-fifth century, but increased considerably thereafter. A fourth century treasury inventory from Delos lists sixty different kinds of vessel. Foreign influences were of course also very active at the time. The enormous booty of gold and silver ware, taken during the Second Persian War, at the battle of Plataea in 479 B.C. exerted a marked influence on Greek *toreutic* (embossing), and, for, instance it popularized a richer variety of *mesomphalos* bowl in Greece and various forms of *rhyton*. The latter was a vessel in the shape of an animal head, long known to the Scythians in the form of a drinking horn ending in a round, sculptural animal form. Formal and stylistic elements from Scythia penetrated Greece via the Greco-Scythian school in the Black Sea colonies, where Greek gold- and silversmiths worked for local patrons; this school flourished in about 400 or 350 B.C., and the *amphora* of Chertomlyk is one of the most beautiful works of its golden age (see page 27).

The evolution of metalwork was not confined to an increased typological variety. During the fifth century stronger tendencies towards plastic forms became clear. For instance, whereas at first the decoration on the *mesomphalos* bowl was restricted to a narrow ornamental band, usually gilt, immediately round the *omphalos* as in archaic times, now it became more and more common to decorate the interior of the vessel with figurative and ornamental reliefs. No doubt the great sculptors of classical times influenced this development. This is known to be true of Phidias, the master of the Parthenon sculptures. Pliny reports that Phidias was the first to have 'opened up the art of *toreutic*' and explained its nature. We know that Phidias executed his great works in very varied materials, stone and bronze, ivory and gold. The shield of his Athena Parthenon, the mighty ivory image of worship in the Parthenon, was decorated with gold reliefs of warriors from the battles of the Greeks and the Amazons, her sandals with lapiths and centaurs. It is not certain whether Pliny's story means that Phidias created the first free repoussé relief, as opposed to earlier ones which were hammered or punched into matrices as in archaic times. What is certain, however, is that an artistic figure such as Phidias, whose work became a criterion for a whole generation of artists, exploited the artistic potentials of metalwork to the full. In addition, Martial tells us that the great sculptors of the fifth century – Phidias, Polycleitus and Myron – produced gold and silver relief vessels which were often copied in later times; this proves again what we learnt of Theodoros of Samos and what has remained valid throughout the centuries until modern times – that major artists who achieved greatness in other artistic media also created or designed works in gold and silver.

For a relatively short period in the history of Greek gold and silver, from around the mid-fifth century, some vessels, in particular the libation cup, were decorated with engraved figurative scenes (plate 2, page 26). The graphic style of these engravings is reminiscent of the linear vase painting of the red-figure period in Greece. But the Greeks abandoned this decorative principle in the fourth century.

At the end of the fifth century B.C., silver plate gradually came into domestic use, at first in the form of smooth, unadorned vessels, closely related to the black-glazed ceramics from Attic workshops (plate 1, page 26). But in the following centuries, it became more and more usual to collect silver plate in a private capacity, largely as a permanent capital investment. Besides utensils that had been rare hitherto, such as ladles and strainers, 'toilet silver' also became more frequent, for example mirrors, strigils and different kinds of little jars and phials for ointments and perfumes. These were all articles that reflected cultivated and luxurious taste.

Hellenism. This takes us to the Hellenistic period, which did not come to an end until the Battle of Actium in 31 B.C. which marked the establishment of the rule of the Roman Empire. Alexander the Great had realized his dream of a great Greek Empire, a fusion of the East and Greece, and had advanced victoriously as far as India. But the thirteen short years of his reign were not enough to secure his vast empire from within. Under the struggles for power of his successors, the Diadochs, it fell apart again. Not until the third century could the great kingdoms of the Diadochs assert themselves – the Seleucids in the Near East, the Ptolemys in Egypt, the Antigonids in Greece and Asia Minor – and determine the future face of Hellenism.

Alexander's father Philip II had opened up the Macedonian and Thracian silver mines, and these were now joined by the rich resources of the Seleucid and Ptolemaic regions. Most classical gold and silver plate was executed in Attic and Greco-Scythian workshops, but now Syria and Egypt became important centres. Their courts were rich and magnificent, and the Ptolemaic and Seleucid rulers outdid each other in enriching the Greek sanctuaries with precious gifts. Temple inventories prove this. It was probably not unusual for the time that Antiochus IV, Epiphanos of Syria, who had amassed a huge hoard of gold and silver plate, should be in the habit of visiting the gold and silver workshops to learn about the latest developments. Antioch and other Syrian cities had important workshops; Alexandria in particular had become a centre of great culture and active scholarship with its world-famous library. The works from there, which we know chiefly from the treasures of Tukh el-Qaramous and Tell Tmai, show strong Persian influences. It was, of course, inevitable that the close contacts with the East after the victory of Alexander should open the door to new influences.

Although the empire of Alexander the Great soon fell apart into individual principalities and kingdoms, the artistic production of the Hellenistic world remained surprisingly homogeneous. This often makes it very difficult to distinguish regional styles or to attribute individual works to particular artistic centres. Close trade relations and the freedom of the gold and silversmiths to move from one centre to another erased any local peculiarities of style.

The luxury of the Hellenistic courts, the wealth of the temple treasures and the prosperous citizens' collections of plate had increased to an extent unknown to the classical period, yet on the whole we only know this from written sources; so little has survived from these late Greek centuries that we do not have the remotest idea of the wealth of the age. With some restrictions this also applies to the era of the Roman Empire. Much more Roman silver has come down to us and comprehensive hoards have given us some idea of the extent of private collections; yet what we know can only be an extremely small part of what originally existed.

Rome. When Greek art began to decline with the loss of creative power in late Hellenistic times, Roman art advanced and took over its heritage. Rome recognized the spiritual greatness of Greek classicism and used classical Greek art as the point of departure for its own creations. Countless works of every kind, which were brought to Rome as booty after the conquest of the Eastern provinces, familiarized the Romans with Greek art. No doubt this link with earlier Greek elements gave Roman art the 'classic' accent that is so clear in the many copies of Greek classical works. But it would be wrong to see Roman art as no more than the last phase of Greek art. When the Roman Empire ruled the world, Roman art also led the field. In other spheres, particularly in architecture and portrait sculpture, Rome created many major original works. Rome was very poor in gold and silver in earlier times. Silver coins were not minted before the third century B.C., and silver plate was rare. The turning point came with the Second Punic War, which brought the Spanish silver mines under Roman control. Even more important was the enormous amount of gold and silver loot that flowed into Rome during the gradual subjection of the Hellenistic world which increased the demand among Romans to possess silver. Even in the last century B.C., i.e. still at the time of the Republic, the passion for collecting was still in full strength, and it was not to decline until the fall of the Roman Empire. We know of households that employed several slaves solely to look after the silver. Silver treasures of a hundred or more pieces were characteristic of a prosperous middle class family. To own no silver at all was a sign of almost disreputable poverty. We even hear that a slave of Emperor Claudius had formed an enormous collection of his own. In view of this wealth and the great demand, which could only be supplied by a trade highly organized for mass production, one can even believe the story about Martial's silver chamber pot encrusted with precious stones.

The original pieces we know from Republican Rome can in no way reflect the immense wealth of the time. On the other hand, the finds in the first century A.D. make this the best-covered period of antiquity. Apart from smaller finds and a number of individual pieces, the most important pieces come from diggings in the towns of the Bay of Naples which had been buried by a sudden eruption of Vesuvius in A.D. 79. In 1895 a hoard of 109 pieces of table silver came to light in a wine vat below a villa at Boscoreale; in 1930 an even greater hoard was found in the Casa del Menandro at Pompeii, 118 pieces wrapped in cloth in a bronze-bound wooden chest. The uniform content and extent of the two finds suggest them to be typical collections of a middle class Roman, perhaps a merchant.

There was a great variety of table silver and eating utensils. The most common were round plates and dishes, quite often in fairly large sets. Some of them were reserved for particular foods, such as fish, fruit or pastry. The meals were carried in from the kitchen on large trays. Apart from jugs, *amphorae* and wine cups, the table plate was completed by sauce boats, ladles, strainers, salt cellars and pepper pots. Silver knives and forks were not used, but spoons were. This domestic plate was hardly decorated, but in addition every household owned a similar amount of richly decorated pieces, purely for display, which served no particular purpose and stood on side tables in the dining room. Often the style of these ornamental pieces with their rich figurative relief remains Hellenistic, and we can see them as copies of earlier works that were probably already common in Republican times. They include lovely handled jugs with trefoil necks and scenic relief on the bodies; the most splendid examples come from the treasure found at Berthouville (page 29). The dishes with a sculptural medallion, an *emblema*, in the centre of the base, which were often a dominating size, are also of Hellenistic inspiration (page 25). But the shallow dishes with a single relief round the interior are an original Roman invention; the earliest examples of such dishes, which were display pieces from the start, do not date from before the first century B. C. The most characteristic and common vessels from this period are cups of various shapes, richly decorated in relief. They occur with and without foot, with one or two handles, and they served both as domestic plate and display pieces. Again the form is Greek and inspired by late Hellenistic works. The chased relief decoration is of an inexhaustible variety. The walls of the vessels are covered with naturalistic branches of myrtle or ivy, foliage and olives, with landscapes, birds and other animals. One finds Nereids and Tritons, Bacchanalian themes, erotic and homoerotic scenes and scenes from religious ritual, Greek mythology and literature; historical scenes leading towards political propaganda also occur, as in the cup showing Emperor Augustus as ruler in war and peace. These cups and beakers have been found throughout the Roman Empire and even outside its borders, in Denmark and Poland. It may be that they arrived there as diplomatic gifts. 'Toilet silver', i.e. the various phials and pyxes and the round hand mirrors with relief on the back, also provided many opportunities for enriching the household treasure. Rich households are even reported to have had silver furniture – tables and couches – and the Hildesheim finds have given us a small silver tripod table. But such objects must have been relatively rare, for even the prosperous citizens usually had wooden and bronze furniture.

Apart from a few small finds, little is known of the second century. However, a series of treasures from the second half of the third century were uncovered in northern France at Chaourse (Aisne), Berthouville, Graincourt-les-Havrincourt (Pas de Calais), Notre-Dame d'Alençon, and the smaller hoards of Caubiac and Chattuzangele-Goubet (Drôme). These treasures were buried before the barbarian attacks and not recovered again. Most of the pieces were made in Gallic workshops and date from the time of burial. But the Berthouville treasure, unlike the others, was not a private collection but the treasure of the Temple of Mercury at Canetonum, or at least a part of it, and includes a number of earlier works. It is made up of ritual dishes and gifts to the Temple of private display pieces, which had been preserved for many years. The dates of the sixty three pieces range over a period of more than two hundred years.

A considerable number of hoards were also buried in the late fourth and early fifth centuries. They were hidden underground when the Western Roman Empire collapsed. Pieces were also discovered further west, in Mildenhall, Traprain Law in Scotland and Coleraine in Ireland. The treasure of Kaiseraugst near Basel was buried within the walls of a Roman fortress. Together with the finds from the Esquiline and from Carthage, which was one of several in Roman North Africa, and the numerous outstanding individual pieces found in all the provinces of the empire, it conveys a good idea of the quality of Late Roman silver work. Naturally, styles had changed over the period and a number of older forms had disappeared. The drinking cup, one of the most common vessels in early times, had been replaced by the glass beaker; similarly, the cup decorated with relief, usually chased in the first century but later cast in a piece, became even rarer. To judge by individual finds, the *amphora* also seems to have become rarer. Instead, a slender, flask-like vessel came into use, sometimes with a handle and serving as a jug (plate 2, page 30). As before, the most common finds were bowls and dishes with engraved, floral ornament or figurative relief work, occasionally measuring sixty or more centimetres in diameter. Besides the usual round shapes, this later age also produced rectangular forms, or round dishes framed by a square or multiangular openwork border. The relief, which sometimes rises almost as high as the rim, as on the Hildesheim cup of Athena, is not seen on these later works, and instead there is very low, though equally extensive relief. Occasionally the relief is cut out of the metal, a process which did not produce the soft modelling of cast and chased works. The fourth and fifth centuries can boast important and very beautiful *nielli;* they are occasionally found in earlier times, but reached a high point here. In parcel gilt, and often decorated with animated scenes, these works achieve an elegant restrained colourfulness with the harmonies of silver and gold and the black of the *nielli.*

This brings us to the final phase of Antique art, although one cannot set a precise or even approximate date to its end, as the decline of the Antique coincided with the rise of the new Christian art, which ushered in what we know as the Middle Ages, the one following the other in a smooth transition.

Early Christian and Byzantine Silver

Late Antiquity. The rule of Emperor Diocletian, under whom the persecution of the Christians had reached great proportions, came to an end in 305. This was also the end of the persecution. When his successor, Constantine, became sole ruler in 313 after long struggles for power, he adopted and officially supported Christianity. The rule of Constantine the Great marks the beginning of the history of the Christian West.

However important the official recognition of Christianity was, it brought no sudden artistic change. It is true that Christian and Biblical themes were represented more and more frequently, in particular on sarcophagi and church mosaics, but the style remained Late Roman. Very often old pagan, Antique forms and images were simply invested with a new Christian content. For instance, the mosaic of Christ in the Necropolis under St Peter's shows him as the sun god Sol who brings light to mankind, a formulation common since late classical times. This fusion of a centuries-old tradition with the new doctrine of Salvation is a very clear example of the smooth transition from Antique to Christian art.

The silver treasures from the fourth and fifth century are the earliest Christian silver works we know. They are no different from other contemporary works in form or style and only the figurative images and the inscriptions tell us of their Christian content. It is difficult to distinguish between works of private and sacred use. Some may have served either. It is rare to find pieces so clearly destined for private use as the piece of toilet silver from the Esquiline treasure with its inscription SECVNDE ET PROIECTA VIVATIS IN CHRISTO. This was a wedding present, showing scenes from the ceremony beside relief portraits of the bride and bridegroom. The rectangular, flat dish found in Risley Park in Derbyshire in the eighteenth century, and then lost again, whose main decoration is Antique hunting scenes, hardly seems to be a piece of church silver were it not for the inscription that tells of a Bishop Exsuperius who dedicated it to a church, unknown today. No doubt much of the silver plate of that time was destined for churches, and many pieces were gifts. Emperor Constantine himself presented the basilica of SS Peter and Marcellinus with a treasure of ten silver vessels, including a bowl weighing fifteen librae, i.e. about 4.9 kilogrammes. A find from Canoscio in Umbria, presumably a church treasure, consisting of twenty-four pieces, gives us an idea of the church silver normally in use. It consists of bowls, dishes, cups and spoons. Other finds have brought to light lamps and candlesticks, incense burners and jugs which were used both for washing the hands and for wine. A small but important group consists of silver reliquaries, which can all probably be dated to the fifth century. Besides pictures of Christ and the Apostles, the walls and lids are usually decorated with scenes from the Old and New Testaments. For instance, the reliquary from Castello di Brivio in Lombardy, now in the Louvre, shows the Adoration of the Three Kings, Meshach, Shadrach and Abednego in the fiery furnace and the Raising of Lazarus.

An event equal in importance to Constantine's adoption of Christianity was the removal of the Imperial capital from Rome to Byzantium, which until then had been a fairly modest Hellenistic colony on the Bosphorus. Perhaps one reason for this move was that Constantine wanted to avoid the opposition of the pagan aristocracy to the official adoption of Christianity; but more important was the need to secure the eastern territories against the threat of attack by Persia, which had always been the greatest rival of Greece and Rome. In 324 he decided to settle in Byzantium, and immediately began work on the extension of the city, which was completed in a surprisingly short time. The new capital was officially consecrated on 11 May 330 and named Constantinople after its founder. For the following century and a half the Empires of the East and the West were ruled together. But soon Rome hat to surrender its place to the new residence in the East, and very few decades later there was no longer any doubt which of the two towns was the most important.

At first the Empire of the West exerted a strong influence on the fairly rapid growth of Constantinople from a provincial town into the focus of the civilized world. The Roman élite settled in Byzantium with Constantine and he granted them special privileges. They brought with them the Roman language, culture, the Roman political and judicial system. Similarly, the artists, technicians and craftsmen who were summoned from the different centres of the Empire created works that can hardly be distinguished from those in the West. But these direct traditions alone cannot explain the close links between the art of Byzantium and that of late Antiquity. The deciding factor was the sense that Byzantium had inherited the legacy of Rome with its lofty, universal concept of Empire and Imperial obligations. Art, which was inextricably bound up with the Imperial concept, also had to recognize the Roman legacy. This even applied in the field of religious art, for the founding of an official state religion meant that the Church also served the Empire. This sense of continuity with late Roman tradition never entirely disappeared until the fall of Byzantium after the Turkish conquest in 1453. We can observe this dependence of Byzantine art on its Antique heritage from early times; it gained strength again in periods characterized by Renaissance forms. A number of works of chased silver survive from the sixth and seventh centuries, usually bowls with mythological scenes such as the assembly of the Gods, Meleager and Atalante and so on, whose style would indicate that they are late Roman except for the Byzantine stamps that indicate they are later works.

Early Byzantine art. This antiquating trend was very soon joined by a new development whose main features were the adoption and elaboration of Eastern influences. Eventually it led to what we call 'Byzantine' art.

The relief scene on the silver shield of Emperor Theodosius I (now in Madrid), dating from about 388, makes the stylistic changes clear. The enthroned Emperor is stiff and strictly frontal, enthroned under an arcade, between his two sons Arcadius and Valentinian II, in turn flanked by two soldiers holding shield and lance. They are portrayed as if they are petrified; all human activity and expression has been sacrificed to a suprapersonal representation. Roman art reached its apogee in sculptural portraits, in notating the minute individual details with relentless realism – but here the individual is avoided entirely. The rigid frontal treatment eliminates all human elements and makes the figures completely unrealistic. They stand isolated in a row, connected only by the architecture above them. This conception is as alien to Roman art as the strictly symmetrical composition. The plastic treatment is equally different. The visible lack of spatial depth, the flat, more linear than sculptural quality, is by no means a result of the consistently low relief, but reflects a new artistic concept.

Works like this shield introduced a movement away from the naturalism of the Antique. Instead of compact, asymmetrical and animated compositions we find a strict symmetry and frontal view, and a loose, additive assembly of isolated pictorial elements. This is the expression of a more abstract creative principle, inspired by the East. By the mid-fourth century, we find works in the Black Sea area which show a similarly rigid treatment of physiognomy, and sculptural effects give way to a more graphic style. Decoration was perhaps even more receptive to Eastern influence yet it seems to have been more affected by Syrian art, which was in turn affected by the art of Persia and Mesopotamia. We cannot assign a definite origin to the new artistic concept. The mutation in style was chiefly a result of the convergence of particular features from the East and the barbarian North.

The Mid-Byzantine Period. The ninth to twelfth centuries were the golden age of Byzantine art, which reached its peak in the tenth and eleventh centuries. Gold and silver, enamel precious stones and ivory were the most popular materials all of them precious and valuable. But, in spite of this love of splendour (life at the Byzantine Court was one of refined luxury and extremely sophisticated culture), costliness was not the only deciding factor in the choice of material. More important was that these materials corresponded to the basic principles of Byzantine art, which is optical and flat with strong colour effects, as expressed in the interplay of gold, enamel and precious stones. The numerous chalices with semi-precious stones and enamel set in silver, for instance, are based on these colouristic principles (page 34). The tendency towards painting became most evident in the numerous enamel works. The decor was almost always cloisonné enamel on gold and the ground could be either silver or pure gold. The enamels were never set in plain silver, for the craftsman was intent on the heightened colour effects produced by gold. The inspiration for such Byzantine enamel work may well have come from late Roman cellular glazing which, although a different technique, has almost the same artistic effect.

The very little enamel pieces that survive from early times until about 900 are difficult to date. On the whole they are rather crude works from the Eastern Byzantine provinces; the pictorial representations are devoid of all corporeal or plastic accents and are reduced to zones of pure colour set into the colourful enamel ground. The tenth century brought a change, which was not confined to enamel work alone. After the Iconoclastic disputes, which lasted from 726 to 843, a critical time for the Empire, the prominent emperors of the Macedonian dynasty brought a new political, religious and artistic revival, which reached its high point under Basileios II (976 to 1025). This 'Renaissance' period is characterised by a stronger adherence to late Roman tradition, and the return to three-dimensional sculptural forms. In enamel work, in which the antiquating tendencies took the form of stronger, more vivid, colours, the sculptural effects were heightened. The folds of draperies are emphasised by broad contrasting bands of colour which give a sense of volume. The gold ground, behind which the figures now always stood, stresses their colourfulness and makes them stand out more clearly by defining their contours more firmly. One of the most beautiful and best known works from this period is the gold staurotheca (reliquary of the True Cross) now in the Cathedral of Limburg a. d. Lahn. The inscription names Constantine VII Prophyrogentos, the very refined, art-loving Emperor, and his son Romanos as donors, which indicates a date around 960. The lovely, high quality, figurative enamel work reflects the new artistic concepts; and the wealth of precious stones, cut so as to produce a smooth, curved surface, on the inner frame of the tabular reliquary give it a new, hitherto unknown, plastic quality.

Late period and decline. Around the turn of the tenth and eleventh centuries a reaction set in to the antiquating style and soon began to gain strength. The return to stylization once more emphasized the linear quality. The uniform network of very fine parallel lines on the gold fillet on the draperies produces a delicate modelling without actually suggesting volume. Occasionally the draperies are decorated with a regular heart-shaped pattern which completely flattens the figures. This is accompanied by subdued colours and delicately modelled features in translucent enamel (page 34,). The course of the eleventh century occasionally brought a coarsening of this style, reflected particularly in a more schematic linear structure with broken up zigzags on the folds of the draperies. This development coincided with declining technical quality. However, the process was slow, and we do not find complete schematization until the thirteenth and fourteenth centuries.

The largest Byzantine enamel work is in St Mark's in Venice; the Pala d'oro, a gold altar panel originally designed as an antependium (an altar frontal) and measuring 3. 4. x 1. 4. metres. It was commissioned in Byzantium in 976 to 978 and extended and repeatedly altered in the course of centuries first in 1105, again in 1209, and finally under Doge Andrea Dandolo in 1345; it has remained unchanged since then. The enthroned Christ is surrounded by different small panels mounted in a fourteenth century Gothic frame and showing a very varied series of saints, angels and Christian feasts (page 38). The enamel work also lacks stylistic unity. It reflects stylistic developments from the late tenth century through the eleventh and twelfth centuries and up to the time when the tendency towards schematism, contrasting colours and a decline in technical quality became apparent. We can no longer judge the former overall appearance of the panel since it has been altered. Yet we may assume that it was not arranged architecturally since this was foreign to Byzantine art. We already find this non-architectural structure in the tabular reliquaries of the True Cross in Limburg and Esztergom (page 33). They have flat panels and the impression of flatness is further increased by the additional decoration.

As well as the numerous enamel works, embossing in gold and silver was also very popular at this time. The position of the relief, mid-way between free-standing sculpture and the visually flat surface, corresponded to the basic principles of Byzantine art. The development of relief work runs almost parallel to that of enamel. The same applies to mosaic work and book illumination. Early Byzantine embossing, as on the silver shield of Theodosius, followed the Early Christian tradition of stiff, two-dimensional

Central panel of the Pala d'oro in San Marco, Venice. After an engraving of 1839

compositions. The lovely gilt, eleventh century paten from the Cathedral treasury of Halberstadt is an example of the antiquating tendencies apparent in the mid-Byzantine period after the Iconoclastic disputes. The sculpturally modelled figures in the Crucifixion group and the severe patterns of foliage, clearly detached from the ground, are a return to the Antique heritage without leading to naturalism. The twelfth century relief panel of the Women at the Sepulchre shows the re-emergence of optical rather than spatial tendencies (page 35). The flatness of the relief and the dense pattern of delicate lines on the draperies echo contemporary enamels, in which a network of very fine lines suggests modelling.

Like the others, the fourth and last crusade originally aimed at liberating the holy places of Palestine from the hands of the unbelievers. Instead, the crusaders simpley set about the conquest of Christian Byzantium. Constantinople fell to them in 1204; they drove out the Emperors and set up a new Latin Empire. But the Latins only managed to maintain their unstable rule for half a century. By 1258 they had been driven out again, and the last Byzantine dynastic, the Palaeologues, assumed power. It is almost impossible to estimate how much plunder fell into the hands of the conquerors. The crusaders looted the immensely rich church treasures and carried them off to the West where they dispersed. Many pieces – chalices, patens, manuscripts and, above all, reliquaries – were preserved, however, when they were given to churches in Germany, Italy and France as gifts. The most extensive Byzantine hoard of precious metalwork is preserved in St Mark's in Venice. Little as we may understand it today, the conquest and looting of Byzantium, a Christian Empire, by knights who had set out to fight the heathens in the name of Christianity, the survival of countless very precious works of art is due to the fact that the crusaders carried them off to the West. Had they remained in Constantinople they would have been lost after the Turkish conquest of 1453, since the Turks had no interest in preserving Christian church treasures, however precious.

It was inevitable that the rule of the Latin Emperors should seriously affect the Empire; the State was impoverished and in art this meant that costly and precious materials could no longer be used. The decline in the applied arts was overcome in the fourteenth and fifteenth centuries, but this did not lead to the emergence of new concepts or to any basic change of style. The artists continued working in the style of the thirteenth century.

It is typical of Byzantine art that it clung desperately to the formal repertory it had once established; this very conservative attitude was one of its basic traits. This is not to say that it did not evolve at all in the course of the centuries, but that the constant creative struggle for a new formal language that characterizes Western art – in Italy, France and Germany – was foreign to Byzantium. Byzantine art never completely denied its Antique heritage,

Decorative dish depicting Athena. Parcel gilt. From the Hildesheim Treasure. Roman, first century A. D. Medallion probably a copy after a Hellenistic work. Diameter 25 cm. Antiken-museum, Berlin

Above: double-handled bowl from the burial of Nymphaneum near Kertsch. Greece, *c.* 400 B. C.; Ashmolean Museum, Oxford. *Below left:* Handled beaker with engraved ritual scenes. From the burial of Solokha near Melitopol. Greece, *c.* 420 B. C.; height 9.8 cm. Hermitage, Leningrad. *Right:* gilt vase from Ithaca. Greece, *c.* 200 B. C.; height 8.6 cm. British Museum, London

Gilt amphora from Chertomlyk. Greco-Scythian, *c.* 350 B.C.; height 70 cm. Hermitage, Leningrad

Centaur, probably part of a rhyton, from the find at Civita Castellana. Probably Pergamon,
c. 133 B. C.; height 18.5 cm. Kunsthistorisches Museum, Vienna

One of a pair of jugs with pictures from the legend of Hector and Achilles; from the Treasure of Berthouville, Roman, first century B. C.; height 29.9 cm. Cabinet des Médailles, Paris

Above: Emblem in the form of the bust of a girl, probably formerly attached to the centre of a dish. Origin unknown, Roman, first half of second century; height 6 cm. Römisch-Germanisches Museum, Cologne. *Below:* secular vessels from the Chaourse find (Aisne). Gaul, *c.* 270. British Museum, London

Left: Lamp stand. Byzantium, fourth century; height 49 cm. The Cleveland Museum of Art.
Right: Vase. Byzantium, fourth to sixth century; height 99.5 cm. The Cleveland Museum of Art

31

Reliquary of St Anastasius. Gilt and *niello*. Three sides with doors. Antioch *c.* 1000; height 39 cm. Cathedral Treasury, Aachen
Facing page: Reliquary of the True Cross. Gilt with cloisonné enamel. Beside the cross, the Emperor Constantine and Helena. Byzantium, eleventh century, the embossed frame added in the fifteenth century; height 35 cm. Cathedral Treasury, Esztergom

Chalice of sardonyx, silver-gilt setting with pearls and cloisonné enamel. Busts of saints on
the vertical bands and on the foot; the bust of Christ in the centre of the bowl. Byzantium,
eleventh century; height 23.5 cm. Treasury of St Mark's, Venice
Facing page: Front cover of a reliquary showing the angel and the Holy Women at the
Sepulchre. Gilt. Byzantium, twelfth century; height 42 cm. Musée du Louvre, Paris

ΦΩϹΕΥΠΡΕΠΙϹΤΑΙϹΓΥΝΑΙΞΙΝΟΑΓΓΕΛΟϹ

ΕΜΦΥΓΥϹΥΜΒΟΛΑΛΥΚΑΘΑΡΟΤΗΤΟϹΤΗΙΟΥΡΦΗΤΕΜΗΝΥΝΤΟΦΕΗ

ΕΙΧΕΔΕΑΓΛΑϹΤΡΟΜΟϹΚΑΙΕΚΤΑϹΙϹ

ΔΕΥΤΕΙΔΕΤΟΝΤΟΠΟΝ
ΟΠΟΥΕΚΕΙΤΟΟΚϹ

ΟΤΑΦΟϹΤΟΥΚΥ

ΝΥΗΕΜΠΕΦΑΝΠΓΚΑΗΛΑΥΓΗϹΦΕΡΩΠΗϹ

ΚΑΙΟΙΦΥΛΑϹϹΟΝΤΕϹΑΠΕΝΕΚΡΩΘΗϹΑΝ

ΑΤΑϹΕΩϹΚΡΑΖΩ   ΙΕΡΘΗΟΚϹ

Reliquary Cross. Gilt with enamel. Byzantium, late twelfth century; height 26 cm. Cathedral Treasury, Cosenza

never moved as far from it as did the West, which had also belonged to the great Roman Empire for centuries. This attitude explains the limitations of Byzantine art but within these limits magnificent works were created. This too is characteristic of the Consistent high quality and high standard of craftmanship in Byzantine art. Byzantium sent strong impulses and retroactive influences to the West. Italian art was largely influenced by Byzantium throughout the Middle Ages. In Germany and France, Byzantine influences were repeatedly adopted and digested until the thirteenth century. The Balkan states, the Ukraine, Georgia and Russia, adopted Eastern Roman art together with Eastern Roman Christianity and clung to it for centuries after the fall of Byzantium.

The Middle Ages

The Carolingian Renaissance. The real beginning of Western art after Antiquity came in the second half of the eighth century. The new impulses that emerged then were indissolubly bound up with the figure of Charlemagne. The Emperor's bold plan for restoring the Holy Roman Empire on Frankish soil was conceived in political and religious terms as well as in art and literature. He deliberately turned back to Antiquity in order to create a new Renaissance that encompassed the whole spiritual life of his times. In art this meant a break with the formal language of the preceding Merovingian age.

Charlemagne summoned artists and scholars to his court to 'breed' a new, noble classical culture, based not on the elaboration of existing elements but on the return to late Antiquity. All this was initiated and supported by the Emperor himself. Georg Dehio has said that no artist has ever exerted an influence equal to that of Charlemagne, who marks the beginning of the history of art in the West. But there was one element which the Carolingians did not take over from Antiquity – the monumental form of the human body. This was as alien to the Germanic tribes as was all large-scale sculpture. 'Their rich ornamental imagination, which was able to develop an entirely non-representational art in purely linear, almost musical, terms, has no sense at all of the corporeal shape of the body' (H. Jantzen). This basic artistic attitude was very important to the development of large-scale sculpture in the North. The Carolingians did not draw on the monumental concepts of Antiquity but began with small-scale art and followed a new, personal path that did not lead to monumentality until the age of twelfth century French cathedral sculpture. This meant that of the most typical products of Carolingian sculpture are small-format works, such as carved ivories and gold works. Both branches of art reached an equal level of production and artistic importance although today we can only judge the artistic standard, owing to the scarcity of surviving gold. The largest and most important commissions for ivories and gold came from the Church, and so it remained until late Gothic times. Most of the orders were for liturgical implements, splendid manuscript bindings, portable altars, reliquaries of the most varied kinds, and finally antependia – decorated frontals for the lower part of the altar. Gold was chiefly used for this throughout the early Middle Ages, while silver was used less and occupied a subordinate position; this was not solely because of the difference in material value between the two metals. It is true that the Carolingians wanted to use the most precious materials they knew – which of course also included countless pearls and precious stones – in the service of God in the same way as they celebrated the secular ruler by his imperial insignia. But the essential reason, typical of medieval thought, was the urge to spiritualize matter 'to make the spiritual content more visible'. Gold was regarded as a reflection of the divine light, so gold rather than silver was the most expressive symbol of divinity.

Although the creative energies of the Carolingian Emperors were inspired by Antiquity, entirely different influences, directly opposed to the 'Classicism' of Charlemagne, were also at work. They were particularly strong in early Carolingian art. A small but significant group of works survives from the last third of the eighth century which is very closely related to the Irish and Anglo-Saxon art brought to the continent by the missions of the Irish monks. They are based on purely ornamental principles, with characteristic motifs of flat, intricately intertwined and interwoven bands of decoration. The most famous piece in this group is the copper Tassilo Chalice, decorated with gold, silver and *niello,* which was presumably dedicated to the monastery of Kremsmünster by the Duke of Bavaria, Tassilo, when it was founded in 777; it is still there today. The cover of the *Lindau Gospels*, made in about 800 and now in the Metropolitan Museum of Art, New York, is such a perfect example of the Irish style that it is difficult to accept it as a Continental work. In Berlin there is a purse reliquary in the form of a bag (page 61), which comes from the convent of Dionysius in Enger near Herford (Westphalia), where the Saxon duke Widukind died, founded by Charlemagne in 807. Some people think this purse may have been a christening present from the Emperor to Widukind. The display side is of gold, covered with opaque cloisonné enamel, some of which has been damaged. The twelve precious stones are grouped on bands of enamel radiating from a central stone – a symbol of Christ and the Apostles. This symbolic arrangement is difficult to grasp today but was very familiar to the medieval mind. The sides, and the back with its chased relief of Christ in majesty between angels and the Virgin flanked by St Peter and St Paul, are worked in silver. The same Anglo-Saxon influences are apparent in the interlaced decoration on the earliest, and unique, surviving secular vessel from this period, a purse-shaped silver cup from a tomb in Pettstadt, northern Franconia; it probably also dated from the eigth century and is now in the Germanisches Nationalmuseum, Nuremberg.

We have no gold or silver works dating from the early reign of Charlemagne which might reflect the ideas of the Carolingian Renaissance. The most important surviving works from this period date from the second half of the ninth century. They were made under Charles the Bald in about 870 in western France, probably in Rheims. They include the cover of an ornate Gospel Book, the *Codex Aureus,* now in the Staatsbibliothek, Munich, and a portable altar, the so-called Ciborium of Arnulf. The altarstone is surmounted by a two-story ciborium rising from columns and covered by two connecting cross-vaults; it is made of wood covered in gold leaf. King Arnulf of Kärnten dedicated both these pieces to the convent of the St Emmeram in Regensburg in 896 before his coronation; when the convent was secularized they came to Munich in 1811.

The arrangement of the cover of the *Codex Aureus* follows the traditional five-part composition of late Antique ivory diptychs, but the artistic effect resides in the contrast between the precious stones in the frame – in tones of green and blue – and the much lighter, uniform, glowing gold of the chased reliefs on the flat areas. It is a magnificent display piece imbued with great pictorial effects ... The drawing of the relief has a vibrant sharpness; the limbs and movements of the figures are wiry and tense, with precise, rather graphic lines. The central plaque shows the enthroned Christ; this is surrounded by the four Evangelists, sitting at their writing desks; finally, on the "periphery", are four relief scenes from the Old Testament. The types and motifs of this magnificent book cover derive from Antique models. But the accumulation of decorative elements which, together with the lively, scenic chased work, creates an effect of quite inconceivable value, can be described as 'characteristically medieval' (W. Sauerländer). Unfortunately the relief on the slopes of the roof of the Ciborium of Arnulf is not very well preserved; stylistically they are related to the relief scenes on the *Codex Aureus,* 'but with their violently agitated, nervous forms they are among the most magnificent achievements in the visual arts of the entire period' (Sauerländer). Unlike the case of the much greater number of surviving ivories, it is very difficult to trace the development of gold on the few surviving examples. The ivories show clearly, however, that we cannot define the general attitude and style of this period as simply derivative from the Antique. The age of late Antiquity was now over and its stylistic features could not simply be transplanted to an entirely different artistic conception and yet remain the same. This means that even in the Carolingian age new tendencies emerged side by side with the 'classicist' style and, to a certain extent at least, reveal the formal language of medieval times. The portable altar of San Ambrogio, made under Bishop Angilbert (824–56), combines both tendencies. The gold frontal of this altar panelling, which covers all four sides, adheres to the late Antique pictorial language with its images of Christ, the Apostles and the Evangelists, and with lively animated figures and their spatial relationship to the relief ground. But on the silver relief on the back, which shows the patron saint of Milan, St Ambrose, and was perhaps made by the Frankish goldsmith Wolvinius, the figures are rigid and the negation of three-dimensional spatial effects is very clear. This rejection of the 'naturalism' of Antiquity was to become the determining factor in art throughout the Middle Ages.

Ottonian art. The art of the Ottonians did not follow on smoothly from the Carolingian period, although it continued to depend largely on imperial commissions and its aims were the same. Here again, in the second half of the tenth century, we find a new departure, a new return to the forms of Antiquity, i. e. a new Renaissance. The Ottonians were also influenced by Byzantine art, but it was elaborated and converted into indigenous forms to a much greater extent than during the Carolingian return to Antique sources. The true medieval language began to emerge and take root in this process of conversion and elaboration. At the same time, the centres of artistic production shifted to the East. New centres began to appear in central Germany in Saxony, the native land of the Ottonian emperors, which had hitherto remained on the periphery of artistic development. Hildesheim, Fulda and Magdeburg quickly gained in importance while the west declined accordingly. France, which remained under Carolingian rule as the kingdom of the Western Franks but was no longer a part of the Empire, declined for a while and took no part in the development of Ottonian art. It is during this period that we find the early beginnings of 'French' and 'German' national cultures. Ottonian art, with its great achievements, remained confined within the boundaries of the German Empire.
Many of these great achievements were due to the goldsmiths, who created some of the most precious and important works of Western art of the time. Gold remained the most popular material. The expressive power with which the craftsmen now imbued it far excelled that of Carolingian works. 'Gold displays power and wealth in objective fashion, embodies them in sensible terms. So gold was put in the service of the sacred mission as the highest vocation of art. But it is not the material value that characterizes gold at the time of the Ottonian empire, but rather a special kind of spiritualization of the metal. No period of medieval German art, or even of recent times had such a highly developed sense of the mysterious power that emanated from this precious metal as the Ottonian age, or managed to imbue liturgical implements with the mystical enchantment that still radiates from these creations nearly a thousand years later' (H. Jantzen). Jantzen's sensitive description of

the virgin in the cathedral treasury at Essen makes it clear how this 'mysterious power' of gold could fuse with the sculptural form to produce a masterpiece of perfect unity and spiritual expression: 'She (the Virgin) is the point of departure for all German sculptures of the Virgin; she is in the language of the late tenth century which is so far from natural, enthroned, her head slightly inclined to the side, her left hand on the shoulder of the divine Child who "sits" diagonally across her lap. Nowhere does one sense more strongly than here how little use the Ottonian images of worship had for the artistic concepts of Antique sculpture, and how this image of the divinity is based on entirely different sources; at the same time it becomes clear how impossible it is to speak of "sculpture" in the original sense of the term here. This art reaches for the invisible, intangible, non-circumscribable. The golden Madonna of Essen does not have the effect of a corporeal artistic image. Although she is shown enthroned, holding the Child, she is remote from any sculptural or anthropomorphic concepts as a glance at her face and eyes will show. Jesus is not conceived as a child, nor as a boy seated on the lap of his mother. The Madonna belongs exclusively to the unapproachable region of the radiant golden light she emanates, like a divinity to be worshipped from a mystical distance. And yet her delicate, fluid contours also express a certain supernatural sweetness and piety.'

This ideal of the interpenetration of material, artistic expression and spiritual conception, all fused into a unified whole, explains why the Ottonians valued gold so highly and silver so little. Not until post-Ottonian times was silver to come into current use again, although even then gold forfeited little of its power.

A considerable number of Ottonian gold and silver works of very high quality survive. Most of them were probably made in the workshops of the large monasteries, convents and cathedral schools, such as Reichenau, Trier, Echternach, Hildesheim and Regensburg, who also produced most of the illuminations. But it is usually very difficult to localize works exactly; only the products from the workshop of the art-loving Bishop Egbert of Trier, one of the most influential centres of the age, bear clear stylistic resemblances and can be related to one another. Their high level of craftsmanship and the colourfulness of the cloisonné enamel and precious stones reflect a magnificence that is never vulgar, and that is far more balanced than in Carolingian works. Similarly, the relief work is more delicate, the figures more restful. Byzantine influences contributed towards this harmonious balance and return to the three-dimensional.

One of the most important works of this period is the gold Basel antependium dedicated to the Minster in about 1020 by Emperor Henry II; it has been in the Musée de Cluny in Paris since the nineteenth century, and although formerly attributed to the school of Reichenau, it has more recently been assigned to Fulda (page 63). Christ stands under a five-part, clearly balanced arcade: He is shown strictly frontally, flanked by the three archangels and St Benedict, who tun slightly towards Him. At His feet are the donors Emperor Henry II and his wife Kunigunde, very small and in an attitude of worship. This was how the medieval ruler, holder of absolute secular power, saw himself before God. The area of wall above the arcades and the projecting frame are covered with Byzantine foliage inset with medallions; the overall structure is clearly defined, but in spite of the arcades the effect is not architectural. The rounded figures stand calm and motionless before a smooth ground. Even where the artist aimed at movement, as in the fluttering ends of the drapery of Christ, the effect is of calm and rigidity. The antiquating spatial effects and animation of Carolingian works are here supplanted by a generously conceived, quiet summarization. The artist took up and elaborated Byzantine stimuli to create one of the masterpieces of early medieval sculpture.

Roger von Helmarshausen. The beginning of the twelfth century saw a development, distinct from that of the preceding century. The art of the Ottonians was 'spiritual to the highest degree', and represented the 'most transcendental phase of the art of the Middle Ages' (H. Schnitzler); it had moved farther away from the 'tangible experience of reality' (Sauerländer) of the art of Antiquity than any other age, including the Byzantine. The Byzantines, in spite of their forceful conversion of spatial and sculptural values into visual pictorial ones, had never entirely denied their legacy from Antiquity. In every case where the art of the Middle Ages was penetrated by Byzantine influences, it still adhered to this same legacy. The same applied in the twelfth century. The increasing affirmation of corporeal and architectural reality quickly led away from the transcendental concepts of Ottonian art.
Hand in hand with this new concept of art came the choice of new means of expression and new materials. From this time onwards gold faded into the background and works of solid gold become increasingly rare. Yet the artists did not abandon the effects of gold; works in silver, and often in copper, were often gilt. Naturally this meant a shift of values; instead of emphasizing the spiritual content the artist concentrated more on superficial effects. The old technique of gold cloisonné gave way to opaque champlevé on copper, a technique which was carried to a high degree of artistic and technical perfection in an almost inconceivable number of works, many of which still survive. One can without exaggerating call the twelfth century the age of champlevé. Both in artistic terms and in terms of production the Rhineland became the leading centre, with the focus on Cologne, and the Maas valley with Liège and the abbey of Stablo also became important centres.
The goldsmith monk Rogerus stands at the beginning of these new formal

developments. He lived and worked in the monastery of Helmarshausen (in the extreme north of what is now Hessen) at the turn of the eleventh and twelfth centuries. His name appears in a record of 1100 in connection with a shrine he made for the cathedral of Paderborn. This portable altar is still there and has been identified as his work. Art historians have managed to detect his style and that of his workshop in a number of other works page 62). They are characterized by their strong, clear structure; the figures have a summary, forceful corporeality. All four sides of the portable altar form the former monastery of Abdinghof depict the lives of the saints in tense, dynamic narrative scenes with dramatic highpoints; they are brought out by a masterly use of *opus interrasile*, i. e. gilt copper plaques cut out like fretwork with engraved and punched designs. Apart from his artistic creations, Roger von Helmarshausen has also left us another very important work, the *Schedula diversarum* artium, a comprehensive technical manual that provides us with a detailed picture of the artistic concepts and practices of the Middle Ages.

The tasks of the goldsmiths in the twelfth century remained the same as before, but a particular form of reliquary, unknown before, now became current, the large shrine destined to house the whole body of a saint. The number of such shrines that were made in the region of the Rhine and the Maas, in particular in the second half of the twelfth century, most of them still in the churches for which they were executed, is considerable. The basic form is a rectangular box up to two metres long surmounted by a cross vault, as found in earlier times though on a smaller scale, but the structure has become more clearly defined, and it eventually became increasingly architectural. This applies especially to the Cologne works. By contrast the shrines from the Maas valley retained the rather box-like shape, like the shrine of Servatius in Maastricht and the two shrines for St Domitian and St Mangold by Godefroid de Claire in Huy (near Liège). They are also more restrained in the use of enamel and less colourful. The shrine of Heribert, dating from about 1170, which is the masterpiece of Cologne silver work in the period immediately before Nicolas de Verdun, still belongs to an earlier phase. Its long walls are decorated with seated Apostles in chased silver, alternating with standing prophets in enamel; the Virgin and St Heribert are enthroned on the gables. The sloping roof is divided into six areas by bands of enamel, following the arrangement of the long sides; each area inset with an enamel medallion with scenes from the lives of the saint. A cast, copper gilt, fretwork comb studded with crystals follows the ridge of the roof. The slopes of the pedestals and edges of the roof are covered in a chased silver foliage pattern with strips of alternate ornamental enamels and little plaques of filigree encrusted with precious stones. Not until the shrines of the last two decades of the twelfth century by the school of Nicolas de Verdun do we find a more determined architectural form, when the long sides were structured by columns and groups of columns detached from the wall of the shrine. They carry simple or quatrefoil arcades which span the figures projecting in high relief (page 65). This period shortly before 1200 is the highpoint of Romanesque gold work.

Before examining these works we must turn to the art centre in southern Saxony around Brunswick and Hildesheim. It is known as the 'artistic circle of Henry the Lion' and produced a series of very important works in the second half of the twelfth century. They form the Welf Treasure, most of which is now in Berlin. What is important in our context is that these works had many stylistic features in common with contemporary English art. This can be explained by the exile of Henry, the rival of Emperor Barbarossa, in England from 1181 to 1185. His second wife Matilda was a daughter of the English king. It is from England, or more specifically from the area around the Channel, that the idea seems to have come of using *niello* rather than enamel as the principal decorative medium (page 64).

Nicolas de Verdun and his successors: The art of the Middle Ages is anonymous. The medieval artist did not see himself as an autonomous creative force, as did artists in periods of increased self-consciousness; instead he humbly offered up the talent he had received from God to the service of God. He would have considered it arrogance with respect to the one and only Creator to sign his name on his work. This is why we know so few names from the Middle Ages, and nothing of the personalities of the artists. It is only from the twelfth century on that we find a few names: Roger von Helmarshausen, Reiner von Huy and Godefroid de Claire in Maasland and Eilbertus in Cologne. We know of them from records rather than from signatures on their works. But the greatest of the goldsmiths of that age, one whose creative ability had no equal and who has been described as the Donatello of the twelfth century, left two works signed 'Nicolas de Verdun'.

He came from Verdun, but where he trained or did his early work we do not know. From 1171 he worked in the convent of Klosterneuberg, where he made an antependium which was completed in 1181 and later converted into an altarpiece, the so-called altarpiece of Klosterneuberg. In three registers it shows fifty-one typologically corresponding scenes from the Old and New Testaments. Here for the first time we find individual scenes from the Life of Christ juxtaposed or strictly related to scenes of the Ark of the Convenant before and after the tablets of the law. 'These scenes in copper gilt with blue and red enamelled draperies are shown against a blue, partly green, accentuated enamel ground. Quatrefoil arcades with inscriptions and decorated enamel panels with busts of angels, prophets and virtues in the corners, tie the scenes to the flat, colourful illusionary architecture. It is proof of the creative imagination of Nicolas de Verdun that his newly conceived scenes stand out from the traditional, well-known type of composition by a wealth of individual features; it is proof of his foresight into the imminent Gothic style that, in the Late Romanesque era, which was marked by the splendour of colourful enamel, he essentially confined his effects to blue and gold' (H. Kohlhaussen).

The forceful and tense corporeality of the figures, stressed by the soft flowing lines of the draperies, is conceived in a masterly and mature fashion. In the plastic figures on the Shrine of the Magi it was to culminate in an extreme, hitherto unknown, monumentality. Nicolas de Verdun went to Cologne to start work on this shrine, the greatest twelfth century shrine in terms of size and structure, after completing the Klosterneuberg altarpiece. The design of the impressive, three-aisled basilica and the lower lateral walls, which were finished by 1191, are entirely by his hand. The rest of the work, which was not completed until 1230, was executed by his extensive workshop after his departure for Tournai (Hennegau), where he completed the shrine of the Virgin in 1205. The great wealth of the immense Shrine of the Magi, with its comprehensive uniform pictorial programme, enhanced by enamel on the relief parts, cannot be described here (cf. H. Schnitzler, *Rheinische Schatzkammer*, vol. II) but we can take a closer look at the silver-gilt prophets on the lower long side, which are the masterpiece of Nicolas de Verdun and of the whole twelfth century. The essence of the great art of Nicolas de Verdun is a forceful, 'close-to-nature', corporeality, very varied, energetic gestures and the individuality of the lively heads (page 65). The mighty figures are solidly planted in the niches, animated – but not violently – by an inner energy. Richly flowing draperies stress the bodies and movement rather than concealing them. They are stretched tight round the shoulders and knees, in tense lines of folds; they fall softly between the limbs, are massed into piles and cling to the heavy upper part of the bodies like wet cloth. The heads, with their individual and differentiated features and lively, penetrating gaze, are truly those of prophets and express all the power of the Old Testament. This forceful, internally inspired, monumental corporeality has been unequalled since Antique times. And indeed it was the Antique heritage that Nicolas had adopted, via Byzantium, and raised to a unique achievement. Nicolas de Verdun's later figures on the Shrine of the Virgin in Tournai no longer achieve this force and pre-eminence. They are more delicate and the attitudes and movements seem rather weary. Presumably this was a late work of his old age.

It is understandable that Nicolas de Verdun's creative powers exerted a retrospective influence on the goldsmiths who worked with and after him. Shrines were made in Cologne in the last two decades of the century – the Anno and the Albinus shrines – whose delicate architecture and tense, clear ornamental designs are essentially derivative. Even the splendid

Shrine of the Virgin in Aachen, completed in 1238, harks back to the shrine of the Magi.

Nicolas de Verdun was not alone in creating figures of an antiquating tendency. From about 1180 to 1230, in the area between the Rhineland, Lorraine and northern France and as far away as southern England, we find numerous works of gold and silver, illuminations and cathedral sculptures, in which the form of the drapery folds can be defined as the 'groove-fold style'. The works of Nicolas de Verdun were certainly an important influence in this style, yet it cannot be explained by this alone. Art historians are still faced with a number of problems, particularly regarding its beginnings, which presumably coincide with the roots of the art of Nicolas de Verdun. The stylistic links between the monumental stone sculptures on the two northern portals of Rheims Cathedral, dating from about 1220, and contemporary gold and silver work in this style once again reveal the creative formal mastery of the goldsmiths of the late Middle Ages – in works which have nothing in common with the 'small-scale art' or applied art of later centuries.

The goldsmith monk, Hugo von Oignies, who worked in the monastery of Oignies near Namur until c. 1240, also belongs to this 'antiquating' stylistic group with his figurative work. But new formal principles obtain in their formal structure. His groin reliquary of 1238 (page 66) has a delicate, elongated solidity that complexly avoids the two dimensional. The ornaments and decorative motifs are subordinated to the clear structure and stress on the vertical, which begins with the lancet of the base. The lovely chalice by Hugo von Oignies also has lancets rising from the base to the shaft, corresponding to the powerful vertical ribs of the nodus. This architectural tension and stress on the vertical are essential elements of Gothic art. So are the complete abandonment of flat, colourful champlevé enamel in favour of *niello,* whose design stands out from the silver ground. Precious stones were still used, but less frequently, and their coloured patterns were more rigidly arranged. On the whole the effect of these works is based on the elegant, restrained harmony of gold and silver, and the black of the *niello.*

The works of Hugo von Oignies, which also include the cover of a Gospel Book, belong among an extensive group of works created in around 1200 to 1250 in the area that is now northwest France and neighbouring Hennegau, and which are all stamped by the Gothic style. The new style had already emerged in 1140 in the French royal domain, the Ile de France, with the abbey church of Saint-Denis in Paris, and was to reach its peak in the northern French cathedrals of the twelfth and thirteenth centuries. As far as one can tell, Artois was already one of the leading artistic regions of Gothic style in the twelfth century, and it seems that this was also the area where the new style was taken up in gold and silver; Arras may have been the most important centre.

In these early Gothic works of gold and silver, the creative powers of the goldsmith once again came into their own. While Germany adhered to the traditions of the twelfth century almost throughout the thirteenth century, with its decorative arrangement of ornamental motifs (page 68), a new development emerged in France in about 1250 which led to the direct adoption of the forms of monumental architecture in gold and silver work. It reached its high point in the reliquary shrine of St Gertrude in Nivelles, executed in 1272–98 and destroyed in the last war (page 67). This work has nothing in common with twelfth century shrines; it is a faithful copy to the last detail of a late Gothic church. Similarly, the style of the figures is based on the Apostles of the Sainte-Chapelle in Paris, which at the time were the most advanced products of monumental sculpture. This style had penetrated to the north by way of Rheims Cathedral. By inclining towards architectural imitation in this way, gold and silver largely forfeited their own particular formal powers.

The fourteenth and fifteenth centuries.
But although the goldsmiths lost some of their creative powers, the artistic quality of their works did not decline. A great number of very beautiful works were executed up until the end of the Middle Ages. However, the art of gold and silver work could no longer attain the high level reached in Ottonian times. It could not boast a figure such as Nicolas de Verdun, one of the greatest geniuses of the late Middle Ages, who inspired some great cathedral sculptures with his figurative work. Other branches of art had now taken over the stylistic leadership and become creative inspirations: architecture, painting and sculpture in stone and wood. This is where we now find the models that inspired the goldsmiths. The numerous, high-quality images of worship and figurative reliquaries followed the stylistic developments of sculpture, even in the case of the most progressive works of the time and the most important artists (page 77). We can see this in the work of Bernt Notke of Lübeck, who was a sculptor himself and achieved his masterpieces in this field, or in the powerful figures of the Hallwyl Reliquary (page 77), which recall the works of Niklaus Gerhard, one of the most important sculptors of his time, who came from Leiden and chiefly worked on the northern Rhine, particularly in Strasbourg. The same applies to the many beautiful engravings often found on reliquaries; many of them echo Master E. S. or Martin Schongauer.
In the thirteenth and early fourteenth centuries, the introduction of new liturgical practices and feasts (Corpus Christi) and the urge to represent the symbol of the divine in sensible form led to the demand for a new liturgical implement: the monstrance. Until the end of the Middle Ages and even later it was chiefly characterized by architectural features.

The basic shape of the monstrance is a broad base with a long shaft supporting a crystal cylinder for the Host, which is flanked by flying buttresses and surmounted by an architectural roof (page 70). We find countless delicate architectural forms in the roof, often interspersed with a number of minute figures of saints in the niches and on the finials; the form of the details and individual motifs closely correspond to the developments in architecture. These monstrances took on a very exuberant, almost confusingly ornate form in the late fifteenth century in Spain. At the same time, the knops of the chalices became disproportionately large and architectural, often with clusters and superimposed rows of little pointed towers and finials. The function of the knops as a grip for the hand when it holds the shaft has disappeared, which meant that one could no longer hold the shaft comfortably. We find a similar form of knop in contemporary Polish chalices.

Opaque repoussé enamel completely disappeared during the course of the thirteenth century. This was partly for stylistic reasons, partly because silver was used exclusively at that time instead of copper. Translucent enamelled silver appeared in about 1300, and reached its climax in the fourteenth century. The technique was either the old champlevé or the new form of *émail de basse taille,* enamelled silver low-relief work. It is not easy to decide whether this enamel work originated in France or in Italy, since it appeared at the same time in both countries. In Italy, where enamelled silver was used until the sixteenth century, Siena, and later Florence, were the main centres of production. What is certain, however, is that wire enamel (enamel plaques in a wire setting) first evolved in Italy, perhaps in Venice; this technique soon became widespread in Italy and also penetrated to the north, particularly to Hungary, and reached its highpoint in the fifteenth century. It is also found, although more rarely, in Austria and Poland.

North of the Alps, Paris, with its high-quality enamelled silver work, was a centre whose influences radiated to England and Germany. The lovely jug in Copenhagen, of about 1335, was made in Paris (page 72). The colours are restricted to red and blue, and the design of the slender, elongated figures with the naked parts of their bodies in gold is delicate and animated. Since a chalice and paten of the same colour, technique and style are in Copenhagen Museum, these three pieces have always been described together, and the jug was regarded as a piece of church plate illustrated with scenes from the life of the prodigal son. It is only recently that it was exposed as a secular work with scenes from a contemporary tale. This also explains the scenes of sports, such as stilts and hockey in the upper register, which would hardly be suitable on a holy vessel. The two lower registers show half-human, half-animal figures. This makes the splendid jug a rare example of secular art from this early period that has left us so little secular silver.

In Germany the main centres of production were in the upper Rhine area, in

Constance and Basel, which evolved a very individual style. A reliquary of the cross in the cathedral treasury of Basel (now in Berlin) comes from an early group, as does the former chalice of Sigmaringer (now in Baltimore). The sharp drawing of the figures suggests that they were executed in about 1320–30 in Constance, which was the leading centre in the first third of the century. A later group from the mid-fourteenth century came from Basel, including the monstrance of Henry II and his wife Kunigunde, of 1347, showing scenes from the life of the imperial couple (page 70).

Towards the end of the fourteenth century, enamelled silver appeared less frequently, and it was hardly used at all in the fifteenth century. Instead, around 1400, we find gold enamel sculpture (émail en ronde bosse) in France and in the Burgundian and Dutch areas; because of their great value, these works were reserved for the exclusive circles of the court and the style did not penetrate to Germany. The masterpiece of this group is the delightful Madonna in the rose bush in Altötting. In the first third of the fifteenth century painterly tendencies emerged in the Netherlands, and this led to a pictorial enamel – a kind of grisaille of silver or gold enamel on a black ground. Its effects derived from the delicate gradations of tone. Works from this group include the so-called Simian Cup in the Metropolitan Museum in New York.

Secular Work in the Late Middle Ages. It is difficult to determine the extent to which the early Middle Ages knew and used silver plate. From the eleventh century onwards book illuminations show tables laid with numerous different bowls and dishes, but it is difficult to say whether they were made of silver. Some certainly must have been. The first rare surviving pieces are from the fourteenth century (page 71). Understandably, little domestic silver survived since it was used so much, and particularly since the forms and decoration were too simple to make it worth preserving. We have a little information from written sources and records such as the description of the comprehensive silver hoard of Duke Charles the Bold of Burgundy, with his great taste for luxury. His table on the occasion of his encounter with Emperor Frederick III was described as follows: 'Fifty extremely valuable vessels of gold and silver were set on the tables, besides the bowls standing on the sideboards; there were also bottles and large jugs, which held twelve or perhaps more quarts' (H. Brunner). He took this silver with him on his campaigns in a trunk (a custom which survived throughout the eighteenth century and led to the formation of a travelling service fitted in a case), until it fell to the federal conquerors at the battle of Grandson in 1476.

The large luxury vessels have survived rather better than domestic plate because of their magnificence. They were designed as table decorations, like the lovely table fountain inlaid with enamels from the end of the fourteenth century (page 73), or were only used on special occasions for ritual libations: reception and farewell drinks, the 'Minnetrunk' (love drink) at betrothals, the round drink after concluding agreements. Some of them must have stood on the sideboards as purely show pieces, as was customary in Roman Antiquity. The 'Katzenelnbogen Willkomm' (page 74) which had passed to the landgraves of Hessen with the estate of the last count of Katzenelnbogen, may, however, have really served a function; in the interior a short tube rises from the centre of the base, to which a sieve is attached on top that presumably contained ingredients for preparing spiced wine. In form it recalls a cooped wooden vat, twined with osier; the spout is attractively curved in the form of a griffin neck. The three feet and the prominent thumbpiece on the handle are shaped like miniature architecture, with windows, alcoves, doorways, portcullises and drawbridges. The body is engraved with a delicate design of late Gothic foliage. This piece already takes us some decades into the fifteenth century. It anticipates the period of the Late Middle Ages in which the Dutch painters discovered the surface of things – their visible nature – while sculpture began to free the human figure from the standard type and introduced a greater realism. If we look at the crucifix on the Hallwyl Reliquary (page 77), with the prominent ribs, the taut muscles of the arms and bony knees, the tendency towards naturalism becomes clear. Bernt Notke's St George (page 76) shows this new realism in the very carefully executed details of the armour, and the artist's love of nature is apparent on the osier work on the wooden fence round the pedestal. The 'wild men' holding coats of arms and supporting the work show the same exuberance; they are hairy, shaggy 'children of nature' who appear throughout the late Middle Ages. Another sign of this new trend is that wooden mazers become double bowls (see page 71) by means of silver-gilt mounts, and that aurochs horns are mounted to become drinking vessels, the 'griffins'. The precious 'Oldenburg Horn' (page 75) imitated the form of these mounted aurochs horns in silver, just as the 'Katzenelnbogen Willkomm' imitated the vat. In the luxuriant, exuberant, intricate foliage work, even the architectural forms of the tower monstrance change into vegetable forms, and what was once shaft and flying buttress now rises as a trunk with branches. This very late phase of Gothic gold and silver work is paralleled by the sculpture and painting of the Danube School.

The Renaissance

The Renaissance that began in Florence in the fifteenth century introduced a new age characterized, in the words of Jacob Burckhardt, as that of the 'discovery of man and the world'. After the long medieval period, which Giorgio Vasari, the famous Renaissance art historian, saw as a dark age in the history of art, a new era was born. This 'rebirth' is most clearly visible in art, but it also revolutionized every facet of human life, science, politics and the economy. Its sources lay in Antiquity, but artists soon began to measure themselves against their models and to think they had exceeded them. Besides the rediscovery of Antiquity, the new feeling for nature was the determining factor. Here the innovations were radical, although the old traditions from the Carolingian and Ottonian Renaissances in Italian art and the partial ties with the Church remained effective. The new movement focussed in Italy in the fifteenth century. The rest of Europe was not affected until almost three generations later. Then the innovations and Italian influences in art were accompanied by overwhelming changes in the spiritual, economic and political fields, leading among other things, to the Reformation in the North.

Italy. We must look at Italian gold and silver in the fifteenth century from two aspects if we want to appreciate it properly. What is preserved cannot give us a sufficiently clear picture. Much was destroyed when it was stolen and looted, or it was melted down, for money in times of war and need, or because later ages, particularly the Baroque, needed material for new works. This may be said to have applied to Italy in this period even more than to other European countries. Records relating to Italian art centres and the numerous courts tell us of immense treasures, particularly of secular silver. The most extensive hoards appear to have consisted of display and table silver, besides pieces of all kinds, including weapons and helmets. The noblemen and men of means were not only interested in increasing the number of display pieces on their sideboards – basins, bowls, dishes and candelabra. This is emphasized by the Neapolitan statesman and writer Giovanni Pontano (1426–1503) in his work *De Splendore*. He requires that the individual pieces, such as cups and drinking bowls, should be both of outstanding beauty and great variety of form, even if used for the same function. Such hoards were tangible signs of the prestige of the mighty; they shared his changing fortunes in the struggles for power that characterize this century. Hardly a single piece from the great display services has survived, although they existed at the courts of the Sforza in Milan and of the d'Este in Ferrara, as well as in the rest of Renaissance Italy.
We know a little more of church plate, but what has survived from the

church treasures still cannot give us a complete picture of the extent of production and variety of forms of the liturgical implements and precious reliquaries.

Florentine gold and silver work took the leading place in the fifteenth century and largely determined the activity at other centres. The Florentine workshops produced the masters who were to direct the course of Italian Renaissance art for several generations to come. Important figures were Lorenzo Ghiberti (1378–1455), the master builder Filippo Brunelleschi and the sculptor Donatello; later they are joined by Andrea del Verrocchio and Antonio Pollaiuolo, to name only the most famous. In the sixteenth century we still often encounter masters who executed works in gold and silver or designs for them distinct from their activity as sculptors.

The frequency of this dual talent and the variety of fields of activity of the artists are an integral feature of Italian gold and silver work. But the interactions that were initially so fruitful a stimulus to both sculptor and goldsmith also meant that more and more artists turned away from gold and silver with the growing importance of sculpture. This was to the benefit of the pioneers of sculpture but deprived gold and silver work of much of its creative force.

In 1401 the cathedral of Florence held a competition for the execution of the second bronze baptistry door. At the beginning of the work which Ghiberti took over in 1403, the two Florentine goldsmiths, Leonardo di Ser Giovanni and Betto di Geri, who were working on the silver altar dossal which was begun in 1366 and not yet completed, were called in to assist in the baptistry door. From 1402 until 1452, when the third baptistry door, the Door of Paradise, was finished, most of the patrons' money and the Florentine sculptors' powers were devoted to this work. The silver altar dossal in this oldest of Florentine churches was not taken up again until 1452.

Ghiberti's life work, the two bronze doors in the baptistry, belong to the sphere of large-scale sculpture. At the same time the many gilt relief figures on the first door and the gilt relief zones on the second door, together with the richly ornamented frame, are inconceivable without the knowledge and experience of the goldsmith Ghiberti. Benvenuto Cellini, his famous successor, who mentions Ghiberti first and foremost in his introduction to the *Tract on gold and silver work* of 1568, said of him: 'Lorenzo Ghiberti was truly a goldsmith, both in what concerns the dainty manner of his beautiful works and particularly in its infinite clarity and precise execution. This man, who must be counted among the outstanding goldsmiths, applied himself to everything, in particular to the casting of smaller works.' Nothing has survived of the works in solid silver or gold which Ghiberti lists in his *Commentarii* – and which included a pluvial clasp for Pope Martin V and the tiara for Pope Eugene IV. But we have two busts of prophets and the statuettes on the large silver altar of Pistoia Cathedral that were made by his rival in the competition for the first bronze door, the architect of the dome of Florence Cathedral, Filippo Brunelleschi (1377–1446), who probably only did little gold and silver work. This altar, with its countless figures and reliefs, is a masterpiece of Tuscan gold and silver. It was executed and enriched by several artists from the thirteenth century on. Among them was Leonardo di Ser Giovanni, who also worked on the more famous silver altar dossal of the baptistry of San Giovanni, the most important work of Florentine silver. In 1402 this altar dossal, which was eventually converted into an altar, consisted of eight large reliefs surmounted by a frieze of thirty small figures. Christofano di Paolo created a tabernacle in the Gothic style for a large figure of John the Baptist in the centre in 1350. The statuette itself was not commissioned until 1452, after work had been completed on the third baptistry door. It was entrusted to the sculptor and future master builder of the cathedral, Michelozzo di Bartolommeo (1396–1472). One can see how the figure (page 81) has been forced into its Gothic frame. But in spite of this sense of confinement, John the Baptist stands in an elegant attitude; in marked constrast to the gravity and stiffness of his gesture. The silver figure, 60 cm high and weighing fourteen pounds, recalls Ghiberti and Donatello in style; Michelozzo had been an assistant in their workshops.

In 1477 several artists were entrusted with finishing the altar with panels on the right and left side walls. The four large reliefs with scenes from the Life of John the Baptist were divided up as follows: the Feast of Herod was executed by Antonio di Salvi and Francesco di Giovanni, who also did the architectural parts. The relief consisting of two scenes, on the left the Annunciation to Zacharias, on the right the Visitation of the Virgin Mary to Elizabeth (page 78), are by Bernardo Cellini. The scene of the Birth of John the Baptist was given to Antonio Pollaiuolo (page 78, below), while Andrea del Verrocchio executed the Beheading of John the Baptist (page 83). A comparsion of the reliefs by Cennini and Verrocchio immediately reveals the immense differences in style and temperament between the two artists. Cennini (born 1415) clearly echoes his stylistic origins in the workshop of Ghiberti, although his figures lack the calm harmony of Ghiberti's; they are formed more as individuals and Cennini has not achieved a unified composition inspite of his use of perspective. Perhaps he followed Verrocchio (about 1435–1488) here; but Verrocchio's forceful organization of the scene on a steep sloping stage and his powerful characterization of the individual, crudely contrasting figures, achieves a quite different and very dramatic effect. The carefully modelled nude figure of the executioner seen from the rear in the centre of the scene and the different attitudes of the warriors and accompanying figures, some of them rather mannered, are almost didactic examples of the sculptural powers of the master. At the same time, the goldsmith's talent for precise detail is apparent in the armour and the ornamental decoration. The monumental concept of the figures, who seem to burst out of the small format of the relief scene, recalls the great bronze casts of Verrocchio. The clear contours of these casts were largely a result of the hand of the goldsmith who chased the surface. The relief of the Beheading of John the Baptist is the only surviving work in silver by Verrocchio, who mainly concentrated on large-scale sculpture and painting.

We know of one other work in silver by the master of the last relief on the silver altar of the baptistry. Antonio Pollaiuolo (1433–98) also executed the reliquary of the cross in the baptistry (now also in the museum of the cathedral), but it was changed in later times, making the animated, crowded scene of the Birth of John the Baptist particularly important to the reader. The assurance of the master is clearly evident in the modelling of the standing, walking, kneeling and reclining figures in antique draperies and elegant attitudes, who fill the lying-in chamber of a Florentine citizen's house.

The figures and style of the relief are, as we have seen, closely related to sculpture. In the various phases of the early Renaissance this style reflects the masters' preoccupation with Antique models and their attempts at naturalism. If we look at small-scale church plate from Florence, Siena, Bologna and Milan we may note that Gothic traditions continued to exert prolonged influence. This also applied to enamel work. Even smaller church instruments aimed at the strong colour effects of enamel, which enhances the glow of the silver altars in Florence and Pistoia. Quite often enamel is the major decorative ornament, on chalices for instance. The form of Gothic liturgical instruments also seems to have exerted a prolonged influence. There were no Antique models for the goldsmiths to adopt or convert here. They did not begin to study Roman stone decoration until the late fifteenth century. The precious small ciborium in the Kunstgewerbemuseum in Berlin, only 21 cm high and created in about 1500, was perhaps based on an Antique vase, with its precise structure and sparse ornamentation (page 86). Other liturgical instruments, by constrast, like the reliquary of St Jerome in Florence (page 84), dated 1487, already expressed the typical architectural forms of the early Renaissance, but the basic Gothic structure remains unmistakable. Smaller reliquary caskets took on the form of sarcophagi and the precious enamelled paxes have architectural motifs.

For many of his works, especially silver book covers, the artist used *niello*, a technique known since earliest times. The art of *niello* – a design incised into the ground and filled with a fused black mass of lead, silver, sulphur and copper – was particularly popular in the fifteenth century. It fell out of use in the course of the sixteenth century. The Florentine book cover now in Cleveland (page 85) is a very good example of the adoption of the Early Renaissance style for ornament and figurative scenes.

Enamel and *niello* are but two of the important techniques known to Italian goldsmiths in the fifteenth century. Their field of activity also touched upon another hitherto unmentioned craft, that of the stone cutter. Here we must begin by noting the Antique gems, whose reliefs became an important source of inspiration to Renaissance artists. These cut stones were often mounted in precious gold or silver settings. The fifteenth century artists who cut stones 'all' antica' – often to give the illusion of antiquity – presumably included goldsmiths. Another new facet of the goldsmiths' work was to cut and set hard, colourful, semi-precious stones, such as amethyst, sardonyx and jasper, in smooth or facetted vessels. The treasure of the Medici in the Pitti Palace in Florence includes some Antique vessels in magnificent gold and silver settings. The early agate and amethyst dishes and vases and sardonyx chalices of Lorenzo di' Medici (also called the Magnificent) give an impression of extraordinary magnificence and value. But it was the sixteenth century artists, particularly the Mannerists, who used these stones to create an extremely bold and fantastic variety of elegant vessels.

Cut rock crystal also forms an important part of stonecutting work, which was mainly executed by the goldsmiths. Valerio Belli from Vicenza (about 1468–1546), who gained great fame in his lifetime, led this art to its highpoint. He worked from designs by other masters or from Antique gems and coins, and rarely executed original works. His masterpiece is a plain, framed casket with twenty rock crystal panels of scenes from the Life of Christ. It was created in about 1530–32 for Pope Clement VII and today it is in the Pitti Palace in Florence. The great altar cross and the two candlesticks in the Victoria and Albert Museum in London (page 81) are presumably early works by Valerio Belli. In structure and details – such as the trefoil forms of the rock crystal cross – they clearly echo the fifteenth century.

The works of another northern Italian artist, Giovanni Bernardi da Castelbolognese (1496–1553), who was a goldsmith, made medallions and vied with Valerio Belli as a stone and crystal cutter, reflect the transition to Mannerism. He began work on the Cassetta Farnese, a magnificent shrine (now in the Museo Nazionale in Naples) in 1543 for Cardinal Alessandro Farnese. The rich figurative and ornamental gold frame clearly shows the influence of Michelangelo, while some of the six large oval cut crystals suggest Antique stones. The crowded figurative scenes are based on mythological, historical and allegorical themes.

Germany. The few surviving pieces of Italian gold and silver work can scarcely give us an idea of the extent of production in the fifteenth and sixteenth century. But from about 1500 onwards, perhaps inspired by the many-sided activity of a number of important artists in different fields which led to a fragmentation of creative forces, works by foreign artists came to be more and more in demand in Italy too. Today we still find German works in Italian collections and church treasures, for example, in the Santo in Padua. Records from the sixteenth century tell us of the considerable activity of German goldsmiths in Italy. No doubt at first this was simply due to influences flowing back again, particularly in the north, but after the end of the fifteenth century the surplus of creative powers in German gold and silver work became so great that it was no particular loss to Germany that some of its artists worked abroad.

We can trace developments in Germany since the fifteenth century very well, especially in the main centres, because of the wealth of surviving material. But very few pieces survive from the equally extensive production of workshops in Paris, Antwerp, Ghent and Bruges. Yet these few works show the excellence and high standard achieved in these towns, some of which had been art centres since the Middle Ages.

The transition from Late Gothic to Early Renaissance first took place in the German towns of Augsburg and Nuremberg. Gold and silver work did not lag behind this development. We already find secular gold and silver plate in the mid-fifteenth century and gold and silver work soon assumed a major rank among the crafts.

We may start our survey of German gold and silver work in the sixteenth century with Nuremberg, which was the indubitable leader in this field also until the beginning of the seventeenth century. The wealth of surviving sixteenth century Nuremberg silver plate would seem to suggest that less was destroyed here in comparison with other towns. To a degree this is true. The Nuremberg goldsmiths were patronized by the patrician families and particularly by German and foreign nobles, into whose treasuries the best works naturally flowed. These treasuries and the museums of art into which some were later converted, headed by the silver vault at the Kremlin in Moscow, then the museums in Berlin, Dresden, Cassel, Munich, Nuremberg, Vienna, London, Paris, Florence and a number of others, still house the richest sixteenth century treasures from Nuremberg. In the years between Late Gothic and Early Baroque, around 1620, more than five hundred goldsmiths were active in Nuremberg. Today we can attribute very few pieces to specific masters, so we must assume that the decimation of what once existed was no less here than at Augsburg, Ulm and other towns.

In the early sixteenth century Nuremberg gold and silver plate still reflected late Gothic forms, although they were frequently enlivened by individual Renaissance motifs, such as were adopted and then converted by artists who had travelled to Italy like Dürer or Holbein the Younger. The large extent of the output is particularly evident in goblets and cups, whose development can be followed almost without interruption. In reaction to the tall implements and vessels of late Gothic, the forms now became much squatter, while the stress on verticals increasingly gave way to a balance in which horizontals predominate. The period between 1510 and 1525 brought a number of transitional variants in the Form of the cup; between 1525 and 1535 a low, broad form developed, and sometimes the vessel was even formed as a double cup with a spreading foot and even broader bowl on a very narrow shaft; although inspired by Italy, this was a purely German creation (page 92). In the 1540s we again find slender, tall cups; they became even taller towards the end of the century and the decoration became more and more exuberant and luxuriant, until the late Gothic tankard was revived in the retrospective phase around 1600.

The art of Albrecht Dürer influenced the work of the silversmiths in Nuremberg and beyond its limits, as it did all other art forms. Dürer himself was the son of a goldsmith and a goldsmith's apprentice in his early years, and he never abandoned this branch of art. He made a number of designs for cups, some in the shape of apples or pears (page 90 and 91) which were executed according to his instructions by the leading master of this period, Ludwig Krug (about 1488–1532). The gnarled branch that forms the stem connecting the round foot, decorated with foliage, with the apple, still echoes late Gothic forms, but the independent form of the fruit shows the emergence of a new trend. A desire for quiet balance is noticeable in the pear-shaped cup where the swelling forms of the fruit are constricted by the careful overall structuring and tautness of form. Dürer also evolved the form of a low cup with broad bowl and spreading foot; the most typical examples are entirely devoided of figurative decoration on the pedestal or lid. An example of this style is the Pfinzing cup (page 100) which was probably made by Melchior Baier the Elder (master 1525, died 1577). The outstanding enamel work on this piece elevates it far above the average work of this kind.

At the beginning of the sixteenth century a great number of painters and copper engravers besides Dürer – such as Albrecht Altdorfer, Hans Holbein the Younger, Heinrich Aldegrever, Hans Brosamer and many of the so-called lesser masters – made engravings and designs for vessels and other objects. Presumably only some of them were intended as actual models for the goldsmith, but as documents of a well-developed artistic imagination they make it clear how great the general readiness was to discuss and develop the new forms of the Renaissance.

The forms of the vessels, the pictorial decoration and the numerous little figures on them prove that the goldsmith was also a small-format sculptor; in addition he had to master the art of drawing. In the fifteenth century the engraved designs on Gothic works already show a vivid pictorial and ornamental intentiveness, from which the technique of copper engraving developed in German goldsmiths' workshops. Peter Flötner (about 1493–1546), although not a goldsmith himself, created a number of designs for ornaments and vessels and designed plastic models for the formal repertory of the gold-smiths thanks to the many facets of his talent. But from the mid-sixteenth century onwards, most of the ornamental pattern sheets and designs were made in the workshops themselves. We may note in particular Matthias Zündt and Jonas Silber, both pupils of Wenzel Jamnitzer, who achieved masterpieces in this field. Other masters of ornamental engraving, such as Virgil Solis and Jost Amman, based their designs on existing works of gold or silver, which they occasionally adapted and elaborated without actually being goldsmiths themselves. Hand in hand with the adoption of newly-developed ornamental motifs, such as the moresque, the grotesque and the scroll which had infiltrated from Italy and the Netherlands but which Germany made its own, we find artists creating almost canonical forms. Once again this is most evident in the form of the cup. In order to establish a definite criterion for the master's examination, the Nuremberg guild of gold-smiths required every master to excute a silver 'Agley cup' after a fixed model, besides two other works, from 1531–35 on – no doubt because of the need to achieve a certain uniformity among the various forms of this vessel that had evolved. Of these Agley cups – that is bossed, lidded cups in the form of a hare-bell – a number survived until they were auctioned in Nurem-berg Town Hall in 1868. Today we know of no more than two dozen. Such regulations as these, which Nuremberg was to observe for a long time to come, are also found in other German towns on the same lines as Nuremberg. Other Nuremberg rules for goldsmiths' work, such as the stamp with the master's mark that was required from 1541 on (together with the city arms), became models for other companies of goldsmiths, such as the one in Breslau – more proof of the leading role Nuremberg played in the sixteenth century. But the regulations of the guilds of craftsmen were not only strict in Nuremberg. In Augsburg, craftsmen who wanted to become masters had to spend a certain number of years as apprentices and journeymen. For instance Christoph Wie-ditz (about 1500–1559 ?), who worked as a medallion maker, sculptor and goldsmith, and had travelled extensively, had to obtain an especial privilege from the Emperor Charles V to be allowed to work in gold and silver under dispensation of the years as apprentice and journeyman. He replied to the difficulties which the Augsburg guild of goldsmiths still put in his way with the proud words: 'Then I will never let this freedom and dispensation be taken away from me, for I have made masterpieces enough, thank God'. Only one of his works in gold, an ornamental dagger signed in full with his name, is intact. But his other works (mainly portrait medallions) give us an idea of his autonomous personality; he was an independent spirit, fully aware of his own powers in a way usually only found in Italy at this time. Indeed, the flowering of the goldsmiths' craft in the sixteenth century brought with it the social rise of the goldsmiths, although they could seldom avoid regulations such as that which forbade the workshop to employ more than two or three assistants. But in Nuremberg we can see how the most reputable goldsmiths became eligible to become councillors and sometimes even obtained the important office of freeman. In the same way the circle of noble patrons they met and the intercourse with princes must have raised the standing of the leading masters.

The main clients were the merchant patricians, the towns themselves and their guilds, and secular fraternities, such as the so-called 'Company of Blackheads' in Riga. The emperor and the princes presumably commissioned the most extensive works, but in terms of numers it seems that members of the rising bourgeoisie were the main customers. But ecclesiastical work diminished considerably. The spread of the Reformation meant that few and simple liturgical instruments were made in protestant countries. At the beginning of the century Cardinal Albrecht of Brandenburg, the mighty Renaissance prince and keen promotor of new art forms, had given numerous orders for reliquaries, monstrances and large paxes for his reliquary treasure, the 'Halle Relics', choosing the most important artists – including the leading Nuremberg masters of the early Renaissance – with a sure instinct. Little of this rich treasure has survived, but the 'Halle Book of Relics', an inventory illustrated with a number of very faithful copies (now in Aschaffenburg) gives some idea of the most outstanding and precious works.

Melchior Baier the Elder, mentioned earlier, created an important sacred work, the silver altar in the chapel of Jagellone in Cracow of 1538; it was commissioned by the king of Poland. The chronicler of Nuremberg artists, Johann Neudörffer, gives us interesting details on the origins of the twelve figurative reliefs on this work in his biography of Baier (1546): 'This Bayr is famous for his chasing, his engraving and large works in silver; he made the king of Poland a solid silver altar-panel, that weighed CCXII Marks; and for this panel Peter Flötner made the design and the figures in wood, while Pangraz Labenwolff cast these same wooden designs in bronze; the silver panels were sunk and chased into these bronze plates'. This division of labour was not unusual for the time. A master such as Wenzel Jamnitzer sometimes used designs or plaques, as we now call these casts, by Peter Flötner although he made models himself and transmitted them to other workshops.

The cup, the favourite form of drinking vessel in this century, presumably originated in the Communion chalice. Its secularization dates from Gothic times. The former custom of offering a greeting or farewell drink in the town halls and guilds was presumably based on a sense of religious community. So we quite often find chased reliefs or engravings of scenes from the Life of Christ on vessels of an entirely secular nature. Conversely, we also find mythological figures and fabulous beings from Antiquity decorating church plate.

We learn of the use of the silver cup and its origins from one of the most important and extensive hoards of German silver, the Lüneburg municipal silver. In 1610 this hoard still consisted of over two hundred and fifty pieces of silver. Thirty-three of them, presumably the most valuable ones, have survived. Since 1874 they have been in the Kunstgewerbemuseum in Berlin. Most of them were actually made in Lüneburg, and they give us a general idea of artistic developments in a medium-sized city from Gothic times until about 1600, and indicate what must have once existed in centres of gold and silver work such as Lübeck, Hamburg, Frankfurt and Cologne. For instance the 'Schoss' cup – a calyx shape with Gothic bosses and engraved Renaissance foliage – made by Heinrich Grabow in Lüneburg in 1522 was used to offer a drink to the citizens who paid their annual income tax (Schoss). The medallion cup with the head of Janus (page 93), in the proportions of the early Renaissance, is a commemorative gift in honour of the patron, like a number of other cups in the municipal silver vault in Lüneburg. The motif of the head of Janus recalls the need for forethought and prudence, as explained by a Latin and a German inscription. The master, Joachim Gripeswoldt, who made the cup in 1536, also made other pieces of the municipal silver, such as the great lion jug of 1540.

The individual guilds and corporations of craftsmen in the towns quite often ordered guild cups with connections to their particular craft. For instance the cup of the guild of seamstresses in Nuremberg was in the shape of a thimble; Elias Lencker executed it in 1580. Examples of this occur in almost all the German towns from Königsberg to Basel and from Danzig to Salzburg.

Another favourite was vessels in the form of animals. Nearly a hundred examples of silver owl cups are preserved from many German-speaking areas (page 96). At times they served as prizes of honour for the companies of marksmen. This is still not the most extensive group of animal cups. The late sixteenth century and later times loved cups made of valuable natural materials set in silver, such as coconut cups, ostrich-egg cups and cups of precious minerals set in silver. A much-quoted later writer, who censured the luxury and drinking habits of this age, gave a critical survey of the variety of cups: 'Nowadays the worldlings and drinking heroes drink from ships, windmills, lanterns, bagpipes, boxes, horns, crosspikes, wine carts, grapes, apples, pears, cocks, monkeys, peacocks, monks, nuns, farmers, bears, lions, deer, horses, ostriches, screech-owls, swans, pigs, elks' feet and other unusual drinking vessels invented by the devil, to the great displeasure of God in heaven'.

The goldsmiths did not only have to satisfy a demand for luxury goods, but also the growing desire for ornaments. A number of portrait paintings show the surprising variety of precious trinkets. The figurative pendants of pearls and enamelled gold, of which a particularly large number survive from the second half of the sixteenth century, display an amazing variety of very

Purse-shaped reliquary. Gold plate and parcel gilt silver over a wooden core with precious stones, pearls, cloisonné enamel and glass. Alemannic (?), third quarter of eight century; height 16 cm. Kunstgewerbemuseum, Berlin

Altar frontal so-called Basel Antependium. Embossed gold plate over a wooden core. Dedicated by Emperor Henry II and Empress Kunigunde to the Basel Minster, possibly on its consecration on 11 October 1019. Reichenau (?), early eleventh century. Height 120 cm, width 177.5 cm. Musée de Cluny, Paris

Left page: Cover of a Gospel Book showing the four symbols of the Evangelists. Gold, copper gilt, enamel, set with precious stones and pearls. Attributed to Roger von Helmarshausen, Helmarshausen *c.* 1100. Height 32.7 cm. Cathedral Treasury, Trier

63

Reliquary of St Oswald. The domed structure nielloed and parcel gilt silver over a wooden core. Circle of Henry the Lion, Brunswick or England, c. 1170. Head probably second half of fourteenth century. The rings of the crown c. 1000 and first half of twelth century. Height (without crown) 44 cm. Cathedral Treasury, Hildesheim

The Prophet Jeremiah, from the left side wall of the Shrine of the Three Kings. Embossed and silver gilt. Parts of the shrine copper gilt, champlevé and cloisonné enamel, brown varnish, precious stones and pearls. Nicolas de Verdun. Cologne, 1181–91. Cathedral, Cologne

Left: Reliquary and rock crystal receptacle. Parcel gilt. France, first third of thirteenth century. Height 28.5 cm. St-Michel des Lions, Limoges. *Right:* Groin reliquary. Parcel gilt and niello, encrusted with precious stones and pearls. Hugo von Oignies, 1238. Height 50.5 cm. Treasury of the monastery of Soeurs de Notre-Dame, Namur

Facing page: Reliquary shrine of St Gertrude, gilt. Nivelles 1272—98. Destroyed in the last war except from for fragments. Collegiate church of St Gertrude, Nivelles

Communion chalice. Gilt, the figures of the twelve Apostles niello. Made for the Black Forest monastery of St Trudpert. Northern Rhein, *c.* 1230. Metropolitan Museum of Art, New York

Enthroned Virgin, Gilt. Westphalia or Brunswick, midthirteenth century; height 40 cm. Cathedral Treasury, Minden

Monstrance of the Imperial
couple, gilt with translucent
émail de basse taille. Statuettes of the canonized pair,
Henry II and Kunigunde,
on the flying buttresses.
Basel, after 1347; height
67 cm. Historisches Museum,
Basel

Above: Drinking bowl of Countess Elisabeth von Rapperswyl. Gilt, the arms of the Rapperswyl on the base of the bowl. Switzerland, *c.* 1300. Length 20.8 cm. Kunsthistorisches Museum, Vienna. *Left:* Covered bowl, so-called Studley Bowl. Gilt. An engraved alphabet runs round the cover and walls. England, late fourteenth century; height 14 cm. Victoria and Albert Museum, London. *Right:* Double bowl. Switzerland fourteenth century; Historisches Museum, Basel

Jug. Gilt, with scenes from a contemporary novel and sports in translucent enamel. Paris, c. 1335. Nationalmuseum, Copenhagen

Table fountain. Gilt with translucent enamel. Burgundy, late fourteenth century; height
32 cm. The Cleveland Museum of Art

Pouring jug, the 'Katzenelnbogische Willkomm'. Gilt. From the collection of Count Philipp von Katzenelnbogen, Middle Rhine, before 1453; height 40.5 cm. Staatliche Kunstsammlung, Kassel

The Oldenburg Horn. Gilt. Music makers and arms bearers in the architectural elements. Southern Saxony, c. 1470. Presumably from the collection of Christian I, the first Danish king, from the Oldenburg house. Height 33 cm. Rosenborg Castle, Copenhagen

Reliquary with statuette of St George. Parcel gilt and encrusted with precious stones. Bernt Notke, Lübeck, *c.* 1480; height 46 cm. Museum für Kunst und Gewerbe, Hamburg

The Hallwyl Reliquary. Shrine silver gilt, crucifixion group gold. The arms of Rudolf of Hallwyl and his second wife Ursula at the top of the cross. Strasbourg, by a successor of Niclaus Gerhard of Leyden, before 1470; height 42 cm. Historisches Museum, Basel

Left: Virgin and Child. Parcel gilt. France, late fifteenth century; height 35 cm. Notre-Dame de l'Epine, Evron

Right: Crucifix. Parcel gilt. South-western France (Toulouse?), mid-fifteenth century; height 17.3 cm. Museum für Kunst und Gewerbe, Hamburg

Clasp for a cope. Parcel gilt, formerly partly enamelled and painted. Reinecke vam Dressche, Minden i. W., 1487; diameter 14 cm. Kunstgewerbemuseum, Berlin

Standing dish. Parcel gilt. Probably south German, c. 1500; height 22 cm. Schweizerisches
Landesmuseum, Zurich

Centre of the silver altar frontal of the Baptistery of Florence with a figure of St John the Baptist. Figure by Michelozzo, 1452; tabernacle by Cristofano di Paolo, 1390. Museum of the Baptistery, Florence

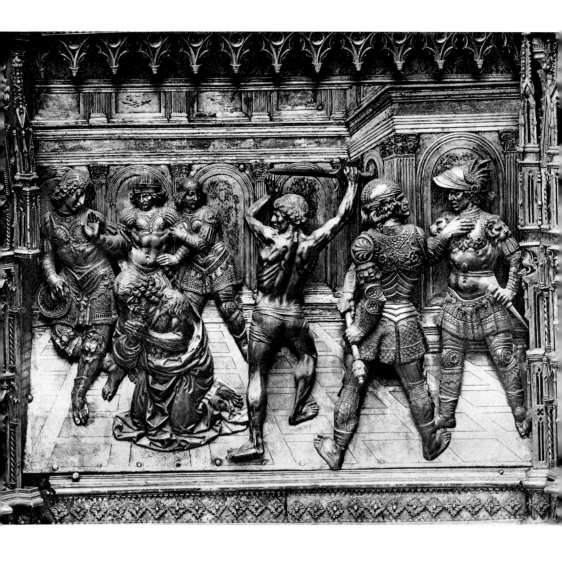

The Beheading of St John the Baptist from the right wing of the altar of St John in the
Florence Baptistery by Andrea del Verrocchio. Baptistery Museum, Florence

Left: Left wing of the silver altar in the Baptistery of Florence of 1480 showing the Visit-
ation of the Virgin *(above)* by Bernardo Ceninni and the Birth of St John the Baptist by
Antonio Pollaiuolo. The architectural frame by Antonio di Salvi and Francesco di Giovanni.
Baptistery Museum, Florence

Reliquary of St Jerome; Partly enamelled. Florence, 1487. Baptistery Museum, Florence

Right: Book cover showing the Annunciation to the Virgin, the Nativity and the Adoration of the Child. Silver and niello. Florence, *c.* 1467—9. The Cleveland Museum of Art

Ciborium. Parcel gilt. Italy *c.* 1500. Kunstgewerbemuseum, Köpenick Palace

Altar decoration. Gilt with enamel foliage work. The cut rock crystal plaques by Valerio Belli from Vicenza, probably also the gold work, *c.* 1510–15. Height of the cross 82 cm. Victoria and Albert Museum, London

Crook of a bishop's staff with a half-figure of St Lawrence. Dedicated to the Basilica di San Lorenzo, Florence, by Pope Leo X in 1520. Probably Roman. San Lorenzo, Florence

Covered dish. Rock crystal, fourteenth century; setting c. 1540 after a design by Hans Holbein the Younger. Treasury of the Residenz, Munich

Cup in the form of an apple. Gilt. Ludwig Krug after a design by Dürer. Nuremberg, c. 1520; height 21.5 cm. Germanisches Nationalmuseum, Nuremberg

Left: Cup. gilt. Ludwig Krug after Dürer. Nuremberg, soon after 1526; height 32 cm. Kunsthistorisches Museum, Vienna. *Right:* Communion chalice. Gilt. Master AK, Prague 1575; height 24 cm. Kunstgewerbemuseum, Berlin

Double cup. Gilt. South German, *c.* 1530–40; total height 33 cm. Kunsthistorisches Museum, Vienna

Coin cup from the Lüneburg municipal silver. Parcel gilt. Joachim Gripeswoldt, Lüneburg 1536; height 47 cm. Kunstgewerbemuseum, Berlin

Covered cup. Partly enamelled, with pictures of the seven gods of the day painted on glass. Attributed to Jacob Fröhlich, Nuremberg, third quarter of sixteenth century. Walters Art Gallery, Baltimore

'Willkomm' of the Holzschuher family, so-called Second Holzschuher Cup. Gilt, arms
enamelled. Elias Lencker, Nuremberg 1564–73; height 40 cm. Germanisches Nationalmuseum, Nuremberg

Left: Salt cellar. Unknown master, London, 1563–4; height 15.2 cm. Victoria and Albert Museum, London. *Right:* Drinking vessel in the form of an owl. Parcel gilt. Germany second half of sixteenth century; height 13 cm. Staatliche Kunstsammlungen, Kassel

Font kettle. Parcel gilt. Augsburg, third quarter of sixteenth century; height 12 cm. Cathedral Treasury, Salzburg

Cover of a Missal. Jerome Mamacker, Antwerp 1543; height 38.5 cm. Abbey of Tongerlo

Communion chalice. Gilt. Guillaume Floch, Morlaix, first half of sixteenth century; height 34.5 cm. Church of St Jean-Baptiste, Saint-Jean-du-Doigt (Finistère)

Pfinzing Cup. Gilt with translucent enamel. Dedicated by the three brothers of Provost Melchior Pfinzing of St Sebald to council of Emperor Maximilian. Probably Melchior Bayer under the influence of Peter Flötner, Nuremberg 1536. Germanisches Nationalmuseum, Nuremberg

fanciful images. Finally we also find the goldsmith engaged on scientific and astronomical instruments, such as clocks and astrolabes. Only the goldsmith could achieve the necessary precision for such instruments, and often he was also the assistant inventor and constructor as well.

Spain. Finally we must speak of a country in which the transition to the Renaissance took place within the traditions handed down by the Catholic Church and where the goldsmiths continued to devote themselves to tradi-

Juan d'Arphe, Custodia of Seville Cathedral. After an engraving of 1587

tional liturgical commissions. What has survived is mostly preserved in the large treasuries of the cathedrals and suggests a prolific output. The gold and silver treasures that flowed into Spain from the newly-discovered lands supplied ample material. We find silver monstrances, lectern crosses and chalices. The developments can best be traced in an instrument found only in Spain, the custodia. This is a tower-like tabernacle that houses the monstrance and is only seen during the Corpus Christi processions. The custodia could be an immense height, and its architectural structure has a wealth of decorative figures and reliefs. The chief master of these magnificent tabernacles was the goldsmith family Arphe, whose most important works were scattered throughout the land. The first of the Arphe family, Enrique d'Arphe (Harp), probably came from Cologne. He created custodias, which were still stamped by the late Gothic style, in Sahagun monastery, and in the cathedrals of Córdoba and Toledo. The Toledo custodia, which rises from a hexagonal base to a height of 2.50 metres, with two hundred and sixty statuettes, was made in 1515–24. The work of his son Antonio, who made the custodias in Santiago (1544) and Medina de Rioseco, allows us to retrace the transition to the plateresque style, a hybrid style which immediately precedes the Renaissance style. The most famous member of the family was Juan d'Arphe y Villafane (1535–1603), who also wrote theoretical works; he was already under the influence of the Italian late Renaissance, and its new concepts of proportion determined forms of his architecturally conceived works. This applies particularly to his custodia of 1580–87 for the cathedral of Seville (page 101). This work is made up of four superimposed temples of strictly classical proportions and arrangements of columns.

Mannerism

The body of the vessel is formed of two mother-of-pearl snails split in two and then reassembled (page 125). An eagle, attacking a large snail on an artfully intertwined swarm of small snakes, supports it on outspread wings. Colourful bands of enamel in the form of two dainty cornucopias nestle around the soft curves of the shell, culminating in a fantastic being, half woman, half monster, armless, with matted hairy claws and tufted serpentine tails, surmounting the bulging vessel and forming its neck. Like a caryatid, this being is crowned by a kind of capital, serving as a lid to close the spout, decorated with the head of a child. The handle curves up from her back, ornamented with foliage and lions' heads, and ending in a ring holding the headscarf drawn back on her head.

The vessel is a jug. Wenzel Jamnitzer created it in Nuremberg in about 1570. The material is precious and the execution outstanding; the composition is complex, imaginative and precise. This seems to contradict its practical function. Although it has all the features of a jug its functional attributes are overshadowed by the modelled details and ornament. The whole is, indeed, conceived from the point of view of the detail. The overall form is built up from the individual, apparently unmotivated, plastic details on the generous, elegant curves of the contours. There are no verticals, no horizontals; a multitude of converging, diverging, intertwining 'S' curves determine the structure. The artist has avoided all symmetry; there are no parallels or hidden vertical axes. He has renounced the idea of static repose, of architectural elements; there is no effect of mass or support. Instead the whole is poised in a tense, apparently dangerous balance. This does not apply to the structure alone. The tension of the juxtaposed and counterpoised assorted materials and forms, the contradiction and harmony of the heavy, hard silver with the fragile delicacy of the shell, the shimmering smoothness of the mother-of-pearl and the detailed, small-scale arrangement of the metalwork surfaces, the introduction of natural forms into artifical forms – all this contributes towards the object's greatness. Its variety of forms also explains the variety of possible interpretations of the piece as a whole. Presumably it was conceived as a jug and it can be used as such; but first and foremost it is an autonomous work of art.

It avoided all that had been typical only a few decades earlier: quiet proportions, clear forms and architectural structure. It was not alone in this divergence from the rule. From about 1520 onwards we find a new trend, starting from the achievements of the late Renaissance, overtaking them and even contradicting them. Again the beginnings are to be found in Italy, where the new generation that had grown up had reached the limits of the formal ideas of the late Renaissance. The new, sceptical, highly intellectualized youth no longer found it possible to reconcile the spiritual needs of a period of crisis with the artistic ideals of the Renaissance which ignored the true questions of existence. In no artist was this conflict so profound as in Michelangelo. He stood at the beginning of the new era, and his successors could not free themselves from his overwhelming example until the end of the century. What happened in the decades after 1520 was not so much a re-creation as a reorientation of accepted values, both from an intellectual point of view and in terms of a concept of art that became increasingly more subjective. The young artists recognized the spiritual and formal achievements of the Renaissance and took them as a point of departure, but they opposed its careful order and harmonious forms and demanded freedom of the spirit and independence of rules. This naturally led to an extension of formal media. The two poles between which artistic creation ran its course in this era are cool speculation and almost limitless genius. It is the age of the incipient cult of the genius and of artistic theory. In spite of all the demands for the freedom of the individual in art, no other age produced as many works on the theory of art as Italy in the sixteenth century. The movement in the decades between 1520 and about 1600 is described as Mannerism. It embraced the whole of Europe.

One of the concerns of the Mannerists was decoration. The art of the goldsmith was a very important form of decorative art; it thus became a court art. The passion of the collectors and connoisseurs made the European courts into focal points of artistic creation to an extent never known before.

Benvenuto Cellini. We know a lot about the artistic activity at the courts, about the intervention of the princes in the works of their artists and of their active part in elaborating programmes of culture. But our most vivid picture comes from the autobiography of Benvenuto Cellini, the most important Mannerist goldsmith in Italy. He wrote his memoirs himself, when he was fifty-eight; Goethe later translated them. Often it is tempting to describe the self-assured words of this proud artist as exaggeration; yet this almost invincible self-assurance is characteristic of the time. Otherwise Cellini could not have dared to confess how far his attitude towards the princes depended on their recognition of his art. The prince was considered not so much a master as a potential patron. If his recognition did not reach the required level, Cellini did not hesitate to censure him – even if he was Pope. Cellini saw himself as an artist pure and simple; craftsmanship was a natural part of his artistic talents.

Born in Florence in 1500, he trained as a goldsmith and then travelled to Rome where he remained until 1540 with a few brief interruptions. He visited well-known Roman artists, continued to study, worked for Pope Clement VII and Pope Paul III, and became papal mint master. His life was made up in equal parts of work and fame, arguments, intrigues, assassinations and imprisonments. He spent from 1540–45 at the court of François I in Paris, where he was soon commissioned to do twelve life-size silver statues of Antique gods which were to decorate the table as candlesticks. He only completed Jupiter; like all the silver of his Roman period, it has not survived. All we have is a drawing for Juno, now in the Louvre. In 1543 he executed the golden salt-cellar for the king, which he had designed some years earlier for Ippolito d'Este. This is the only work of gold that can definitely be attributed to Cellini; it is also the earliest and most important piece of Italian gold work, which fully and purely expresses the style of the age, both in its plastic concept and in its design (page 118).

'In order to show how the sea links up with the earth I made two figures ... that sat face to face with intertwined feet, just as the arms of the sea embrace the earth. The sea, in the form of a man, held a richly worked ship, which could hold an ample quantity of salt; I had given the earth a female form, as beautiful and attractive as I could imagine and execute. I had placed a richly decorated temple at their feet on the ground beside them to hold the pepper.' This is how Cellini himself described his *concetto,* whose pedestal is extended by reclining figures, inspired by Michelangelo, of the four times of day and relief busts of the four winds. It did not seem too erudite to this age to incorporate the condiments used at the princely table into a cosmic system with the help of an extensive allegorical theory. In spite of all the joy in minute detail, the sculptured forms rise above the level of applied art into the realm of the monumental. The mastery of the human figure, derived from the experiences of the late Renaissance, reaches an extreme virtuosity: the elongated, cool bodies are subordinated to the ideal of formal and linear beauty to an extent that almost makes them unreal, in accordance with the contemporary view that art should be not the pupil but the mistress of nature. These figures make it unterstandable why Cellini very soon turned to large-format bronze casting. His Perseus in the Loggia dei Lanze, which he cast for Cosimo I. de Medici in 1553-54 after his return to Florence – and which is only one of his monumental sculptures – proves his sculptural powers beyond any doubt.

The conversion or even convulsive transformation of the human figure into an eternal form remained the central concern of Mannerist art, particularly in Italy. This may explain the strong plastic tendencies of Italian silver at the time. Even in the decoration on the sides of the vessels, the human figure dominates all the ornament. Not much has come down to us in the way of pure silver vessels, although we know that a great many existed. Most of the Mannerist vessels that have survived belong to the field of the glyptik. These are vessels of semi-precious cut stones, which are mounted on enamelled gold and shaped as pots, vases and cups. Their inexhaustible formal variety, the beauty of the material and the assurance and quality of the workmanship exert an attraction that well justifies the passion of the age for collecting. We have a number of designs for gold and silver plate, some by the hand of important artists who were not necessarily goldsmiths themselves. This art received lively stimuli from the publication of Antique finds from the excavations which were increasingly undertaken in Rome in the early sixteenth century and aroused further interest. The damaged pieces were restored in the graphic reproductions, usually very freely; very animated human figures – satyrs, tritons, nereids – were added as handles or spouts on the vessels. This naturally meant that their forms were often adapted to the style of the time. The series of Antique vases published in 1543 by Enea Vico seem much more Mannerist in style than Antique. From the point of view of historical truth, this extensive adaptation must be considered as falsification, except that the sense of history that has become an unquestioned part of our intellectual attitude to the present since Romantic times was alien to earlier periods, so we cannot speak of a *falsifying* interpretation. A series of drawings by Francesco Salviati adheres more closely to the *modo antico* than the works of Vico, and was widely published. These drawings exerted an immense influence on the goldsmiths, for whom some of them were intended; but we must not forget that the Antique models were not worked in metal but in marble. Silver was not hoarded in Roman times. Another non-goldsmith who made designs for gold and silver plate, as had already occurred in the Renaissance, was Giulio Romano, the pupil of Raphael. His drawings are often based on a bold design embracing not only the detail but the whole body of the vessel, like his conversion of a dolphin into a decanter. Some of these designs were executed for the Gonzaga family in Mantua, where Giulio Romano was court architect and painter and designed the Palazzo del Te.

The School of Fontainebleau. In 1530 François I called on the Florentine artist Giovanni Battista Rosso, known as Rosso Florentino, and two years later on the Bolognese painter Francesco Primaticcio, who had worked under Giulio Romano on the Palazzo del Te in Mantua, to furnish his palace at Fontainebleau. This step was of enormous importance to the transmission of Italian Mannerism north of the Alps; besides this, the school of Fontainebleau made a decisive contribution to the formulation of a new ornamental style which continued to characterize northern European Mannerism until the early seventeenth century. Rosso designed a sculptural stucco frame for the paintings in the Galerie François I, in the form of scrollwork, together with numerous, sometimes violently agitated, figures, garlands and hanging fruits. Scrollwork consists of flat bands imposed on the wall which detach themselves from it at the ends and unfurl freely into space, thus completing their two-dimensional character by three-dimensional spatial effects. The surprising feature of this ornamental form is that, though brought to the North by Italians, it was only consistently developed in France where it became extremely widespread, while it was scarcely adopted in Italy itself, where the grotesque remained the predominant ornament.

The school of Fontainebleau does not appear to have directly influenced French gold and silver work. The fact that the king fetched Cellini to Paris ten years later confirms this. Cellini himself did not think much of the ability of French goldsmiths as a whole, and preferred to employ Italian and particularly German assistants in his extensive workshop. Here again the French nobility does not appear to have shared the King's predilection for Cellini's art, or for Italian art in general, for Cellini's main customers were Italians who had settled in Paris. So it would be risky to draw any conclusions from the distressingly few works that have survived from sixteenth century France, although we may affirm that they had very little connection with the work of Fontainebleau. The so-called golden Cup of St Michael, of about 1530–40 (now in the Kunsthistorisches Museum in Vienna), which was dedicated by Charles IX to Archduke Ferdinand of Tirol together with Cellini's salt cellar and an onyx vessel set in gold, expresses the Mannerist style in a certain overabundance of decorative ornament rather than in the actual design, whose stress on verticals and horizontals is still typical of the Renaissance. In the same way, the lovely casket dating from the third quarter of the century, with its sparse ornament and sharp but delicate contours reflects a restrained version of Mannerism (page 120); in fact, the elegance and the classicism of the overall effect and detail are marked expressions of the French spirit of the age.

Meanwhile the ornamental engravers had shown themselves receptive to the new stimuli from the school of Fontainebleau. France became the leader in spreading the style to the rest of Europe. Besides Jacques Androuet Ducerceau, who had adopted the style of Fontainebleau in his maturity and was ceaselessly engaged in making engravings for every branch of crafts most other engravers did their main work for goldsmiths, like Etienne Delaune, whose engravings and drawings are particularly pleasing. A series of engravings of table plate, by René Boyvin, are the best expression of the spirit of Fontainebleau: jugs, candlesticks, salt cellars, a table fountain and a container for napkins in the form of a boat, as well as a series of jewellery. Tradition has it that they were engraved by the Flemish artist Léonard Thiry, a colleague of Rosso, who died in Antwerp in 1550.

We do not know when Thiry returned to his native country or what part he took in spreading the Fontainebleau style there. It is possible that he exerted a considerable influence on the leading masters of Flemish Mannerism. Around the mid-century Antwerp was a rich, flourishing harbour town, whose extensive trade relations with all parts of Europe made it easy for Mannerist forms to penetrate abroad. The lively and direct stimuli from Italy and the ornamental style of Fontainebleau became the main sources of inspiration and point of departure for the flourishing art of the goldsmiths in those years of wealthy bourgeoisie.

Ornamental engravings. It was mainly the painters and sculptors who converted the new ideas into an ornamental form of their own in the North in about 1540. They were soon widely known and popularized by engravings. Cornelia Bos, born in Herzogenbosch in 1510, who left for Rome very early on to work as an engraver at the workshop of Marcanton Raimondi, published a series of prints in about 1546 which introduced a new ornamental style in a combination of scrollwork and Raphaelesque grotesques; a very animated crowd of naked satyrs and nymphs is shown frolicking in a three-dimensional framework of scrollwork festooned with bulging fruit. These creatures have little of Italian classicism or French elegance; they are forceful and earthbound, expressing their constant *joie de vivre* in acrobatic games. Even more fantastic and bizarre are the drawings and designs of Cornelis

Floris. He had also been to Rome, where he may have worked with Cornelis Bos. As a sculptor he employed a large workshop; as an architect he was the builder of the town hall in his home town Antwerp. The first of his pattern books was aimed at the goldsmiths, and he took up and elaborated the models of Enea Vico. The designs include twenty jugs and bowls, 'a ghostly confusion, the basic form usually consisting of bent, twisted and sawn-up nautilus and snake bodies; the stems, spouts and handles largely made up of figures who seem to have sprung from a madhouse of Antique beings, like a sneer at all sensible construction, and yet conceived in a unified, self-conscious spirit' (P. Jessen).

A series of preserved nautilus cups is presumably based on these drawings, although they seem much less imaginative (page 117). This appears to be a general rule, as the drawing that transcribes an artistic idea can free itself from all technical and material limitations. Several features of Floris' designs would have been difficult for a goldsmith to realize. Moreover, the artist had to take his client into consideration, and had to restrict himself in terms of the expense of the material and labour if his work was to be sold. Naturally this also affected the artistic form. The costly luxury plate, by contrast, was almost always made on commission, and the goldsmith's design had already been decided to the last detail and fully discussed with the patron. The published engravings served as stimuli and offered the artist an opportunity to adopt certain individual motifs, and to choose freely from the formal repertory they offered. Indeed, no other period has left us as many designs for goldsmiths' works as Mannerism; again many of them are by artists who were not trained and did not themselves work in this medium. The variety of forms and complex structures as well as the frequent inclusion of the human figure, made model designs necessary. Some passages from Cellini's memoirs tell of this goldsmith's talent for original designs. On one occasion when Cellini received a commission from the Pope for an artistic coin, in the presence of the sculptor and pupil of Michelangelo, Baccio Bandinelli, the latter remarked rather scornfully: 'We have to do the drawings for these beautiful works by the goldsmiths'. To which Cellini replied that he did not need his (Bandinelli's) drawing; in fact that he hoped he would soon outdo him with his own drawings and works. The ability of Cellini obviously excelled that of most of the goldsmiths of his time. When he was only fifteen and training at the workshop of the Florentine goldsmith Antonio Sandro, his father arranged with the latter that he should not be paid for his work, as was customary, so that 'with his natural bent for art', he might also draw when he felt like it – which he then did extensively. Later, when he studied and copied the Raphael frescoes in the Villa Farnesina in Rome, the house of the Chigi, Porzia, the sister-in-law of Gismondo Chigi on one occasion asked him wether he was a painter or sculptor. She would not believe that he was a goldsmith, since 'he drew too well' for this. The ability to draw meant, therefore, going beyond mere technical mastery of a craft and creating a work of art. 'The drawing' was a design, the result of a creative sense of form, the transcription of an artistic concept. To train as a goldsmith did not necessarily go beyond the framework of craftsmanship. The rise from craftsman to creative artist was a question of the ambition and personal development of the individual.

The hard Dutch scrollwork on the ornamental engravings, particularly in the form evolved by Floris' pupil Johannes Vredeman de Vries, became very widespread in northern Germany as the 'Floris style', but it was not the only valid ornament any more than the distorted forms of Floris were the only valid ones in the overall structure of ceremonial vessels. Several beautiful ewers and basins preserved in the Louvre and in the British Museum in London, dating from the late 1550s and 1570-71, clearly reveal the influence of Italian forms, based on Antique vases, with their handles and spouts in the form of satyrs or fantastic animals. The sides are entirely covered in chased friezes, mythological scenes or lively processions of tritons, while the ornament is based on the grotesque. The design of these works is as outstanding as the execution.

The reason that so little of the infinitely rich output of the southern Netherlands has survived is because of particularly rigorous melting down in the time around 1794. The aspiring young Flemish artists, whose centre was Antwerp, had come to assume an important part in European Mannerism. But this rapid development was suddenly interrupted by the political situation. Alba's reign of terror forced many of the Flemish to emigrate, particularly between 1567 and 1569. A considerable number of goldsmiths left for England.

Mannerism had never really taken root in England. English gold and silver plate adhered to the Renaissance in form and idea. In the 1530s, Holbein had designed a few pieces for the king which had markedly Mannerist features; but the exclusive court circles for whom he worked seem to have prevented the style from spreading, and Holbein's drawings were never published. It is strange that the many immigrants from the continent still only managed to introduce Mannerism in a moderate form, nor did a specifically English style evolve. Individual pieces of a more pronounced Mannerist type are so close to the style of the continental schools that they can only have been executed by immigrants. For instance, the lovely salt cellar (page 122) with the London assay mark of 1576, must very probably be attributed to a French master because of the elegance of its delicate architectural structure and in particular because the motif of columns rising not from the corners but from the centre of the sides is also found in contemporary French furniture. Since the beginning of the unrest in France, more specifically since St Bartholomew's Night massacre in 1572, many Huguenot goldsmiths lived in England and their influence probably determined the form of this salt cellar.

Wenzel Jamnitzer. No other country has left us such a wealth of gold and silver and signed masterpieces as Germany. The major centres of production lay, as before, in the south, and Nuremberg remained the centre of activity. Although a variety of influences penetrated from Italy and the Netherlands, the Mannerism that evolved here was unmistakably German. The 'naturalistic' tendencies that evolved in late Gothic times, the conversion of architectural elements into vegetable forms and the network of foliage on the bodies of the vessels now became concentrated into a particular style of Mannerist art, the *'style rustique'* or rustic style. The stress on naturalism meant that casting from nature became a legitimate artistic medium. The works of the most important of the sixteenth century German goldsmiths, Wenzel Jamnitzer, expresses this style in its earliest and also most complete form.

Jamnitzer was born in Vienna in 1508. We do not know where he trained or travelled. But in 1534 he settled in Nuremberg, where he remained until his death in 1585. He achieved great recognition, became town councillor and worked as court goldsmith for Emperor Rudolph II, King Ferdinand I and Archduke Ferdinand of Tirol. Like Cellini, he was a past master in the art of freehand drawing and made studies from the Antique; he was also a scholar and wrote manuals on mathematics and physics and constructed an instrument for the study of perspective. His friend, the writing and arithmetic teacher Johann Neudorffer, described the activity of Wenzel and his brother Albrecht, who worked with him: 'They both work in gold and silver, have a great knowledge of perspective and measurement, both cut coats-of-arms and seals in silver, stone and iron. They enamel glass in beautiful colours and have brought etching on silver to a fine art. But the silver moulds they make of little animals, little worms, herbs and snails, with which they decorate the silver vessels, are such as have never been seen before. They have honoured me with a pure silver snail, surrounded by all kinds of moulded little flowers and herbs, and the little leaves and herbs are so subtle and so thin that they would break at a breath. But they do all this to the honour of God alone'.

The casts from nature described here play a very important role in the work of Wenzel Jamnitzer. A number of little snakes, frogs, snails and beetles, flowers, herbs and all kinds of grass copied from nature occur on his work. The artistic aim behind this is most clearly evident in the 'Merkel Centrepiece', which was not a commissioned work. The town council bought it when it was completed in 1549. In 1806 the Nuremberg merchant Johann Wolfgang Merkel saved it from the melting furnace by buying it at an auction of the municipal treasure, and it was subsequently named after him. After a number of intermediate stages it eventually reached Amsterdam, and it is now in the Rijksmuseum (page 124). 'It is a work which shows us all the facets of Jamnitzer's many sided artistic personality. The most varied formal elements occur. His repertory of ornamental motifs is like a grammar of the decorative forms of the period and of his artistic circle. The figure of Mother Earth is a small-scale sculpture which hardly has an equal in the mid-sixteenth century. The influence of contemporary northern Italian art was decisive; one senses something of the spirit of Sansovino' (E. Kris).

The wealth of detail on this masterpiece is inconceivable. The lovely female figure of Mother Earth, of which there is a wooden model in the Kunstgewerbemuseum in Berlin, is shown gazing on a tangle of grass and branches at her feet, in which there are all manner of small insects, a similar arrangement to the upper rim of the bowl. Nothing is left to chance, although the arrangement seems haphazard; strict order and a precise system dominate the small-scale, lively swarm. Here 'the use of the cast from nature corresponded to a clearly circumscribed artistic aim – the legacy of Dürer can be seen in the lively area of turf – to an artistic intention that was closely bound up with the development of German gold work in the sixteenth century' (E. Kris).

But these casts from nature, which Jamnitzer also continually used in other works, and which are particularly dominant on the ewer and basin in the cathedral treasury of Ragusa, cannot be related directly to the development of German gold work since the late Middle Ages. They are a particular feature of Mannerism. Bernard Palissy, the French potter and landscape gardener, and a contemporary of Jamnitzer, often used casts from nature in his ceramic work. They can be related to the garden grottoes of the same period, for example in Castello, in the Boboli Gardens in Florence and in the designs by Palissy. Created artificially, they were intended to resemble natural rocks and were peopled by all kinds of animals. Such naturalism deliberately opposed the 'canon types of Antique architecture'. Even if we can trace its preliminary stages to the preceding century, this naturalism in the sixteenth century emerged as an independent 'Movement'.

The princely art cabinets. This movement coincided with the birth of princely art cabinets and miracle cabinets. With easier access across the great oceans to distant lands, what was alien and remote began to seem attainable and desirable. The passion grew for collecting colourful objects such as ostrich eggs, nautilus shells, coconuts, rare stones, mineral ores and exotic animals and preserving them in the cabinet of miracles. The attraction of the rare and unknown, together with a considerable regard for the occult, made these things into extremely precious possessions, worthy of the most beautiful setting. Mounted in silver gilt, the cabinet pieces were displayed at feasts (pages 111, 117, 119, 125, 128). Whatever seemed rare and beautiful was collected passionately, art and nature were juxtaposed without distinction. No princely court remained untouched by this fashion. The most magnificent collection was that of Archduke Ferdinand II of Tirol, who possessed all that seemed of value at the time. The prototype, however, of the brooding, eccentric collector was Emperor Rudolf II, and his residence in Prague became the reservoir of spiritual and artistic life. The Seychelle nut cup (page 128) shows the value he put on an individual piece and how much care was taken in giving it a worthy artistic setting. 'This nut comes from a palm only found on two islands of the Seychelles in the West Indian Ocean, and was already considered miraculous in the Middle Ages. One of these nuts came into the possession of a Dutch admiral in 1602 as a gift from a Javanese prince, from whom Rudolf bought it for 4000 Gulden. This still did not mean that it was worthy of presentation at court. Only when it was carved with tritons and nereids and mounted in a fantastic figurative and formal silver setting of scalloped tritons, with bands of masks and a sculptural lid of Neptune on a gilt sea-horse was its rarity given the seal of artistic nobility. The final aim of the artist is only apparent when we look at the forms that converge and resound in the colourful triple harmony of gold and silver and dark nut' (Kohlhaussen).

If we look back at the great number of outstanding goldsmiths working at this time – for instance, two more generations of the family of Wenzel and Albrecht Jamnitzer, which reached a new peak with Christoph Jamnitzer, worked in Nuremberg, as did Hanz Petzolt, Jonas Silber and Elias Lencker to name only a few – we must also note a master who worked far from the well-known centres of gold and silver, Anton Eisenhoit, who lived in Warburg in Westphalia and created works worthy of the imperial workshop. He was born in Warburg in 1553–54, went to Rome in about 1580 where he worked as an engraver, returned in 1585 and settled in Warburg again, mainly working for the bishop prince of Paderborn. Unfortunately, little of his work survives, but what is left reveals artistic talent comparable to that of Wenzel Jamnitzer. His style was quite independent of that of the major centres. His works reached a level of artistic excellence that is unique in Westphalia at that time (page 123).

The seventeenth century

Germany. The activity in the workshops of the goldsmiths and silversmiths was at its liveliest and most varied in the towns of the 'Holy Roman Empire of the German Nation' at the beginning of the seventeenth century. Augsburg now equalled Nuremberg as a leading art centre, but the art of the goldsmith in towns such as Breslau, Hamburg, Danzig, Cologne and many others at the same time experienced a great revival. For some time now the princes had not only been commissioning their precious table silver and jewellery from the Nuremberg and Augsburg workshops; at the Saxon court in Dresden, native production gained in extent and importance as the output of the Munich masters had since the days of the art-loving Duke Wilhelm V (who died in 1597). Another artistic centre of the first rank, where a number of German masters received commissions and worked side by side with Italian and Dutch artists, was the court of Emperor Rudolf II (who died in 1612) in Prague. But many of the works for the famous imperial art treasure were still ordered from the famous Nuremberg and Augsburg artists.

We know of a number of masters of gold and silver work who continued to work in the style of the late Renaissance and Mannerism until well into the first decades of the seventeenth century. But some of the masters who began with Mannerism evolved the beginnings of new styles towards 1600 which, for the immediate future at least, were to set the fashion. The new trends included a retrospective tendency, whose most important representative was the Nuremberg master Hans Petzolt (1551–1633). Petzolt turned his back on Renaissance decoration and returned to the form of the Gothic tankard. This return to preceding styles by Hans Petzolt resulted in such new types of vessel such as the cup in the form of grapes or pineapples, whose bowl is formed of a continuous bossed wall. Petzolt supplied at least a dozen of these knobbly drinking vessels in the form of grapes for the silver treasure of Nuremberg in 1610–12. The grape cup supported by a figure of an emperor, now in the Kunstgewerbemuseum in Berlin, is a magnificent example of his work.

The return to Gothic features and to the Dürer period was by no means confined to gold and silver work in about 1600. It was rather a general phenomenon of German art. But at the same time other forces were preparing for the Baroque, which spread from Italy from about 1580 onwards. Besides the Dutch masters whose development will be considered at another point, there were some goldsmiths, particularly among the Germans, who aimed at translating and elaborating the new tendencies that they had encountered during their travels in Italy in their own national language. The early seventeenth century brought the incipient adoption of Italian Baroque, which promised to evolve into a native German style; but the development of gold and silver work in this century eventually took a different course. At the end of the seventeenth century we do not find mature works based on a uniform style but, instead, a renewed dependence on foreign models: French art under Louis XIV. It is not until 1700 that we find the rapid growth of a new forceful and individual movement in German art; at the time of Late

Baroque and Rococo this led to a general and rich flowering of art, to which the goldsmiths made an important contribution.

The first German goldsmith who can be considered a Baroque master, Christoph Jamnitzer (1563–1618), shows the level of development at the beginning of the seventeenth century. By a fitting coincidence the year of his death was also the year of the outbreak of the Thirty Years War, which was to put an end to the first flowering of German Baroque. Christoph Jamnitzer, grandson of the famous Wenzel Jamnitzer, grew up in the tradition of the Nuremberg goldsmiths; he was familiar with all the techniques of silver, and combined experience of life and genius with outstanding craftsmanship. Journeys to Italy, which presumably took him to Rome and Florence and acquainted him with the works and also doubtless the personalities, of Italian artists, exerted a decisive influence on his art. He made the designs for his work himself, and these reveal his mastery. He could, for example, invent and develop a nude figure independently and did not rely on models.

A drawing like the Bacchus in Erlangen (page 115), which was a preliminary sketch for a drinking bowl with figurative handle, shows that he was also one of the leading draughtsmen of his age. As in the case of his two globe cups in Stockholm, his source was Italian sculpture; but he managed to elaborate his model and to stamp it with his own personal style. The figurative decoration on his works is not the only important aspect of his creation. Christoph Jamnitzer also proved himself to be an outstanding ornamental artist. His book of grotesques of 1610, 'invented and engraved' by him, shows him to be a precursor of Jacques Callot. His originality and talent emerge most clearly in the ceremonial plate he executed for Emperor Rudolf II – the bowl and pot now in the Kunsthistorisches Museum of Vienna, both masterpieces, as are the dragon jug in the Grünes Gewölbe in Dresden and the war elephant in the Kunstgewerbemuseum in Berlin. The Vienna 'Triumph Jug', so called because of its relief scenes of the triumph of Time, Truth, Death and Fame, display an almost immeasurable wealth of individual details; the body of the vessel is partitioned up and decorated with reliefs, it is extensively ornamented, with an intricate scalloped handle and grotesque foot; this composition closely approaches Baroque.

Besides developing the ornamental form of the grotesque, Christoph Jamnitzer was also one of the first German artists to make use of cartilage work, and yet he did not exert the same, almost didactic influence on his pupils and contemporaries at Nuremberg as Hans Petzold the Elder had done. The works of a Dresden master, Daniel Kellerthaler (c. 1575–1651), who also came from an important and well-known family of goldsmiths, have very similar forms, which were perhaps due to personal acquaintance with Jamnitzer. There is also evidence of internal stylistic relations between this equally widely travelled Dresden court artist and Jamnitzer in the frequent similarity of some of their compositions, particularly in the way the body of the vessel and the figures and ornaments are set off against the reliefs and in the organization of the whole. Kellerthaler's baptismal font of the Wettiner of 1615 (Schloss Moritzburg near Dresden) and the rosewater fountain of 1629 (Grünes Gewölbe, Dresden), are very reminiscent of Jamnitzer's bowl in Vienna, but the main resemblance is in the sculptural powers they both reveal, which were perhaps the main stimuli to the development of

Christoph Jamnitzer, design for the shaft figure of a drinking bowl. Pen and ink drawing, 1597

German Early Baroque gold and silver plate. Kellerthaler's many-sided talents also recall Jamnitzer; like him he was also a draughtsman and executed jewellery and valuable armour.

We shall discuss a few examples from the great number of towns and masters who gained an important reputation in German gold and silver work at the beginning of the seventeenth century. The town of Leipzig in Saxony experienced a considerable flowering with Elias Geyer (master 1589, died 1634). He made drinking vessels, sometimes grotesque in form but already Baroque in conception, in the shape of ostriches and horses, and chased basins and ewers, most of them executed for the Dresden Kunstkammer (now in the Grünes Gewölbe). In Hamburg, Jacob Mores the Elder (died c. 1610) created the foundations for a far-reaching artistic development and rich output, which was hardly affected by the Thirty Years War. This flowering was stimulated and promoted by the extensive orders to this Hamburg master for silver plate by the courts of Denmark and Sweden. They served the ambassadors of these countries as diplomatic gifts to the Russian Tsar's court; today, although much was sold in the first half of this century, the silver vaults of the Kremlin still give an idea of the ability and output of the Hamburg silversmiths in the seventeenth century. In 1644 King Christian IV of Denmark presented the Russian Tsar with a sweetmeat tree as a centrepiece (page 134); this extremely individual work was made by Dietrich thor Moye. The different parts, i. e. the figures, shells and branches, are still arranged in a very loose order, but the composition already anticipates the solutions of the Baroque although the latter were more unified. In few towns did gold and silver work in the seventeenth century experience such a calm and broad development as in Hamburg, where besides large works, a great number of smaller and more modest works such as table services was made for the middle-class home.

This art took a different course in Cologne because of the political situation. Cologne was the centre of the Counter-Reformation and of the accompanying development and flourishing of the Church. Works such as the Shrine of Engelbert of 1633, made by Conrad Duisberg in 1633 (master c. 1597, died 1643 or 1644), have no equal in wealth or magnitude, and it can count as the most outstanding example.

Augsburg became the leading centre of German gold and silver work in the beginning of the seventeenth century. Although its quality evidently declined in the war years and later, its masters established the roots of the international reputation of Augsburg Baroque gold and silver work in the eighteenth century. Scholars have wanted to attribute the excellence of the Augsburg work to the fact that in 1615 one hundred and eighty five goldsmiths were active in Augsburg as opposed to only one hundred and thirty seven bakers. But we must remember the words of the Augsburg writer Paul von Stetten who introduced the chapter on goldsmiths in his *Kunst-Gewerb- und-Handwerks Geschichte der Reichs-Stadt Augsburg 1779,* with the words: 'Not all goldsmiths are artists. I am far from presenting as artists those who only make ordinary domestic plate, well and skilfully executed but only, so to speak, according to the rule, without excelling by any particular refinement, draughtsmanship or taste. By contrast we cannot deny honour to those who stand out, partly by cast or beaten pictures, vessels, etc., partly by chased work, partly by enamel work, or even hammered work, sometimes with very beautiful gilding, and who have achieved outstanding works in this way'.

The artistic quality of gold and silver was determined by great masters throughout this century. Most of them came from families, such as den Gaap, Gelb, Drentwett, Kilian and Biller, who had worked as goldsmiths for gen-

Nautilus cup. Gilt; the shell with coloured wax and mother-of-pearl inlays. Unknown master, Antwerp, late sixteenth century; height 25 cm. Staatliche Kunstsammlungen, Kassel

117

Salt cellar. Gold, partly enamelled. Benvenuto Cellini. Designed for Ippolito d'Este in 1540,
executed for François I of France in 1543; height 29 cm. Kunsthistorisches Museum, Vienna

Left: Statuette of the Apostle Peter (counterpart to Paul), Parcel gilt. Attributed to Alessandro Vittoria, Venice, *c.* 1560 (?); height 52.5 cm. Museum Boymans — van Beuningen, Rotterdam. *Right:* Altar candlestick (from an altar fitting). Antonio Gentili da Faenza 1581, commissioned by Cardinal Alessandro Farnese for the high altar of St Peter's in Rome. Treasury of St Peter's, Vatican

Casket. Gilt with panels of rock crystal. France, third quarter of sixteenth century; length 30.5 cm. Victoria and Albert Museum, London

Covered cup. Gilt. Unknown master, Antwerp 1545. Emmanuel College, Cambridge

Salt cellar. Gilt. Standing figure of Neptune in the centre of the five-sided rock crystal receptacle. Unknown master, London, 1576. The Worshipful Company of Goldsmiths, London

Right: Cover of a missal showing the Passover feast and allegorical figures. Anton Eisenhoit, Warburg/Westphalia, *c.* 1592; height 35 cm. Wenemar Freiherr von Fürstenberg, Herdringen

VER · VER

ÆSTAS · ÆSTAS

Ceremonial pot. Gilt, partly enamelled, mother-of-pearl snails, Wenzel Jamnitzer, Nuremberg c. 1570; height 32.5 cm. Treasury of the Residenz, Munich

Left: 'Merckel Centrepiece'. Gilt, partly enamelled. Wenzel Jamnitzer, Nuremberg c. 1549; height 100 cm. Rijksmuseum, Amsterdam

Automaton, representing the Triumph of Bacchus. Gilt, partly cold enamel paint. Augsburg, first decade of seventeenth century; height 43 cm. Kunsthistorisches Museum, Vienna

Triton and Nereid. Gilt ornamental vessel. Johannes Lencker, Augsburg *c.* 1600; height
34 cm. Rijksmuseum, Amsterdam

Pot made of carved Seychelle nut in parcel-gilt silver mount. Anton Schweinberger, imperial court workshop, Prague, c. 1600. Kunsthistorisches Museum, Vienna

Standing dish with Apollo and Daphne as shaft. Adam van Vianen, Utrecht, 1620; height 18 cm. Centraal Museum, Utrecht

Basin belonging to the ewer *(facing page)* representing the Bath of Diana, surprised by Actaeon. Paul van Vianen, Prague, 1613; length 32 cm. Rijksmuseum, Amsterdam

Ewer (cf. *facing page*) with relief of Jupiter and Callisto. Paul van Vianen, Prague 1613; height 34 cm. Rijksmuseum, Amsterdam

Dish with rural scenes representing the four seasons. Joannes Lutma, Amsterdam 1651; diameter 35 cm. Hallwylska Museet, Stockholm

Above right: Small basket for baby clothes. Probably Amsterdam 1660, Master GB; length 63.5 cm. *Below:* Dish with relief of Archduke Wilhelm of Habsburg (1614–62). Southern Netherlands c. 1650, attributed to Matthias Melin; height without frame 16.5 cm. Both pieces Rijksmuseum, Amsterdam

'Sweetmeat tree'. Parcel gilt. Dietrich thor Moye, Hamburg 1644; height 53 cm. Gift from Christian IV of Denmark to the Tsar of Russia. Kremlin, Moscow

Left: Agley cup. Gilt. Franz Vischer, Nuremberg mid-seventeenth century; height 78 cm. Museum für Kunst und Kulturgeschichte, Dortmund. *Right:* Drinking vessel in the form of a boat. Gilt with remains of cold work. Esaias zur Linden, Augsburg, first third of seventeenth century; height 33.5 cm. Staatliche Kunstsammlungen, Kassel

135

STAATLICHE KUNSTSAMMLUNGEN

Altar pot. Parcel gilt. Attributed to Markus Jeger, Lübeck 1644; height 37 cm. Heilig-Geist-Hospital, Lübeck

Equestrian statuette of King Gustav Adolf of Sweden. David Lang II, Augsburg c. 1635.
Horse's head detachable. Portrait probably based on the bronze bust by Georg Petel.
Museum für Kunsthandwerk, Frankfurt/Main

Above left: Cup in Roman form. Gilt. Unknown master, Nuremberg *c.* 1680; height 10.1 cm.
Right: Lidded bottle with portraits of Roman emperors. Parcel gilt. Johannes Scheppich (?),
Augsburg 1655—60; height 18.7 cm. Both pieces. Udo and Mania Bey Collection, Sarlhusen.
Below: Covered bowl. Parcel gilt. P. Saller or Paul Hildebrand Sprockhoff, Augsburg
c. 1670—80; height 12 cm. Kunsthandel Ritter, Munich

Tankard with relief of a Bacchanalia inspired by Rubens. Parcel gilt. Probably a replica of a lost original by Georg Petel. Hans Peters, Augsburg *c.* 1660; height 28.7 cm. Udo and Mania Bey Collection, Sarlhusen

Centrepiece. Sebastiano Juvara, Messina *c.* 1670; height 28 cm. Victoria and Albert Museum, London

Jug from a toilet service. Gilt. Nicolas Delaunay (orfèvre du roi), Paris 1697; height 33 cm.
Poitiers Cathedral

Left: Lamp-scissors and stand. Master TB (Thomas Brydon?), London, 1696–7; height of stand 10.8 cm. Victoria and Albert Museum, London. *Above right:* Knife, fork and spoon from a travelling service. Gilt. Master TT, England *c.* 1690; length of spoon 17.8 cm. Victoria and Albert Museum, London. *Below:* Covered cup. John Chartier, England 1699; height 24 cm. Ashmolean Museum, Oxford

Twelve-branched candelabrum of Ebba Brahe. Andreas Wickhardt the Elder, Augsburg mid-seventeenth century; height 140 cm. The leaves added to the branches in 1674. Church of St Nicholas, Stockholm

Baptismal font of the Swedish royal family. Designed by the French sculptor living in Sweden Bernard Rouquet and executed by the Frenchman Jean François Cousinet in Sweden 1696—1707; height 102 cm. Palatine chapel, Stockholm

Silver buffet of Elector Friedrich III of Brandenburg, from the knight's hall of the Berlin Palace. Most of the pieces made by members of the Biller family, Augsburg c. 1698. The major part now in the Kunstgewerbemuseum, Berlin, Schloss Köpenick

Ivory throne of the Danish kings and three lions silver in front. Copenhagen *c*. 1660. In the background two smaller silver guéridons, Hamburg *c*. 1660; the large guéridon in the corner (one of four) Augsburg *c*. 1740. The silver candlesticks on the guéridons Copenhagen *c*. 1730—40. Rosenborg Castle, Copenhagen

Throne and foot stool of Tsarina Anna Ivanovna (1730–40). Nicholas Clausen, London 1731–2; height 178 cm. Hermitage, Leningrad

Figure of Omphalos from the group of Hercules, Omphalos and Aphrodite. Parcel gilt. Christoph Drentwett, Augsburg *c.* 1700; height 28.5 cm. Staatliche Kunstsammlungen, Kassel

erations. Countless technically outstanding masters also mastered all the variety of traditional styles, often only adding fashionable new decorative motifs to the formal types evolved in the sixteenth century. An example is the drinking vessel in the form of a boat (page 129), whose slender proportions and elegance are enhanced by the smooth surfaces and sparse decoration. On the other hand, famous masters not infrequently modelled their works on Italian Renaissance bronzes, for instance for figurative centrepieces. They could either make direct casts or slightly adapt their model, as with the famous Diana Automaten, of which there existed more than twenty copies, by Matthias Wallbaum (died 1632). His work also became a model for lesser Augsburg masters. Johannes Lencker (died 1637) copied an old bronze in his Europa jug showing Europa on the fleeing bull. The magnificent equestrian statuette of Gustav Adolf of Sweden (page 131), some 40 cm high, is based on a group of horsemen made in Innsbruck in 1620. The artist, Daniel Lang (died 1635), tried to translate his bronze model into a work of gold by adding an ornamental pedestal and richly gilt bridle, and by contrasting the silver and the gilt areas, so it is not surprising to find that this statuesque piece is a drinking vessel, the detachable horse's head allows one to fill it or pour the wine.

This use of a small-scale bronze model and the sophisticated differentiation of the surfaces by the contrast of gold and silver recurs again and again until the end of the century. We may assume that Christoph Drentwett (died 1706) based his group of Hercules, Omphalos (page 142) and Aphrodite (now in Kassel), on similar, perhaps Italian' bronzes. Besides works which derive from a foreign model, there are also a number of silver reliefs, some of them large, that must be original works. The masters of the art of the chased silver relief deserve special mention. The most important of them is Johann Andreas Thelot (1655–1734), who continued to work until well into the eighteenth century. A number of large-format reliefs and panels of crowded, figurative, allegorical and battle scenes which he designed and drew himself have survived. His work reveals an assured mastery in the composition of large surfaces and virtuoso treatment of individual figures, together with very delicate gradations of spatial depth and masterly use of the technique of chasing.

The activity of Augsburg goldsmiths in the secular field was immense if one considers the vast number of domestic and ceremonial plate, and the varied requirements of the broad circle of customers. Multi-part table services, tankards (page 133), bowls, goblets, drinking cups, screw-top bottles (page 132, above right) and candlesticks, assume the most varied forms and styles. From the mid-century onwards, the development of what were at first scarcely decorated, purely functional types of vessels led to 'swollen' forms spilling over with acanthus and fruit decoration. The Catholic Church now became an important customer. Communion chalices, ciboria, baptismal fonts and, above all, the magnificent radial monstrances, took on more original forms than secular plate. An example is the monstrance in Salzburg of 1652 by Andreas Wickhardt (who died in 1661), which is already stamped by Baroque pathos, made with the assistance of a painter and a wax embosser. The same master executed the twelve-branched candelabrum in Stockholm (page 137) – an example of the goldsmith undertaking the kind of work that was usually confined to the bronze caster.

The flowering of prestige art and courtly art on the model of the art of Louis XIV became a general phenomenon in the second half of the seventeenth century. This can be traced back on the more simple works and on the large commissions for silver plate by the electors of Saxony and Brandenburg who were aspiring to the throne. This desire for princely prestige is perhaps most splendidly illustrated in the surviving pieces from the Berlin silver buffet, (page 139). King Frederick I of Prussia had it made by Augsburg goldsmiths from the Biller family when he was still Elector of Brandenburg in 1695–98. From about 1703 onwards, this multi-part display plate still stood on consoles on an impressive pyramidal curving pedestal 5 metres high in front of the mirror wall of the knights hall in the Berlin palace. The magnificent decoration of this room, which was the throne room of the Prussian kings, was executed by Andreas Schlüter; it is possible that he also designed the silver buffet.

The great gilt basins, wing-handled kettles, chain bottles, bowls, basins and handled pots were no longer designed as functional objects but for display; together with the throne they were intended as tangible evidence of the wealth and power of the new Prussian Empire. During the rigorous melting down of precious works of silver at the time of Frederick and Napoleon, this prestige value must have played an important part in their preservation. The splendid vessels, whose figurative work was cast in solid silver, are decorated in the style taken over from France with acanthus, rows of pearls and granulation, etc., which renders the squat, dumpy, forms of the pots and kettles even heavier.

Another even more extensive Augsburg work mainly consisting of silver plate, the cabinet of art made in Pommern in 1610–16 (the cabinet itself was destroyed by fire in 1945 but the contents are in the Kunstgewerbemuseum, Berlin), clearly had a different function and shows the different interests of the client; it is a result of chronological differences and the changes that took place during the course of the century. The Pommern art cabinet was a complete work intended to display to its princely owner, Duke Philipp of Pommern, the very varied forms and achievements in art and culture in spendthrift magnificence. Silver table ware and cutlery, little flasks, technical instruments such as clocks and astrolabes, silver playing cards, precious enamelled boxes and playing boards inset with silver were its main contents.

The Netherlands. A glance back to the early seventeenth century will recall the variety of individual trends and styles, which the events of the Thirty Years War seriously impaired in Germany. Except in Augsburg, Germany was to lose its leadership in Europe for a long time to come. In the first half of the century, the goldsmiths of the northern Netherlands took over the primacy.

The high standard of Dutch gold and silver work in the first half of the seventeenth century is best seen in the works of the Van Vianen family of goldsmiths. Paulus van Vianen (about 1570 – about 1630), and Adam van Vianen (about 1569–1627) were the sons of the Utrecht goldsmith Willem van Vianen who died in 1603. After serving his apprenticeship Paulus had visited the German centres of Nuremberg, Augsburg, Salzburg and Munich, which gave him very varied inspirations. His many figurative reliefs reveal the influence of the late Renaissance Nuremberg plaque masters, Hans Jamnitzer and Jonas Silber. In 1609 Paulus made a medal of Hans Petzolt, which suggest that they were personally acquainted. From 1609 to 13 he was goldsmith of honour at the court of Prague.

His brother Adam, who does not appear to have travelled, adopted the cartilaginous style for his silver, and developed it consistently, together with figurative accessories, into a unified style. This is very clear in the drinking bowl in Utrecht (page 123). From a pedestal of rich cartilage work rises Daphne, turning into a laurel tree, pursued by Apollo; this group grows into a scalloped bowl of cartilaginous forms with wide grimaces like a picture-puzzle. The inside of the bowl has a beautiful chased relief of Eros and Apollo with the vanquished python. Another drinking vessel in Amsterdam shows the young Bacchus with putti around the scalloped rim of the bowl; here too the ornamental combines with the figurative to form an elegant unity. Around the mid-century, Adam's son, Christian van Vianen, who also worked in Utrecht as a goldsmith, made a series of ornamental engravings after designs and works by his father.

Contemporaries seem to have valued Paulus' work more highly. Joachim von Sandrart, who only mentions few goldsmiths in his *Teutschen Academie* that appeared in 1675, says of him: 'Paulus had a great passion and love for allegories and histories, whose profound meanings he was very eager to fathom, which is why he then left for Rome where like a bee he drew whatever was the choicest honey of knowledge from the Antique so that, with his hammer alone, he created whole pictures in solid silver, great table plate, lovely handbasins, and also the bath of Diana with a number of naked female figures, animals, and landscapes of perfect decoration, drawing and beauty, so that it is not without cause that he has been honoured and proclaimed a fountainhead of all this art'. The Bath of Diana mentioned here appears on a basin which, with its accompanying ewer, is now in Amsterdam (pages 124 and 125). The cartilage work of Paulus serves even more clearly as the ornamental setting for the relief than in the work of Adam. The forms and contours of Paulus' vessels have a firmer architectural structure, while in Adam van Vianen's works the luxuriant ornament largely dissolves the contours.

Another development of the cartilaginous style is found with Joannes Lutma (1584–1669), a master from Amsterdam, who continued the work of the two Vianen brothers. But his cartilage work shows rigidity of style, as one can see on the dish in Stockholm (page 126); the ornament and the figurative relief crowd closely together and almost anticipate the over-decorated Dutch works of the second half of the seventeenth century (page 127, above).

France. Unlike Germany, where the Thirty Years War interrupted promising development, seventeenth century France experienced an upsurge of political, economic and cultural life which culminated under the absolute rule of Louis XIV (1632–1715, crowned in 1661). Again unlike in Germany, the major forces were concentrated in one centre, and unlike the many larger and smaller domains of the fragmented German nation, the king of France not only disposed of the high nobility of his land, but also surrounded himself with arts and artists in order to glorify his own power and greatness. From the 1680s, however, the steep rise gave way to a sudden economic decline, resulting from the king's ambitious power political plans and the costly wars. The flowering of the arts had given French gold and silver work, which was given to the service of king and court rather than the Church, an importance and influence that affected the whole of Europe. Unlike other art forms, however, the work of the goldsmiths was almost entirely destroyed by the king's edicts of 1689 and 1709, which demanded the surrender and melting down of all objects of precious metal. Louis XIV had all the royal table silver melted down and everyone had to follow his example; even the Church had to make great sacrifices. The silver hoards of earlier times were also affected by these pitiless measures, so that it is hardly possible to gain an idea of previous French output.

Some of the inventories of legacies in the last third of the seventeenth century show the amount of table plate and domestic silver the nobility and even the bourgeoisie must have owned. Fortunately, engravings and designs are preserved which tell us of the precious table plate of the court and of a number of other gold and silver works, otherwise we would have no idea of the appearance and splendour of these works in the Louis XIV style.

The function of displaying the magnificence of the French court determined the character of all the arts, as it did that of the goldsmith's work. These display pieces in their decorative frames – in the form of artfully constructed credences and buffets – had to have a noble 'classical' form, primarily determined by aesthetic principles.

The interior decoration of the palaces was based on an overall plan. The 'Manufacture royale des meubles de la Couronne' (1662), a state concern for the decorative arts specially founded by order of Colbert, and directed by Charles Lebrun (1619–90), also gave a place to goldsmiths. Some goldsmiths were ordered out of their studios to take up residence in the Louvre, such as Mellin, Delaunay and Montarsy, of whose work, however, little survices. Our main information comes from the ornamental engravings of Jean Lemoine (*Livre d'ornements*, 1676), Gédéon Légaré (*Livre de feuilles d'orfèvrerie*) and particularly Jean Bérain (1640–1711), who supplied most designs to the state workshops after the death of Lebrun in 1690. A sheet from one of his books of engravings shows designs for the typical silver plate of the display buffet: tankards, a guéridon and various ornamental and lidded vases (page 155). Their heavy and ornate forms, enhanced by decoration mainly derived from the Antique, are characteristic examples of the Louis XIV style.

An important survival from the late period of this style is the gilt ewer by the court goldsmith Nicolas Delaunay (master 1672, died 1727), now among the silver treasure of the Cathedral of Poitiers (page 135), which was probably once accompanied by a basin. It is less weighty and structural than the designs by Bérain; the varied decoration in several registers seems to rest lightly on the surface of the slender ewer. This stress on the form of the vessel marks the beginning of a new development.

The European influence of the French goldsmiths working in the Louis XIV style was based on the wide circulation of engraved designs, but also on the activities of many French goldsmiths abroad – they left France after the Edict of Nantes in 1685, which abolished religious freedom, or they sought new customers in England and elsewhere after the surrender and melting down of French silver. This is exemplified in outstanding works such as the baptismal font in Stockholm (page 138) and by a smaller silver cup executed by John (Jean) Chartier in London (page 136, below right). The cup shows the influence of the style of the English masters.

The modern history of the decorative arts in England begins with the restoration of Charles II in 1660. The arts and the sciences suddenly burst into flower, among them the art of the silversmith During the previous twenty years, much silver had been melted down to finance a civil war, and with the restoration, prosperity had produced a new volume of demand twice as great. The opening up of the East began to have a broad effect, and produced new social habits, among them the drink called tea. The new style of *Chinoiserie* came into fashion. And about the same time coffee was introduced from the Near East and chocolate, 'that excellent West India drink', from the Americas came into favour. These new social customs required new silver forms, and emphasized the greatest interest of the period, silver for the table. Forks in sets were gradually accepted as something more than a laughable oddity like chopsticks. Porringers and caudle cups became popular. Tankards were produced in great numbers as well as punch bowls and mugs. Other popular objects to satisfy a new luxury were toilet sets, ink-stands, sconces, candlesticks in great numbers, silvered furniture, and fire grates. Forms of decoration ran the gamut – embossing, chasing, engraving and applied devices with the Dutch taste dominant (Charles and his court had spent much of his exile in Holland). During the succeeding reign of William and Mary forms were continued changed only by the application of surface decoration in the French taste following the influx of Huguenot refugees fleeing France after Louis XIV's Revocation of the Edict of Nantes in 1685.

In the American colonies, the seventeenth century was a period of active commercial expansion. The absence of banks presented a security problem and domestic silver objects fashioned from coins brought in by clients provided a combination of utility and a measure of safety when a piece doubly marked with owners' coat-of-arms and a legible marker's name served as identification in case of loss or theft. The earliest American silversmiths in New England, particularly in the Boston area which remained the undisputed centre for two hundred years, worked closely in the English manner since they were either trained in England or had visual models before them in the shape of English silver imported by the more affluent immigrants.

The development of the art of silversmithing at an early date in the American colonies, still largely wilderness, was enhanced by a strict system of apprenticeship brought over from England where it had been mandatory since the thirteenth century. Apprenticeship assured not only a reliable supply of able craftsmen but a continuity of impeccable standards. The young apprentice learned from his master all the steps of the craft, melting of coins, raising of forms, casting, soldering, chasing, engraving and polishing. In Boston as early as 1660 the selectmen passed an ordinance which decreed that no one could open a silver shop until he had reached age of twenty-one and could present evidence of a seven year apprenticeship. Other cities and towns followed suit.

Silversmiths during the period of Boston's domination of the art were men of substance prominent in community life such as justices of the peace, judges, soldiers, surveyors, and even governors. Because of the precious nature of the material, silver was rarely poorly wrought and because of the esteem in which it was held, owners regularly insisted on its being fashioned in the latest London style. In New York (New Amsterdam till 1674) both Dutch settlers and their descendants clung to their rich cultural heritage until well past the

J. Berain jn   3   P. Giffart Sculp

Jean Bérain, goldsmith's models for decorative vessels. After an engraving before 1700

mid-eighteenth century. By 1692 New York was a much richer city than Boston. A polygot centre, its patrons showed an interest in adaptation of European designs, and particularly in richness of pattern and ornamentation, in contrast to New England pieces where simple designs reflected stern Puritan taste. New York silver had an individuality reflecting the taste of luxury-loving prosperous burghers and the lordly 'patroons', lords of manors which covered thousands of acres. Its roster of silversmiths was filled with Dutch and Huguenot names, and their products were by far the most 'European', stylistically, of any executed in the American colonies.

Gold and silver plate remained in the background in seventeenth century Italy, and other art forms seem to have chiefly inspired the goldsmiths' work. A masterpiece of Roman silver, the Communion chalice for Pope Alexander VII, of about 1655 (now in the Kunstgewerbemuseum, Berlin), based on the design of a Roman Baroque master, Pietro da Cortona, plainly reveals the decisive influence exerted by architecture and monumental sculpture. The splendid silver centrepiece by Sebastiano Juvara (page 134) clearly recalls Venetian bronzes of the late sixteenth century in its structure and figurative detail.

The eighteenth century

Silver furniture of the seventeenth and eighteenth centuries. Around the middle of the seventeenth century Ebba Brahe, an old flame of King Gustav Adolf of Sweden, and her husband Marshal Jacob de la Gardie commissioned the ceremonial Baroque candelabrum shown on page 143 from Andreas Wickhardt the Elder of Augsburg. It was 1.4 metres high. On their death in 1674 it came to the church of St Nicholas in Stockholm, where it remained (page 143). Its twelve radiating voluted, intricately interwined arms are arranged in two superimposed circles. At the points where they grow out of the powerful baluster sit nude male and female figures, with strong bodies that reveal southern Dutch influence. Putti frolic at the ends of the branches. The arms of the candelabrum and the baluster are executed in a firm, balanced, auricular style. The Stockholm goldsmith who added the dedicatory inscription in 1674 thought the piece needed modernizing, and added leaves to the arms which slightly impair the clarity of the curving contours. Shortly after, Wickhardt made a second candelabrum in Augsburg, very similar to this one, but of a more advanced style and with an additional circle of arms. In 1663 Queen Hedwig Eleonora gave it to the Riddarsholmskyrka, the burial place of the Swedish kings. A third Augsburg masterpiece of this period also came to Stockholm: the throne made by Abraham I Drentwett, which the son of Ebba Brahe, Magnus Gabriel de la Gardie, one of the greatest men of his time and the favourite of Queen Christine, gave the latter on her coronation in 1650. Since then it has been the throne of the kings of Sweden.

These works were the first of a series of silver furniture and extensive decorative pieces that continued far into the eighteenth century. They combine richness and splendour with their function of princely representation, and their heightened Baroque forms have never been equalled before or since. Today, so much pomp and display may seem rather perverse in a time when war and need reigned over the German and other peoples, during the Thirty Years War and after. Yet one must try to unterstand the attitude of the princes in terms of the spirit of the age; the young French 'Sun King' was living his life before the world, as its centrepoint and his subjects also felt this display to be justified.

Nothing survives of the wealth of silver furniture commissioned by Louis XIV. He himself had it melted down again in order to pay for the Spanish war of succession. But perhaps the lovely baptismal font of the Swedish royal house can tell us something of the style. It was made by two French artists living in Sweden, Bernard Fouquet and Jean-François Cousinet, in about 1700 (page 138). Its generous form with the lovely Hermes figures emanates a calm and yet animated sculptural quality characteristic of the 'classicist' style that began in France in the second half of the seventeenth century.

In Restoration England, silver furniture was a status symbol. Charles II was, after all, the cousin of Louis XIV whose extravagance in that direction set a trend for all the crowned heads of Europe. In the dressing room of the Countess of Arlington, the famous diarist John Evelyn remarked that there were 'silver jars and vases, cabinets, and other such rich furniture as I have seldom seene'; and in the apartments of the Duchess of Portsmouth, *maîtresse en titre* to the King before Nell Gwynne, 'massy pieces of plate, whole tables and stands of incredible value' and 'great vases of wrought plate, tables, stands, chimney furniture, sconces, branches, braseras ect. all of massiv silver, and out of number'. The fact that the silver was in fact usually plated over wood or iron and therefore not solid does not make the list any less impressive. Several mirrors also still exist in England in collections such as Windsor Castle, Ham House and Knole. In 1713, the throne with accompanying footstool for the Tsarina Anna Ivanovna was made in England by the London goldsmith Nicholas Clausen; it is now in the Hermitage in Leningrad (page 141); it has been wrongly described as having been made for the Tsar Peter the Great.

Apart from these secular pieces, gold and silver were still extensively employed, in Italy and other Catholic countries, for ecclesiastical furniture. Shrines, altars, relief decorations depicting scriptural themes, candlesticks, religious statues, engaged a number of silversmiths in Rome in the mid-eighteenth century. The most renowned of these was Luigi Valadier (1726–85) who became official silversmith to the Sacro Palazzo Apostolico, and made the silver table vessels for the Pope, and a complete table service for Prince Borghese in 1784.

Luigi Valadier's father was a French silversmith who had settled in Rome. Luigi was born in Rome, apprenticed to his father and later sent to Paris for further trainig. He eventually controlled a large workshop with a huge output – at one time he had one hundred and eighty assistants. This indicates that, like Matthew Boulton of England with his great factory at Birmingham, industrialisation of an ancient craft was under way. In contrast to Boulton, however, Valadier produced more pieces of a purely decorative nature. Among his most imposing works are the high altar in the Cathedral of Monreale outside Palermo, and the large model of Trajan's column, incorporating a clock, and made with the help of two German assistants, which is now in the Schatzkammer der Residenz, Munich.

The coronation hall of the Danish kings in Rosenborg Palace in Copenhagen houses an extensive series of silver furniture dating from various periods and of varied origins (page 140). It includes the three large rounded sculptural silver lions from the seventeenth century. These singular objects are set up in front of the ivory and gilt coronation throne as watchers, probably in memory of the description in the Bible of the ivory and gilt throne of King Solomon. There, two lions are said to have stood beside the armrests, and another twelve on the steps leading up to the throne.

But silver furniture was not only a royal privilege. Smaller courts also indulged in similar expensive furniture. In Calenberg near Hanover there is a set of furniture with the coat-of-arms of Brunswick-Wolfenbüttel, which was made in Augsburg towards the mid 1720s. It consists of two large mirrors, which may have been made by members of the Gelb family, two tables belonging to Johann Ludwig Biller I or II, four chairs and an armchair belonging to Philipp Jakob Drentwett VI, and four guéridons. As a rule such furniture was made of wood and cased in chased silver. However, Duke Eberhard Ludwig of Württemburg bought his wife a set of solid silver furniture in Augsburg in 1697–8 which, together with a gilt table service cost some 18,000 florins.

A number of other plate belonged to these furnishings, like the many silver fire-dogs. Intimately connected with such works, and a reflection of their final heightened form, is the enormous silver buffet which belonged to Frederick I in Berlin (page 139), which we discussed in the previous chapter.

France. The art of the eighteenth century is a "society art". Although all art reflects a certain class of society, by which it is upheld and which it upholds, this is not only one aspect of French eighteenth century art, but the essence of its creative content. It reached ist most noble and perfect form in the creation we call the 'salon'. This was the highest form of social culture man has ever realized; it was an epicurean culture, but its taste was also unshakeable, even intolerant and of that high tone that combines pride and brilliance. The highest criterion of taste – and of tact – was elegance. Its realm was society. Society evolved highly sophisticated manners, forms of honour and respect, of greeting and of conversation; in fact social life involved very precise demands and obligations – the rules of the game for an extremely refined form of human intercourse.

These principles of social life were embraced in all forms of this world, its public, religious, political, social, domestic and private life, its literary, philosophical, musical, and artistic creations. Everywhere, refinement was set up as the higher sphere of reality, with all the breadth and depth this sphere can contain when it can mould reality to its image' (K. Bauch).

Once or twice a week each lady who had a salon gave a great supper. This was an essential part of social life, informed with the same high tone and culture as everything created by this society. The glow of the table silver and the elegance of its form corresponded to the easy gesture, the bright conversation, the well-lit room with its curved mirrors; it corresponded to the light colours of the painting by Watteau, to the pastel tones of Boucher. For the first time silver was to shine forth in its pure state.

Just as everything France produced in the eighteenth century reflected a refined taste and culture, silver achieved a perfect beauty. Refined table manners and the introduction of new foods and drinks had already led to the creation of new, complex forms of table plate at the end of the previous century; they now reached their full flower. Although the transition from the seventeenth to the eighteenth century was a smooth one at first, the new formal concepts soon asserted themselves. The works became lighter and more elegant, and their elastic, curving contours set them apart from the more compact, earlier pieces. The delicate engravings, related to the spirited small-scale surface ornament of Jean Bérain, and the sparse, flat appliqué work were never overpowering and were always subordinate to clarity of design. These early works have a quality of elegant restraint. But a lovely tureen by Nicolas Basnier, of 1726–7, is decorated with forceful, sculptural ornament that anticipates the development of silver in the decades to come: the restless plasticity of Rococo.

Juste Aurèle Meissonier was the greatest master of Rococo and its most original exponent. He was born in Turin in 1693 and worked in Paris as draughtsman and designer for the king from 1723 until his death in 1750. His designs, which he engraved himself and compiled into a magnificent work, include silver plate, candlesticks, furniture, ornaments, interiors, ceremonial plate and Baroque altars for Gothic choirs. 'In the 1720s he had already mastered all the aspects of the mature Rococo style: its forceful and yet supple plastic accent, the lines surging in every direction, the frames overflowing with curves, the small scalloped work and the sheafs of plants; at first sight a drunken confusion seems to reign but the connoisseur will recognize a wonderful, self-assured kingdom of form. The engravings make it understandable why their all conquering creator was not only adored by the young and the independent, and above all by painters, but why even the architects and academics could not entirely ignore him. Traces of his great inspiration can be found in all the branches of art' (P. Jessen).

Meissonier was a goldsmith, although he did not translate any of his designs into silver himself; others, however, did (page 163). These pots, tureens, cups, tea pots, and candlesticks resemble free-standing sculpture by their forceful modelling. The structures derive from the ornamental form of the shell, which encompasses the whole body of the vessel and fills it with dynamic movement. All symmetry is avoided. Meissonier already used rocaille decoration, which was to become the main ornamental form of Rococo and soon found its way to all parts of Europe and developed into an equally forceful, asymmetrical dynamic form. The shafts of many of the candlesticks consist of a lively animated figure or group of figures, while the lids of the tureens are surmounted by putti and animals. Other artists were very soon to adopt these sculptural tendencies. The entire oeuvre of Thomas Germain, the most important goldsmith of the next period, was determined by them. The wine cooler he made in 1727–8, with its soft diagonals that inform the whole body of the vessel, is a direct successor to the work of Meissonier (page 161). A more modeste piece, such as the teapot in the Louvre (page 163, below), has the same tendencies; the spout is twisted like a rope, the handle is clearly modelled and the lid has a rotating movement.

His father, Pierre Germain, was also 'orfèvre du roi', and in 1725 Thomas became 'orfèvre attiré'. In 1728 he obtained his first large commission, a series of table plate for the royal court of Portugal. When he died in 1748, his son François Thomas continued work on this commission until 1766. Very little of this work by Thomas Germain has survived. Much of it came into the possession of Pedro I of Brazil in 1820 and was sold and melted down owing to an administrative error. One centrepiece from this service can definitely be attributed to him, although it is signed on the base by his son and dated 1757 (page 165). The upper part bears his masters's mark and the Paris year mark 1730–31. Perhaps his son signed the work later or made additions to it. In his works and those of his son, the sculptural form predominates over the functional aspect. And yet the pieces really are table plate. It required a great artist to balance this lively plastic wealth with the form and function of the vessel, so that they mutually determined one another and fused into a unified work of art. François Thomas Germain was also 'sculpteur et orfèvre du roi aux galeries du Louvre,' where he sometimes employed up to eighty assistants. He was flooded with commissions, and yet went bankrupt in about 1765. The works he supplied to the Russian court are preserved in the Hermitage in Leningrad.

Besides the Germain family, a number of other highly talented goldsmiths worked in Paris: Joubert, Regnard, Duguay, Balzac, Bailly and Outrebon, to name but a few. They executed a large number of excellent works. In fact French silver plate in the eighteenth century is generally of very high quality. The wealth of formal and decorative styles can only be appreciated by comparsion of the various pieces. The richly sculptural accent that characterizes the work of the Germain family is even more striking in the work of François Joubert (page 171), Balzac and Bailly, but on the whole it is less well-developed and usually remained restricted to details, such as the handles of jugs. Instead we find clear elegant contours of particular beauty. But on a pot such as the coffee pot by Charles Donze of 1768–9 (page 163) the jagged, broken-up, sculptural body of the vessel and the steep, twisted fluting which avoids all symmetry are still elements which characterized Meissonier's designs at the beginning of this style, although here they are achieved by other means and are less vehement.

Paris was not the only place where the goldsmiths were active. The provinces also had an extensive output of very beautiful works which were by no means slavish copies of Parisian models. On the contrary, particular characteristics and preferences evolved in the respective areas and distinguished them from one another. For instance, a very lush, vegetable ornamental style (page 173) evolved in Toulouse, and gilding was used more at Strasbourg than anywhere else.

Germany. Just as all the countries of Europe adopted the formal repertory of Rococo, goldsmiths came under the influence of France. The goldsmiths of Augsburg, who retained their leadership in this century too, had already adopted the classicism of the Louis XIV style at the end of the seventeenth century, and it still dominated their work after 1700. The new century brought a brief phase marked by strong colourful tendencies, before the artists turned to pure silver. From this era come Augsburg tea services covered with enamel painting, and a series of agate services in silver gilt settings, whose forms and ornaments are closely interrelated. These works are still very close to the spirit of the Baroque art cabinets. A number of other art cabinet pieces appeared in these decades at the court of Augustus the Strong in Dresden, by the hand of the goldsmith and jeweller Johann Melchior Dinglinger. They include the Court of the Grand Mogul, the Bath of Diana, and others. These works combined gold and silver, semi-precious stones, ivory, jewels and enamel in unrivalled splendour. But non-gilt domestic silver soon became the dominant form. In terms of output, it seems that Augsburg was the indubitable leader. In the decades until the middle of the eighteenth century, more than two hundred and fifty masters appear to have worked there almost continuously, and their number only dropped to slightly under two hundred later. But if one considers the number of commissions that were given, including many for large-scale works, it still seems surprising how they could have been undertaken without the quality of the work declining. The fame of Augsburg silverware spread far and wide. 'We would be very silly to praise ourselves: so we much rather refer to the praise of others who know their trade, and to the works of art of goldsmiths ... that have found approbation not only in Europe, but also in other parts of the world whence they were commissioned and sent, and where they were set up and honoured in the palaces of the highest monarchs to their splendour and ornament...' wrote the Augsburg goldsmith Philipp Jacob Jäger the Elder in 1740 in his history of the crafts (after S. Rathke-Köhl). All the German princely courts often gave orders of considerable dimensions to Augsburg. They delivered their commissions via dealers, who were often goldsmiths themselves; the dealer then transmitted them to the Augsburg masters, undertook the delivery and settled the financial question. We shall give a few details to give an idea of the extent of these orders.

The most important commissions came from the Prussian court. In the years between 1730 and 1733 alone, the court was supplied with silver furnishings – including sixty-eight wall candlesticks – and plate to the sum of over 35,597 marks. While the material value came to more than 605,165 florins, the total cost of manufacture was more than double this, about 650,719 thaler. 'After 1733, the Augsburg goldsmiths were hardly ever given commissions by the Prussian court. Frederick the Great only patronized masters from Berlin in order to promote native manufactures ... The enormous sums which this soldier king, well-known for his economy, spent on these luxury articles must be considered primarily as capital investment – which was very useful to his son, Frederick II during the Silesian wars and the Seven Years War. The king seems to have paid little attention to artistic questions.' The relations between the Saxon court and the Augsburg goldsmiths dated back to well into the sixteenth century and were maintained during the eighteenth century too. But this does not mean that Dresden was inactive, as shown by the two outstanding coffee urns made here in 1722. Balthasar Permoser probably designed the figurative ornament (page 159).

The court of Bavaria gave so many commissions to Augsburg that a goldsmith from Munich complained that 'the notable work was being executed outside the land, much to the prejudice of the native citizens'. Evidence is a presentation service made in 1719 for the sum of 20,000 florins, two toilet services for over 5876 florins in 1747, and a table service made in 1751 for 2389 marks.

The most important purchases from Augsburg were commissioned by Duke Eberhard Ludwig (1693–1733) of Württemberg. From the firm of Greiff a solid silver room furnishing and a gilt table service were bought in 1697–8 for the duchess at a price of some 18000 florins, from Matthias Fahrner; at the same time plate, and from Credemann in 1699 furniture and plate. The goldsmith Bartholomäus Seuter supplied silver frames in 1709–10, the firm of Benz and Loschge supplied silver plate in 1717–18. The dealer Johann (Karl?) Gutermann supplied the court with silverware in 1724–45. In 1728, when a large table service was melted down, "models after the most recent fashion were ordered for assay in wood, tin or metal from Augsburg, the designs, however, were ordered in Paris" for a new table service. In 1733 the dealer Creidemann received an order for a service worth 13,774 florins. The main supplier in this period was the silver firm of Rauner, who was paid some 100,000 florins in 1706–12 for goods supplied, and some 200,000 florins in 1712–37. These included the lustres bought in 1736–37, the largest of which cost some 15,000 florins, which dated from the reign of Duke Karl I Alexander (1733–7). In times to come the relations with Augsburg continued uninterrupted as shown by two travelling services owned by Duke Karl II Eugen (1737–93).

Outside the borders of Germany, the main output of Augsburg silverware was in the north and east. The royal courts of Denmark and Sweden had already been supplied since the seventeenth century, and they were joined by the Tsar's court in the eighteenth century. Lively relations were maintained with Poland, Switzerland, and apparently also Italy. France and England with their native, rich high-quality products declined as markets. By contrast, it is said of the Augsburg goldsmiths, in particular those who made fancy goods, that 'Many of them only visited England as a school of art for a short period, and then settled here [in Augsburg] and worked to such credit that their work can be compared to English work'. Besides orders for secular silver, there were also commissions for church plate, and we find this as far as the Rhine province and the Saarland on the one hand, Switzerland on the other. Over and above this, work was also commissioned for the fairs in Frankfurt and Leipzig and by numerous smaller towns that were visited by the dealers in silver (all these details from S. Rathke-Köhl).

We find no outstanding artists in Germany in the eighteenth century – not even in Augsburg, although the general standard of work there remained equally high. Domestic silver ware – bowls, boxes, tureens, tea and coffee pots – is rounded, richly scalloped, supple in contour. S-shaped, curved, soft fluting often runs across the bodies of the vessels in a vertical direction. Chased or engraved foliage and rocaille are the main decoration, unless the walls are left plain. The elegance of the French is lacking in these vessels, yet they have a solid, simple beauty of their own. The sculptural elements are hardly developed. Even the charming Augsburg centrepiece in Frankfurt (page 169) is free of sculpture tendencies; instead the graceful, small scale structure clearly reflects its graphic model.

Church silver, by contrast, is often more plastic, its contours and details more animated, with crowded, intersecting rocailles. The tendency to luxury is unmistakable. Accordingly we find the outstanding sculptures of this century in the religious field, such as the life-size votive figure of Elector Max Joseph of Bavaria by Wilhelm de Groff, which Elector Karl Albert gave to the Holy Chapel of Altötting in 1737 after the recovery of his ten year old son from a serious illness (page 166), or the statuette of St Nepomuk (page 167) made by Ignaz Franzowitz after a model by Ignaz Günther, whose counterpiece is a St Florian. Günther also designed the figures of the Virgin on the monstrances in Munich and Geppersdorf (Bohemia). They are among the most beautiful Rococo sculptures in Bavaria. But one must not forget that these are not really goldsmith's works but sculptures which were transposed into the other material, silver, from the wooden model, in a masterly fashion.

England. Silver plate in eighteenth century England evolved from the work of the Huguenot immigrants. Most of them had come to England from the larger provincial towns of north and west France after the suspension of the Edict of Nantes by Louis XIV in 1685. Here they were given citizenship and permission to work. No doubt it was not always the best masters who left France, yet they had all enjoyed an extremely good training in their craft and their influence was to have a retroactive effect. For one thing, they introduced the Louis XIV style into an England that still lay under Dutch influence; for another, they brought technical practices that were not usual in England. While English vessels were usually chased with very thin walls, the French preferred casting and very thick walls, which rapidly gained popularity among the buyers. The English goldsmiths very soon learned this solid workmanship and it brought England the reputation of outstanding quality during the entire eighteenth century.

During the reigns of Queen Anne and George I (1702–1727), the native English preference for simplicity reasserted itself. In silver, plain squat forms, unobtrusively ornamented in a fashion reminiscent of "Queen Anne" furniture dominated (page 157). The emphasis on silver drinking vessels waned with the rising popularity of glass for general use. Tankards and mugs for drinking ale and beer were still in vogue. But new interest centered around the tea table and more and more on table silver. There was a growing use of teapots, cream jugs, covered sugar bowls, tea caddies, trencher salt cellars and casters as well as silver-handled table and cheese knives and spoons and forks made in sets.

In America, during the "Queen Anne" style of 1715–1750, elaborate embossed forms were replaced by forms whose simplicity of line and graceful shape

Ewer in Gilt. Paul de Lamerie, London 1741; height 37.5 cm. The Worshipful Company of Goldsmiths, London

Tea pot. Johannes van der Lely, Leeuwarden (Friesia) 1714; height 20 cm. Museum Boymans — van Beuningen, Rotterdam

Coffee urn. Gilt. Johann Jacob Irminger, Dresden 1722. The figurative work probably after models by Balthasar Permoser; height 39 cm. Grünes Gewölbe, Dresden

167

Tea urn and réchaud. Charles Kandler, London 1727—37; height 33.6 cm. Victoria and Albert Museum, London

Wine cooler. Thomas Germain, Paris 1727–8; height 22 cm. Musée du Louvre, Paris

Above: Inkstand with bell. Antoine Bailly, Paris 1750—51; length 38.4 cm. Metropolitan Museum of Art, New York, Wentworth Collection. *Below:* Covered dish. Gabriel Tillet, Bordeaux 1724—5; length 30.5 cm. Metropolitan Museum of Art, New York, Wentworth Collection

Above: Coffee pot. Charles Donze, Paris 1768—9; height 20 cm. Metropolitan Museum of Art, New York, Wentworth Collection. *Below:* Tea pot. Gilt. Thomas Germain, Paris 1735—6; height 13.5 cm. Musée du Louvre, Paris. *Right:* Three-branched candelabrum, after a design by Meissonier, Claude Duvivier, Paris 1734—5. Musée des Arts Décoratifs, Paris

Above: Wine cooler. Paul de Lamerie, London 1719; length 96.5 cm. The Minneapolis Institute of Arts, Minnesota. *Below:* Part of a tea service. Gilt with enamel. Unidentified master's mark MB, Augsburg, early eighteenth century; height of tea pot 14.5 cm. Staatliche Kunstsammlungen, Kassel

Above: tureen and stand. François Thomas Germain, Paris 1757; length of stand 58.4 cm. Made together with a large service for King Joseph I of Portugal. *Below:* Centrepiece from the same service. Thomas and François Thomas Germain, Paris 1730 or 1757. Both from the Museu Nacional de Arte Antigua, Lisbon

Votive figure of Elector Max Joseph of Bavaria. Wilhelm de Groff, Munich 1737; height 94 cm. Elector Karl Albrecht gave the 41 lb. votive statuette on the recovery of his son from a serious illness in 1737 to the Holy Chapel of Altötting. Pilgrim's Chapel, Altötting/Obb.

Left: St Nepomuk. Parcel gilt, with two reliquaries (sight glass). Counterpart: St Florian. Ignaz Franzowitz, Munich 1766. After a wooden model by Ignaz Günther; height with base 69 cm. Parish church of St Maria, Niederaschau/Obb. *Right:* Abbess' staff. Silver and copper gilt, encrusted with precious stones; double enamel image of St Benedict and Bernhard. Brother Felix Dreissig, Metten 1741; height of curvature 40 cm. Cistercian abbey of Seligenthal, Landshut

Wermut salver. Gilt with inset porcelain cup (Meissen) and cut glass. Johann Jakob Adam,
Augsburg 1755—7; height 10.5 cm. Kunstgewerbemuseum, Berlin

Centrepiece. Unidentified master's mark LR. Augsburg 1757—9; height 40 cm. Museum für Kunsthandwerk, Frankfurt/Main

Wall candlestick. Unidentified master's mark IGS, Bruchsal *c.* 1760; height 43 cm. Slg. Udo and Mania Bey Collection, Sarlhusen

Left: Egg cup. Unknown master, Paris 1786–7; height 4.4 cm. Metropolitan Museum of Art, New York, Wentworth Collection. *Right:* Condiment box. Pierre Aymé Joubert, Paris 1748–9; length 14.3 cm. Metropolitan Museum of Art, New York, Wentworth Collection. *Below:* Sauce boat. François Joubert, Paris 1754–5; length 21.3 cm. Made for the Marquise de Pompadour. Musée des Arts Décoratifs, Paris

Above: Tea pot. Kilian Kelson, Stockholm 1755; height 18.5 cm. Nationalmuseum, Stockholm. *Below:* Covered dish with plate. Jonas Thomasson Ronander, Stockholm 1766; height 12 cm. Nationalmuseum, Stockholm

Ewer and basin (plan view *above*), Louis Samson, Toulouse 1761–2; length of basin 39.4 cm. Musée des Arts Décoratifs, Paris

Tea urn. Thomas Whipham and Charles Wright, London 1767–8. Lid restored. Height 53.3 cm. Victoria and Albert Museum, London

Above: Cake basket. Matthew Boulton, Birmingham 1788; length 32.4 cm. Assay Office Birmingham. *Below:* Decorative urn. Gilt. William Holmes, London 1776; height 47.6 cm. Walker Art Gallery, Liverpool. *Right:* Chocolate pot. Henry Greenway, London 1777–8; height 32.4 cm. Victoria and Albert Museum, London

Above: Tea pot. Gilt. Andrew Fogelberg and Stephen Gilbert, London 1784–5; height 14.6 cm. Victoria and Albert Museum, London. *Below:* Sauce tureen. Matthew Boulton and J. Fothergill, Birmingham 1776–7; length 15.4 cm. Victoria and Albert Museum, London

Six-branched candelabrum. Gilt. Martin Guillaume Biennais, Paris 1809; height 99 cm.
Musée du Louvre, Paris

Tea and coffee service. Marc Jacquart, Paris 1809—19. Height of coffee percolator 68 cm.
Metropolitan Museum, New York

Tea urn. Abraham Nyemann, Copenhagen 1808. Kunstindustrimuseet, Copenhagen

Reliquary in the form of a radiating monstrance. Gilt with enamel inlays. Made by the
goldsmith J. Moser and the jeweller F. v. Mack, Vienna 1872. Museum für Angewandte
Kunst, Vienna

were enhanced by fine moldings and cast ornament. Boston, in particular, was extremely close to England in fashion, dress, furniture and silver. Extensive travel by merchants and wealthy patrons to and from England insured London decorative fashions an appearance in Boston within three or four months of their acceptance in the mother country. Coupled with increased facility of travel came stiff competition to American silversmiths, either in the form of special orders executed in London, or in direct imports advertised for sale in shops in all major cities of the Eastern seaboard. Following a considerable advance in increased comfort in domestic interiors, American silver appeared in greater number and in a greater variety of forms. Flatware appeared in sets. The porringer was increasingly popular, as were cider tankards. Mugs followed the general form of the tankard, but lost their popularity after the introduction of the can, an open drinking vessel, usually of pint capacity, with curved sides and a rounded bottom with a single scrolled handle. Casters in sets of three, sauce and butter boats and salts supported on three "Queen Anne" cabriole legs were innovations of this period. Chocolate drinking declined, although coffee was still popular. But the rage was tea drinking whose elaborate ceremony involved new forms in silver. As in England utensils considered absolute necessities for the tea table were a cream or milk jug, a sugar dish based on the china tea bowl of the Orient with a low domed cover, and a tea kettle. Another new form introduced with the service of tea was the cannister, or caddy, found in sets of three, with the largest for sugar, all contained in a box whose lock emphasized the cost of these luxurious imports. The introduction of the secretary-bookcase with candle slides, as well as the enormous popularity of gaming tables, is reflected in the numbers and variety of surviving lighting fixtures. Silver tobacco and snuff boxes are reminders that women as well as men smoked pipes and took snuff. Like England, the generous plain surfaces of the Queen Anne style were ideal inducements to fine engraving. In no other period did this special branch of the silversmith's art approach such technical skill.

Silver during the reign of George II (1727–1760) combined simple outline with lavish ornament that developed into an expression of English Rococo, a new style in which richness of effect was paramount. Ornament became higher in relief and increasingly naturalistic. As the style progressed, embossing became a most popular technique. Forms once simple and straight now swelled into apple, pear, or inverted pear shapes.

The Rococo style, developed in Paris in the 1720s, was popularized in England by Paul de Lamerie (active 1712–1751). He was the most important goldsmith in England in the eighteenth century – a superb craftsman who was always in the *avant garde* of the newest styles. (Occasionally, English Rococo has even been called the 'Lamerie style'.) His ewer, commissioned by the Company of Goldsmiths in London in 1741, together with a basin, reflects an early phase of Rococo with its asymmetric foot and intricately interwined and overlapping curves (page 157). Sculptural festoons, which became an important ornament in this period, cling round the body of the vessel. The centrepiece by Roger Newdegate, of 1743–4, in the Victoria and Albert Museum in London, has similarly arranged foliage work round the rim of the bowls; it is free and easy, very fresh, and either spills irregularly over the rim in sculptural forms or is embedded into the ground in low relief. This ornament breathes the joyful spirit of the age.

As once before (in the seventeenth century) a taste for things Chinese (chinoiserie) spread in England; but while at that time figures and scenes were always engraved, they were now set against the vessel walls in low relief. They are lively and animated and were often surrounded and framed by scrolls and rocailles, and usually occur on vessels connected with the preparation of tea, such as tea caddies and tea urns (page 174).

During this period patronage began to shift from the Crown to old landed aristocrats and new moneyed capitalists who set up little "courts" on their vast country estates. A series of able prime ministers maintained comparative peace and prosperity which created an ideal climate for the growth of an immensely wealthy leisure class. Motives of ostentation, imitation and rivalry among clients kept the silversmiths busy as never before, and many new types of silverware appeared. The most important new types were additions to the dining table. They included the elaborate centrepiece known as the épergne, fruit dishes, cake-baskets, sauceboats, soup tureens, and entrée dinner services. Candelabra, though known before, came into vogue for lighting, and candle-sticks increased greatly in height and importance. Three-tined (pronged) forks, in use by the beginning of the eighteenth century, gave way to the modern standard four-tined fork in about 1750.

In the late 1730s in America, too, plain shapes associated with the so-called "Queen Anne" style were gradually discarded for those based on the Rococo mode. The typical asymmetrical forms, sinuous S and C curves, and restless ornament composed of fantastic rocaille, shells, scrolls, and leaf and floral patterns dominated the silver of the times, which was executed in engraved, chased, pierced and cast forms. In the colonies, where closer political relations with England were brought about by a common cause, the French and Indian Wars (1756–1763), London fashions were more and more in vogue. Ever-increasing imports of English silver for the masses supplied models for the new fashion. The long popularity of the inverted pear shaped form in vessels for the tea table is due to the fact that little silver was made during the Revolutionary War. The famous patriot, Paul Revere, the silversmith, was, of course, in government service as Lieutnant-Colonel of an artillery regiment. As always, American taste modified London fashions. The most ornate silver pieces made in Philadelphia, the showcase of the American rococo style, were still restrained compared with those fashioned by Lamerie in London in the 1750s. Much of the rococo style in American silver was expressed not in applied decoration but in rocaille engraving in which coats of arms are set out in asymetrical cartouches, surrounded by shell ornament, enriched by capricious pattern of C scrolls and delicate sprays of realistic leaves and flowers.

Classicissim

The classic revival of the late eighteenth century came about because of two factors – the inevitable reaction against the excesses of the Rococo style, and the international interest in ancient architecture and decoration aroused by archaeological discoveries. The excavations of Herculaneum begun in 1738, and Pompeii, begun in 1748, caused tremendous excitement. Rococo curves began to give way to straight lines and right angles: the new aim was balance and austerity. In England, the classic revival taste was first seen in silver in 1770. Its originator as a style was Robert Adam, who began designing interiors in an antique style after his return from Italy and Dalmatia, in 1758. These designs include a few drawings for silver vessels, some of which were executed. The new style was expressed in form, or ornament, or both together. Vessels were made with a contrast of straight lines and long sweeping curves, using Greek or Roman models. Lightness of form was matched by a new thinness of metal. It was a style ideally suited to the new industrialization of the silversmith's process.

Besides London, Birmingham and Sheffield had become important centres of silver work in the 1760's, and from Sheffield two decisive innovations were introduced: machine production, and 'plated ware', a process in which copper is impressed with a layer of silver under great pressure. This produced works that forfeited something of their beauty but were less costly. Machine production, too, was at the expense of a multiplicity of forms. In London where the traditions of handcraftsmanship had remained alive, formal variety also survived (pages 175 and 176).

As a result of the new manufacturing methods, operations could be speeded up, and complicated forms and processes typical of the Rococo were not adaptable. The new vogue for simplicity was, however, and silver and Sheffield-plate makers were quick to take advantage. Urns and vase forms in silver became common, together with plain or deeply fluted sides. Decoration usually consisted of classic-derived motifs, such as beading, formal foliage and drapery, reeding, and festoons interspersed with classic animal and satyr heads in relief.

The later Adam period saw a revival of engraving in the technique known as "bright-cut." The sideboard, a new piece of dining room furniture, encouraged the making of matching tea services.

In America, the Federal style (1785–1810) based on the English and French classic revival styles was a natural expression of a new republic, whose national motto, eagle emblem, decimal currency, form of federal government as well as public and domestic architecture, were all based on early Roman forms. As in England, American silver employed straight structural lines, emphasized by delicately engraved parallel bands of bright-cut ornament, beaded or reeded mouldings, ovoid and elliptical shapes, both plain and fluted, and urn-shaped finials. The source of American silver forms was English imports, since America, however independent politically, was still culturally and artistically dependent on the mother country. Chauvinism had always run high among American craftsmen in the eighteenth century, and newspapers in all the principal cities were filled with pleas to "buy American". Typical is the advertisement of the silversmith Daniel Henchman, which appeared in Boston in 1773. Henchman promised his customers he would "make any kind of plate they may want equall in goodness and cheaper than any they can import from London, with the greatest Dispatch". And he complains bitterly of importers whose activity hurts "townsmen who have been bred to the Business". In spite of rapidly growing patriotic sentiments, such well-known figures as Franklin and Washington were ordering silver direct from London in the 1750s. And, with the cessation of hostilities, the president of the young republic was once again ordering from London in the 1780s, now the new Sheffield plate.

The establishment of American free trade in European and Asiatic ports following the Revolution led to an increased influence of ceramic shapes in silver of the period. Among the commonest was the Liverpool jug, whose extreme simplicity of shape and functional form appealed to prominent silversmiths such as the patriot Paul Revere. The omnipresent teapot followed closely the contemporary London style and was elliptical in plan, with a straight spout and sides. The body was generally decorated with horizontal delicate bands of bright-cut floral or acorn patterns, or by engraved swags of tasselled drapery in the best Adam style. The teapot was usually accompanied by a footed tray to protect furniture from the heat of an unfooted vessel. A matching cream jug was generally of helmet shape with an elegantly slender "classic" handle. The typical sugar dish was inspired by a Roman funerary urn. In addition, also in urn form, were newly introduced large spouted containers for coffee or tea.

It was inevitable that the simple but very beautiful and elegant forms of "Adam silver" should exert a broad influence extending beyond the boundaries of England to radiate to Germany, Holland and Scandinavia. Denmark in particular, produced works whose extremely simplified forms have a convincing power (page 179).

In France, classicism began in about 1770 with the Louis XVI style, which adopted forms from the Antique and had a much cooler, more serious effect than Rococo while retaining its elegance and lightness. The increasing faithfulness to detail was accompanied by an increasing strictness which entailed a loss of animation but achieved a more monumental effect. This is the period known as "Empire", which began before the Revolution and lasted until after 1820, and thus beyond the Napoleonic age. Unlike contemporary England, we find great names again in France: Henry Auguste, Martin Guillaume Biennais, Jean Baptiste Claude Odiot and Marc Jacquart. The court gave the most important commissions. Napoleon's sense of imperial power was matched by the monumental style, the legacy of the Holy Roman Empire; and it was not chance that the effect of the ceremonial plate was heightened again by gilding. The tea and coffee service by Marc Jacquart can hardly be equalled in splendour, costliness and monumentality (page 178). It was a final highpoint before the decline into the historicism of the nineteenth century.

No similar flowering of classicism occured in Germany, nor did Germany experience an early preliminary phase like the Louis XVI style. The new style did not emerge until the time of the Empire, and always remained restrained, with smooth and often cylindrical forms.

The nineteenth century and the present

Schinkel. It is not without reason that the silver cup by Carl Friedrich Schinkel is at the beginning of the illustrations from the nineteenth century (page 201). This piece reflects the changed situation in craftsmanship and the applied arts after the French Revolution. The Revolution had brought great changes, and the birth of the new century coincided with the birth of a new epoch in world history. The industrialization that had already begun in England became the new, all-determining factor, and the machine became the beacon of the century. The middle classes were the new clients who determined the quality and form of art. In no other time was the image of the world changed so suddenly or so overwhelmingly as in the past century.

As an artist Schinkel was one of the great transformers of man's environment. This architect of the Prussian king was also the designer of the cup for the government surveyor Redtel. He was not a goldsmith and did not realize his design; the executor was presumably the Berlin Gewerbeinstitut, a concern for the promotion of arts and crafts. Just as the architect Schinkel always conceived his work with a view to the whole, so too as an artist he wanted to reform the entire visual world according to an overall concept. He sketched chandeliers, ovens, seats, tables and cupboards for the palaces he built. He drew designs for tapestries and embroideries, designed vessels, glasses and glass windows for the royal porcelain manufacture. He published eight volumes of designs for jugs for the Royal Iron Foundry in Berlin between 1815 and 1833. Pattern books for gold and silver works followed in 1837. This was the beginning of a new era of applied art, in which the designer moved into the forefront and the craftsman, the goldsmith, no longer determined the shape of his work independently. Schinkel's cup betrays the architect in its structure. The individual formal elements are assembled according to architectural principles; they have not evolved from the process of manufacture. The foot, shaft and bowl contrast. The figurative wreath reflects Baroque traditions and has statuesque features. The generous contours and clear beaker form of the cup give the work a monumental character as a unit.

Biedermeier. Schinkel's cup has a function outside the everyday, although not unusual; it stands in the tradition of the gift of honour. But contemporary art for domestic use adhered more closely to general stylistic tendencies. While pieces from the Empire period and in the Empire style were aimed at a non bourgeois market, the applied art of Biedermeier – the style evolved in Germany between 1820 and 1850 – was more closely connected to the wishes of the aspiring bourgeoisie. Good materials, solidity and usefulness were important now, with a preference for clear forms with cubic elements, or segments of circles or ovals. For pots, the producers and owners preferred squat, dumpy proportions. It is easy to establish their stylistic links with the popular utensils of past centuries. The harmonious and balanced structure of the coffee percolator from Vienna (page 202) is a perfect example of this type of silver. The precious material challenged its maker to join dainty handles to the squat vessel, and he added the elegant delicately distributed decoration in order to raise the vessel out of the realm of the everyday.

In England the Adam style persisted till about 1820 in spite of a popular neo-classic style now called "Regency", then called "Greek" or "modern". The new style was classic, but with an important difference, or differences. On the one hand, the inescapable influence from France of Napoleon's Empire promoted silver producing using forms and motifs based on the pomp and grandeur of Imperial Rome. On the other hand, newly unearthed antiquities and a soaring cost of living made simplicity fashionable. In English silver there appeared an obvious dichotomy of taste. While the Greeks employed simple ornaments and pure forms, the Romans were intent on overwhelming the spectator by the sheer weight on works already scaled up to impress the beholder. The pioneer in England in outmoding the Adam style was Tatham

(1772–1842) who in 1806 in his *Designs for Ornamental Plate* complains that 'instead of *Massiveness*, the principal characteristic of good Plate, light and insignificant forms have prevailed, to the utter exclusion of all good Ornament whatever'. The message resulted in the heavier weight of metal, and the low forms and heavily sculpted ornament that was now in vogue among all classes.

Great Britain was established at the Congress of Vienna (1815) as the most powerful country in the world, and London was the greatest city. It was to be expected that some monumental pieces of silver were in demand with titled or the very wealthy patrons at the same time that advances in mechanical techniques gave rise to great quantities of simple, inexpensive plate being produced for an ever-growing market of comparatively wealthy merchants and professional people. The early simple early Roman style of Adam was more and more abandoned in favour of heavier elaborations of Imperial Rome, sometimes combined with motifs from Egypt, such as the sphinx, aping French silver, after the Battle of the Nile. An added and important change in the manufacture of English silver was the application of power-driven machinery in the output of Sheffield plate which effectively widened the gap between the knowledgeable taste of the hand artisan and the blind output of an automaton. Regency designs drew on a multitude of motifs – Roman, Greek, a vulgarized Rococo style, Neo-Gothic, a coarsened "Chinoiserie", mixed with popular pseudo-Turkish and Persian ornaments.

Greater imports of tea and sugar from India resulted in falling prices and the increase of the numbers of tea sets produced during the period, and teapots with greater capacity. Their shapes and ornaments showed great variety, but in general they were heavier, squatter, and coarser in detail. The introduction of Sheffield plate and weighted bases in the last quarter of the eighteenth century allowed candlesticks to be made in a more grandiose scale, at low cost, using less silver, so that sets of a dozen were common. Complete matching dinner services appeared, usually consisting of one or two dozen large and small plates, four entrée dishes, a pair of soup tureens and four sauce tureens with ladles. Paul Storr (active from 1792 to 1821 as a designer and craftsman) is a name associated with all the best in silver production of the Regency period. His pieces in general avoided the prevailing taste which floundered in a profusion of ornament and the inability to leave any surface undecorated.

In America the Monroe Doctrine of 1823 proclaimed the New World's independence from Europe. The Greek War for independence in 1824 fanned enthusiasm for that country's past. And about the same time the opening of the Erie Canal made the American public increasingly aware of the vast potential of their land. Westerward expansion, the factory system, and the enormous growth of mechanization led to the foundation of or the extension of a number of great American fortunes. New wealth created a demand for new homes and furnishings. The classic revival of the earlier Federal era, elegant and restrained, seemed too reminiscent of Europe; Americans turned to "Greek" models which seemed more appropriate to a democracy based on the limitless possibilities of the individual. The Greek Revival style was the predominant national style from the 1820's until the Civil War. The mania for things Greek spread to domestic architecture, (the Greek temple form was ubiquitous from Maine to the South and Midwest), furniture and silver. In silver a coarsening in the scale of ornament followed not only current London fashions but the Parisian French Empire style following the War of 1812. Taken from both were banded laurel ornaments, applied sphinxes and winged claw foot, as seen on the late Duncan Phyfe's furniture. By the 1850s increased travel in the Near and Far East and the popularity of travel books were responsible for a wave of "Persian" and "Turkish" fashions in architecture and the decorative arts. Gradually all-over repoussé floral patterns smothered pseudoclassic shapes in jungle masses of naturalistic forms. The nadir of taste in American silver was prominently displayed at the 1876 Centennial Exhibition.

The style of Biedermeier, by contrast, was the final example in the nineteenth century of compact applied art; it reflects the calm spirit of an unsentimental, lower-middle-class world, which led, unnoticed, to the political and economic confusion of the 1850s. The Dutch table ware (page 203), teapots and milk jugs from the 1840s reflect this compact, self-sufficient world. The silversmith has created a plain and well-balanced pot, serving the refined eating habits of people that were receptive to everything artistic. The municipal and domestic culture of Holland during its flower in the seventeenth century adhered to traditional principles.

Crisis and Renewal in Arts and Crafts. The crisis first became apparent in the great world exhibitions. The prelude to this series of displays of products from all the civilized countries was the 'Great Exhibition' held in London in 1851. The building, the great glass hall of the Crystal Palace, by Joseph Paxton, later destroyed by fire, made of prefabricated iron and glass, was entirely modern. But the goods on display were a confused mass of derivative styles – which is often looked upon as the only real artistic expression of the nineteenth century. The silver in this exhibition, as in the many similar later ones, was no exception. The famous French goldsmith Froment-Meurice showed ceremonial cups, thick-bellied bottles and tall, stiff bowls with abundant appliqué Gothic ornament inset with sculptural and relieved groups of figures. The English manufacturers Messrs. Elkington and Mason proclaimed that their silver was imitated from 'Antique' forms. Galvanized copies of famous antique silver vessels, plated with electrolyzed silver, were also commended. The Russian goldsmith Ignace Sazikoff based his cups on the work of the Augsburg and Nuremberg goldsmiths of the seventeenth century. Then there were Oriental influences, evident both in the decoration and the form of the silverware. The English architect A. W. N. Pugin, who had furnished the new Houses of Parliament in London, had vessels of this kind made according to his designs by Hardmann & Co. in Birmingham.

The Great Exhibition of London was followed by many others in the European capitals. Here the bourgeoisie who attented them *en masse* – in 1851 over six million people visited the Crystal Palace – found its inspirations and formed its 'taste'. The exhibitions offered an abundance of machine-made *kitsch*, which then flooded the house of the bourgeois. The craftsman, who had designed his own forms until the nineteenth century, now had to obey the wishes of his new patrons. The many printed pattern books, such as the *Formenschatz der Renaissance,* supplied him with the preferred models in his workshop. At the same time the world exhibitions marked the beginnings of criticism of what was in show and attempts at innovation. The English realized that the true basis of art could only be topical and contemporary, and they were the first to oppose the variety of stylistic repetitions. The Pre-Raphaelite Brotherhood, a group of seven painters, founded in 1848, resolved to sign its works with the mysterious letters 'P. R. B.'. Its aim was to renew the whole of art and to liberate it from the chains of academicism and rigidity of theme. The artists declared that it was necessary to observe nature so closely that they could learn to express it. They also promised to acquire a true sympathetic understanding of all earlier art in so far as it was an expression of immediate, serious and strong feeling. They opposed anything that seemed merely derivative, complacent or mechanical. The spiritual father of this group was the London painter Dante Gabriel Rossetti.

The Pre-Raphaelites exerted a strong influence on English arts and crafts. Just as the royal architect Schinkel had not conceived his buildings in terms of total environment, the members of this group were not content simply to paint or sculpt. They equipped their homes with furniture and materials they had designed themselves. The friends realized that furniture design came into the legitimate sphere of activity of the creative artist. After this beginning, they decided to found a business concern under the name Morris, Marshall, Falkner & Co., which would devote itself to making objects of craftsmanship based on the ideals of the Pre-Raphaelites. William Morris was the leading force of this enterprise. Its founders made money available besides their artistic talents.

The ban was broken. These men had realized that only a common effort between the artist, the designer and the manufacturer could lead to satisfactory results. The prospectus that was sent out when the firm started explicitly included metalwork of all kinds, including decoration, on its programme. Soon the firm was simply called Morris & Co., under which name it became world-famous.

Morris' ideas determined the new course of the arts and crafts movement. At the beginning of the twentieth century the 'workshops' still unabashedly used his ideas for their own work. Morris said he could not imagine why art should remain the privilege of the few, any more than that culture and freedom should remain the privilege of the few, and believed that beauty could manifest itself equally well in the palace as in the hut. Many a young artist, architect and even dilettante was penetrated by this insight and decided to dedicate his life to the arts and crafts.

Christopher Dresser, whom Nikolaus Pevsner rescued from oblivion in 1937, was one of the typical reformers. He began as a botanist, after training at the School of Design at Somerset House. Between 1859 and 1862 he began to make designs for manufacturers and supplied them to firms throughout England. Hundreds of drawings have survived. Usually they are sketchy ideas for forms, series of variations on the same theme, and they are all the work of the 'designer', not the craftsman. In 1877 he travelled to Japan. Here he studied Japanese arts and crafts, which had first been seen in Europe at the world exhibition in London 1862. The fruits of his encounter with eastern Asian culture in its native country were designs reflecting its influence. The silver-plated tea pot (page 204), made by James Dixon and Sons of Sheffield in about 1880, has no predecessor in European art, and its forms derive from Eastern Asia. The cylindrical body of the vessel, abruptly adjoined by an angular spout like a modern vent pipe, is completely plain. The handle of black ebony, whose angle and form are purely functional, serving for lifting and pouring, is an equally abrupt adjunct. Alf Boe described this tea pot in 1957 in his book *From Gothic Revival to Functional Form*, and ascribed it a high place as incunabula on the road to the modern, creative, 'industrial design' of our time. Dresser's designs for glass, materials, etc., usually have the same precise, modest, entirely functional character. So Christopher Dresser can be considered the first 'industrial designer'.

Richard Redgrave, who made the small christening cup (page 204, above), was also a figure of outstanding importance for English arts and crafts at the time. He began his artistic career like many others as a painter, and was also an art historian. He was commissioner for the department of art at the Great Exhibition of 1851. Together with Gottfried Semper, he also founded the Victoria and Albert Museum. He remained faithful to painting until his death, besides his activity in the arts and crafts. His designs for glass are particularly important. According to his character, he conceived the christening cup in a 'painterly' way. The baptized child, added to the slender beaker in relief, is shown kneeling among plants, protected by angels with crossed hands hovering above him.

A lidded jug in London, made in 1826-7 (opposite the christening jug and above Dresser's tea pot, page 205), recalls the high traditions, uninterrupted in the nineteenth century, of English and specifically London silver work. English silverware had not become a mass product in the previous century, largely because of the rarity of silver. It still combined the task of representation with a clear functional character. Since the seventeenth century the rising English bourgeoisie had joined the aristocracy as customers for 'domestic silver' for their beloved tea and coffee. The jug is an example in the tradition of good 'utility forms' that were valued in nineteenth century middle-class homes and could also be found throughout the continent.

In the German-speaking area, Gottfried Semper was the chief figure to concern himself with the state of arts and crafts in his time, although usually in a theoretical way. In his essay, published in 1856, *Über die formelle Gesetzmäßigkeit des Schmuckes und dessen Bedeutung als Kunstsymbol* (on the formal legitimacy of ornament and its meaning as an artistic symbol), he pointed out that nature offered an abundance of models. He further pointed out the different technical processes possible, and showed how the use of different materials could achieve a number of varied effects in the making of an object. 'So metal can be hammered, forged, cut and cast: in all three or four different treatments its appearance will be fundamentally different.' With these fairly obvious realizations – which at the time had evidently dropped out of sight – he opposed the violation of the material, the illusion of craftsmanship by machine methods, and the imitation of precious substances by cheap *ersatz* materials. Like Redgrave, Semper worked at the Great Exhibition of 1851 in London, where he remained as a political emigrant until 1855. At that time he formulated ideas towards a practical aesthetic system, chiefly concerned with the technical aspects of his age. He was one of the first to recognize the problems that would come with the industrialization of society and its enormous consumer power. He fostered the creation of museums of arts and crafts and propagated the idea of including art schools to train industrial artists. The decanter made by Joseph Angell in 1854-5 exemplifies Semper's idea of taking natural forms as models (page 205). Semper's requirements are fulfilled even more clearly in the vessels exhibited in London in 1851 by Messrs. G. Grainer & Co., such as the ceramic coffee service based entirely on the forms of leaves and ears of corn, or the pot formed of closed waterlily petals. Angell's tall silver wine decanter reflects the artist's effort to free himself from the cycle of derivative styles, in order to find a new kind of decoration: the body of the vessel is decorated with vines and grapes and little figures of an unashamedly narrative quality.

We have deliberately omitted those products of silver that are derivate of past styles. The advertisers by no means tried to disguise their 'style'. '"Willkomm" in medieval form, a highly ingeniously calculated and effective union of glass and metal' is the description of a silver cup by Lobmeyer of Vienna at the Paris Industrial Exhibition of 1864. The goldsmith August Schleissner of Hanau was considered the 'rediscoverer of the art of embossing in precious metal' in Germany at the time. After 1861 he turned to 'making *objets d'art* in the taste of the Renaissance, designed by his own hand'. In 1903 the adress and handbook of German goldsmiths still quotes as the speciality of the firm Schleissner Söhne: 'Embossed table plate . . . in the Antique manner'. So the highly praised skills of the goldsmiths were a result of their adoption of old works as models. The craftsmen had studied the methods of manufacture of these pieces thoroughly. They refined their tools and were proud of their perfect mastery over old processes such as embossing and chasing. In the technical realm as well the situation was ripe for a new departure, for the age of artistic independence with its new aims at the close of the nineteenth century. This stylistic movement of the turn of the century launched the twentieth century.

The new style. The World Fair in Chicago in 1893 can be taken as the turning point and point of departure in the search for a new style in arts and crafts. This was the first time that the Americans had organized a world exhibition, and they naturally took part in it. Their engineering skill had produced technical masterpieces. The great bridges, stations and exhibition halls were perfect constructions in iron. The first skyscrapers announced the triumph of technology in architecture. Louis Sullivan's skyscrapers had already excited attention; in 1893 he built one for the exhibition in Chicago.
In 1893 a new great name emerged in the new style: Louis G. Tiffany. His father Charles L. Tiffany, ran a silver workshop in New York. His oldest son took over and expanded it. He had trained in New York and Paris, at first trying his luck as a painter. The turning point came in 1879 when the thirty-one year old painter changed to the field of 'decorative' art. He immediately designed and executed large house and room furnishings. From 1893 on he made glass for window decorations and glass vases and announced his patent for his newly invented iridescent 'opalescent' glass. Later he also turned to ceramics. The silver vase set with pearls (page 206) made in his father's firm dates from 1893. These vessels attracted attention at the arts and crafts exhibition in Turin in 1902, as they had at the Paris world fair in 1900. The German review *Dekorative Kunst* which exerted a considerable influence on the spread of the new art, together with other contemporary reviews, described the main effect of the Tiffany gold and silver in 1902 as deriving from their 'solidity and weight'. It described 'Tiffany decoration' as no more than a reliable sign of wealth. The 'new technical wonders' from America were judged more positively; these were the 'mixed metals', alloys of copper, silver gold and steel. 'Typically American' features were already

emerging here; terms such as 'function, convenience, industrial production' were used in connection with American objects. In the meantime, the famous Favrile glass of Louis Tiffany had become world famous and was imitated by many European manufacturers. The silver vase of 1893 is typical of a large number of these pieces in which, for the first time American artists participated in a style contracting all of Europe, and this was evidence of the world-wide importance of the new movement. The large, open wine decanter that is ascribed to Tiffany (page 209) exploits the effects of two different materials. The red glass shimmers through the broken up silver casing. The simple, tall and slender form of the decanter is heightened by the rising forms of silver grape vines with luxuriant bulging grapes. It has a well-placed, clearly defined plain silver handle.

Towards the end of the century a new group of English artists contributed towards the evolution of English industrial art. The architect Charles Robert Ashbee, who had also founded a teaching workshop for architecture and interior design, founded the Guild of Handicraft in London, thus following the tradition of Morris and Ruskin, and like them he also devoted himself to printing, establishing the Essex Press in 1901. Ashbee was equally sucessful as an interior decorator and as a designer. The small mustard pot and spoon (page 211) was executed according to his designs by the Guild of Handicraft. Ashbee managed to create an ideal connection between the decoration and the task of casing the glass cylinder by means of stylized foliage. The lid rises to a knop in an elegant curve.

As in the past, Paris remained the focus of handicrafts in Europe around 1900 too. Whole rooms were furnished in the new style of Art Nouveau. This style seemed like a liberation from an unreal world, and the newly formed objects in the shops and exhibition halls seemed to emanate a breath of fresh air. The new style embraced the whole sphere of environment. 'Art Nouveau' became the slogan in Paris. Parisian goldsmiths of the turn of the century had mastered their craft perfectly, and the stimuli for new forms fell on fruitful ground. As in America, there were great names in the French capital, among them the jeweller René Lalique who quickly achieved international fame. His silver plate was also in demand. In his jewellery and vessels he strove to convert natural models into works of art, stylizing the contours of animals and plants.

The chocolate pot and sugar bowl by Cardailhac, made in Paris in about 1895 (page 207) have similar tendencies. Stylized plants decorate the simple forms of the vessels. They do not seem as though imposed but appear integral to the form. We can observe the same harmony between decoration and form in all the branches of the arts and crafts.

Paris catered for the demands of a bourgeoisie of sophisticated, fastidious and cultured tastes. In Germany it was mainly the independent, active and committed younger generation that created a platform for their new ideas in reviews such as *Jugend* and *Pan* and acted as inventor, producer and consumer of 'modern' art. In Germany the new style was called '*Jugendstil*'. It celebrated its greatest triumph at the Paris world fair in 1900 at which Germany was also well represented. It aroused notice with a reception room entirely furnished by artists from Darmstadt. In 1899 Archduke Ernst Ludwig had hit upon the idea of summoning seven artists from Germany-speaking areas to his small town. He hoped this would lead to a revival of the arts. This Maecenas' hopes were fulfilled, even surpassed. Two great figures exerted a particularly decisive influence in the language of the artists' colony at Darmstadt, Joseph Maria Olbrich and Peter Behrens. Olbrich was the only professional architect in the group. He had trained at the Akademie der bildenden Künste in Vienna. From 1894 to 1899 he collaborated with Otto Wagner and was co-founder of the '*Secession*' in Vienna, whose exhibition hall he designed. His opposite number, Peter Behrens, began as a painter, studying at the academy in Karlsruhe and under F. Brütt in Düsseldorf. He qualified as an architect and designer in Darmstadt. His stay in Hessen as member of the Darmstadt artists' colony was only a temporary one. From 1902 to 1907 he acted as director of the Kunstgewerbeschule (school of arts and crafts) in Düsseldorf. His main talents emerged in his buildings, of which the Turbine House of the AEG in Berlin, constructed in 1909, was his real break-through to modern architecture. He also designed the entire graphic advertising work of the AEG. In Darmstadt Behrens evolved a precise 'angular' style in typography and as decoration, based on the austere, elongated lines of the Glasgow 'Modern Style' group. He disliked the vegetal curves of French Art Nouveau, and lines, right angles, additive squares and sharp corners are the hall marks of his decorative style, while the forms stressed the functional aspects. The cup (page 208), gilt on the inside and made in 1899, shows his struggle to discover new forms. The bowl opens widely above a lightly indented body formed like a trunk with abstract cartilages.

Joseph Maria Olbrich's silver candelabrum of 1901 (page 213), made for the house he built and furnished for himself on the Mathildenhöhe in Darmstadt, and which, like the other artists' houses, was opened to the public for the exhibition 'Ein Dokument Deutscher Kunst' in summer 1901, is a perfect example of the basic style of this architect and designer. Olbrich could not deny his origins in the Wiener Werkstätte in his architecture or in his designs for the arts and crafts. As architect, he 'built up' the candlestick systematically and structured it carefully. It is based on his concept of man as the measure and basic essence of all artistic creation. Delicate lines, that do not give the impression of applied decoration, stress the structure. The precious metal, enhanced by a semi-precious stone, is an integral part of the effect of the object.

At the Darmstadt exhibition of 1901 the artists' colony had already turned away from the luxuriant convolutions and scrolls that decorated all the products of Art Nouveau. They disliked this 'surface art' and struggled against the continually decreasing standards of mass production. Art, said the serious protagonists of the new style, should not simply satisfy aesthetic needs, but rather it should contribute towards recreating the whole of life. The artists felt themselves called upon to reform every sphere of human life, thus continuing the ideas of their English predecessors in the mid-nineteenth century. Their efforts were in fact crowned by success. In 1907 the 'Deutscher Werkbund' entered the picture and formulated its aims as 'the spiritualization of work in the collaboration of art, industry and trade through education.' This association of active artists with the powers of 'progress' saw it as one of their tasks to 'recreate manufactures and installations, shops and commercial printing, factory buildings and workers' colonies, in a spirit of the most authentic modernity.' Born of the impulses of the German *Jugendstil*, the 'Deutscher Werkbund' followed the road of the turn of the century movement which led into the twentieth century.

A solitary figure, Henry van de Velde, had evolved similar aims as the Werkbund from the very beginning. Although his early work can be described as floral Art Nouveau, even these works show the beginnings of an independent artistic style which sought to free itself from contemporary rigid uniformity. Like Tiffany, Behrens and others, Van de Velde also started as a painter. His first incentive for designing works of applied art came when he saw the products of the English firm of Liberty & Co. in a shop window in Brussels in 1891. By 1893 we find him acting as co-editor of a Flemish avant-garde review, *Van nu en Strake*, which joined the other art reviews of the movement in fighting for recognition of the new art. Henry van de Velde furnished his house in Uccle entirely himself. The furniture and other decoration all have a marked emphasis on the fluid lines of the new style. This artist, who also trained as an architect, had more success in Germany than in Paris. His furniture was enthusiastically praised at the Dresden arts and crafts exhibition in 1897. He designed all the advertisements and packaging for the German consumer firm Tropon. Soon afterwards, we find him in Berlin, and then in Weimar where he spent many years as director of the academy of arts and crafts. He was a co-founder of the Deutscher Werkbund. In Weimar he became a leading figure in the princely court, which was receptive to all forms of art and deliberately retained Van de Velde in the land, proud of possessing one of the great spirits of the age.

Van de Velde had his hands full at the Weimar school of art. The ceramics factories called for new forms, new combinations of colours, new decorations. The weavers wanted textile designs, the textile firms demanded designs for furniture covers and curtains. Indeed he managed to do what the Darmstadt artists' colony had also wanted – to reform the whole environment and all the objects of daily and festive use. The tea kettle on the spirit burner (page 212) immediately reveals the creative touch of the great designer. Van de Velde managed to fuse the spirit of the age with a harmonious beauty of form. There is no break between shape and function, decoration and form. The supports for the tea kettle spring dynamically and organically from the ornamental curved open base, from the centre of which rises the wick of the round spirit burner. The kettle itself has a bulging shape, that continues into the spout without break; it seems almost to hover on its supports. The tall wooden handle rises above the flat, graduated lid like a construction from the world of technology. This is not a staple product of *Jugendstil;* it is immediately perceptible as a unique work of art, unmistakable and inimitable. The slightly later tea service (page 210) has similar, very plain spherical forms. Like the kettle, the spouts are an integral part of the body, which stands on a flat circular base. The handles are joined to the body at functionally apposite points. These two examples of vessels designed by Van de Velde illustrate the vision of the artist at the turn of the century, which was to lead him on to the twentieth century.

Van de Velde's tea service dating from about 1922 (page 216) shows a consistent evolution in his forms. There is no decline in creative power, and the vessels have attained a perfect artistic form which can almost be viewed apart from their function as objects of daily use. This is the end of the 'fin de siècle' taste; decoration, which appeared no more than ballast and superfluity, has disappeared. Van de Velde's vessels are the realization of what the Viennese architect Adolf Loos demanded again and again, that the form of the vessel should spring purely from its function. It was Loos who wrote the much-quoted, and at the time much-scorned, essay *Ornament und Verbrechen* (ornament and crime) in 1908. Loos said only too clearly what many artists of the time realized unconsciously: 'The ornament that is created today has no human connections at all, no connection with the order of the world ... The modern decorator, however, is a straggler or a pathological phenomenon'.

The Wiener Werkstätte. The new efforts to achieve 'form' by means of 'deformation' are apparent in the tea and coffee service by an unknown designer around 1900 (page 210); similar efforts were made in tin ware. But the results were inconclusive; as one can see on the objects covered with layer upon layer of Art Nouveau ornament, this path led to a dead end in the field of arts and crafts, and particularly in the design of articles of domestic use.

The artists in the great European centres of art joined into groups around the turn of the century, calling themselves the '*Secession*'. Here they discussed and exhibited their works, and were informed of the most recent developments. Many of these groups inspired revivals in the arts and crafts. Ashbee's workshop community of artists and craftsmen, the Guild of Handicraft, was

Cup. Inside of bowl gilt. After a design by Carl Friedrich Schinkel in 1820 for the municipal surveyor Redtel. Presumably made in the Berlin Gewerbe-Institut 1826; height 31 cm. Kunstgewerbemuseum, Berlin

Coffee percolator. St Mayrhofer, Vienna 1825. Österreichisches Museum für angewandte Kunst, Vienna

Above: Tea pot. P. de Meyer, The Hague c. 1840. Gemeentemuseum, The Hague.
Below: Tea pot and milk jug. J. M. van Kempen, Utrecht 1842; height 10.1 cm and 9.8 cm.
Stedelijk Museum De Lakenhal, Leiden

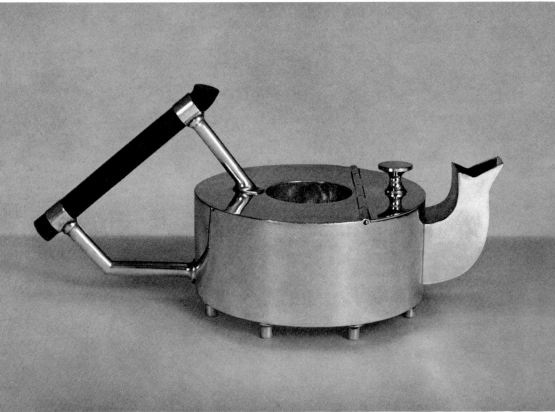

Above left: Christening cup. Richard Redgrave 1848. Manufacturer Harry Emanuel, London and Chesnau for Summerly's Art Manufacturers; height 13 cm. *Above right:* Covered jug. Unidentified master's mark C. P., London 1826–7; height 11.7 cm. both pieces: Victoria and Albert Museum, London. *Below:* Tea pot. Silver gilt. Christopher Dresser, *c.* 1880. Manufactured by James Dixon and Sons, Sheffield. Height 14 cm. James Dixon and Sons, Sheffield

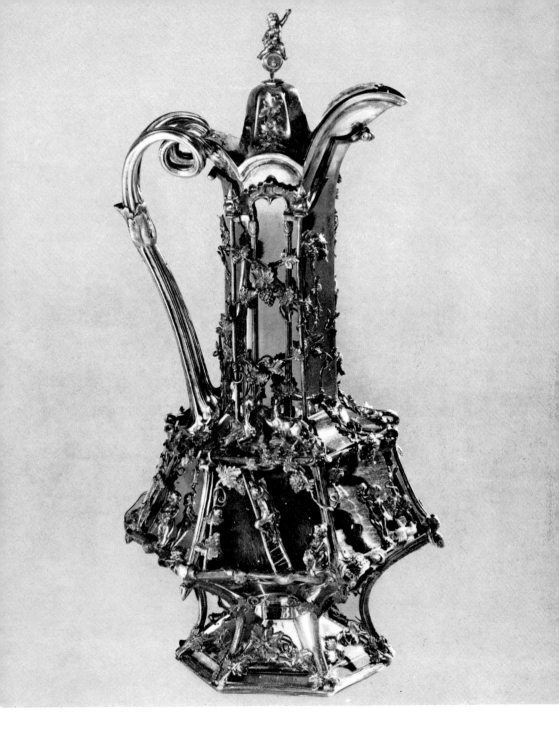

Decanter. Gilt. Joseph Angell 1854–5; height 32 cm. The Cooper Union Museum for the Arts of Decoration, New York

Vase encrusted with pearls. Charles Lewis Tiffany & Co., New York, 1893. Height 17.8 cm.
Kunstgewerbemuseum, Berlin

Chocolate pot and sugar bowl. Cadailhac, Paris *c.* 1895; height 21 and 18.5 cm. Kunst-industrimuseet, Oslo

Cup. Gilt interior. Peter Behrens, Dresden 1899; height 10 cm. Landesgewerbeamt, Baden-Württemberg, Stuttgart

Wine decanter. Glass with perforated silver casing. Attributed to Louis Comfort Tiffany, New York 1903; height 27.5 cm. Kunstgewerbemuseum, Berlin

Above: Tea service and tray. Henry van de Velde, *c.* 1905. Executed by the court jeweller Theodor Müller, Weimar. From the personal collection of the Van de Veldes. Kunstgewerbemuseum, Zurich. *Below:* Coffee and tea service. Unknown designer, *c.* 1900. Manufactured by Orivit-A. G., Cologne-Braunfeld. Height of coffee pot 24 cm. Staatliche Kunstsammlungen, Kassel

Mustard pot and spoon. Charles Robert Ashbee before 1900. Manufactured by the Guild of Handicraft, London. Kunstgewerbemuseum, Zurich

Tea kettle and réchaud. Henry van de Velde *c.* 1902. From the bequest of the Van de Veldes. Kunstgewerbemuseum, Zurich

Left: Silver vase with inlaid glass. Joseph Hoffmann before 1906. Manufactured by Dresdner Werkstätten; height 20 cm. Landesgewerbeamt Baden-Württemberg, Stuttgart. *Right:* Two-branched candelabrum. Joseph Maria Olbrich *c.* 1901. Manufactured by P. Bruckmann & Söhne, Heilbronn; height 34.7 cm. Hessisches Landesmuseum, Darmstadt

Tea service. Eduard Joseph Wimmer 1912. Manufactured by Wiener Werkstätte. Height of tea pot 14.5 cm. Österreichisches Museum für angewandte Kunst, Vienna

Coffee service. Dagobert Peche 1920—22. Manufactured by Wiener Werkstätte. Height of pot 33 cm. Private collection

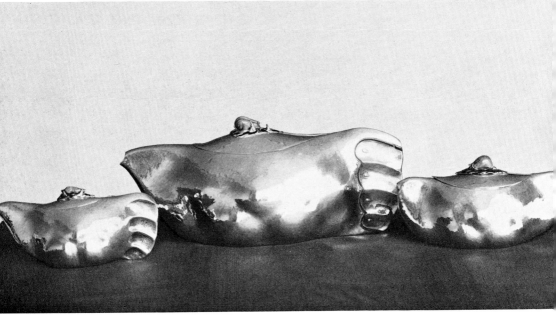

Above: Tea service. Henry van de Velde *c.* 1922. Manufactured by F. Jerdingstad. From the bequest of Van de Velde. Kunstgewerbemuseum, Zurich. *Below:* Tea service. J. Steltman 1925. 'Grand prix' at the 1925 Paris world fair. Height of pot 10.5 cm. J. Steltman, The Hague

Above: Casserole. Henning Koppel, 1961. Manufactured by Georg Jensens Sölvsmedie A/S, Copenhagen. Landesgewerbeamt Baden-Württemberg, Stuttgart. *Below:* Tea service. Robert Welch, 1962. Manufactured by Wakely & Wheeler Ltd., England. Height of pot 14 cm. The Worshipful Company of Goldsmiths, London

221

Iced-water jug. Handle cased in wood. Sigvard Bernadotte, 1952. Manufactured by Georg Jensens Sölvsmedie A/S, Copenhagen. Height 16.3 cm. Museum für Kunst und Gewerbe, Hamburg

Triangular water jug. Gerald Whiles. Manufactured by Silver Workshop Ltd., 1966. University of Sussex

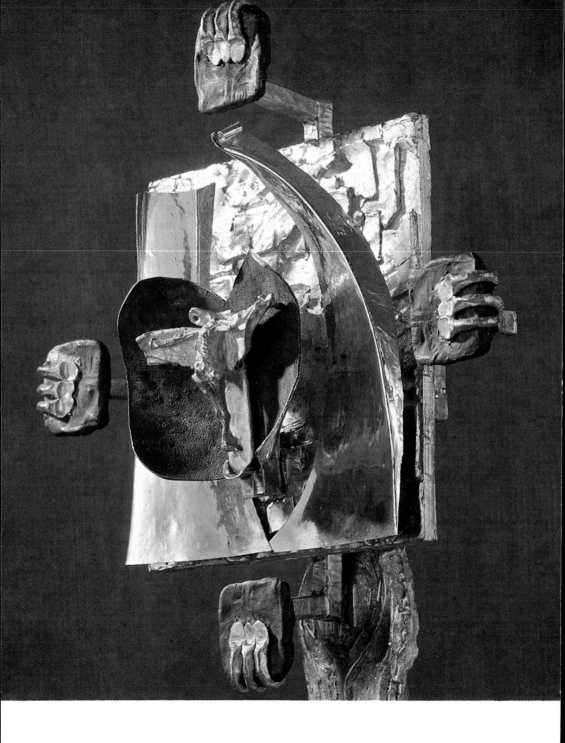

Part of an altar cross. Silver, gold and niello. Graham Sutherland and Louis Osman, 1964. Height 106.5 cm. Collection Mr and Mrs Emery Reves

the direct model of the 'Wiener Werkstätten Produktiv Gemeinschaft von Kunsthandwerkern' in Vienna in 1903 (Vienna workshops' productive association of artist-craftsmen). Fritz Warndörfer was commercial director, Josef Hoffmann and Kolo Moser were artistic directors. Almost all the artists of the Viennese *Secession* worked for the Wiener Werkstätte. Some hundred workers, including thirty-seven masters and craftsmen, offered their services at the outset. With its rise to international fame, the concern became ever larger; people were proud of the newly created 'modern' Viennese style. As the Darmstadt exhibition, 'Ein Dokument Deutscher Kunst', had done, so the artists of the Wiener Werkstätte opposed the way the ornament uninhibitedly overgrew all forms. Adolf Loos prepared their way. Geometrics became apparent in the Viennese products. In the beginning, squares and lines were the only tolerated ornament; later even these disappeared almost entirely. The highpoint before the First World War was the Stoclet Palace, built by Hoffmann in Brussels, for which Gustav Klimt executed his magnificent mosaic frieze. The love of geometry, of smooth surfaces and cubic forms, celebrated its triumph here. Our illustration, the tea service dating from 1912 (page 214), was made by Eduard Joseph Wimmer. From 1907 to 1932 he was one of the leading members of the workshop and directed its fashion studio between 1912 and 1922. The forms of the tea service anticipate the angular style of the post-war years, which was inspired by the pronounced and forceful lines of German Expressionism. Unlike Van de Velde's balanced forms, Wimmer tried to give expression to the artistic spirit of the age with broken-up, squat forms like the angular breaks of his tray and tea caddy. But he did not omit to leave the hammered metal its own effects. Dagobert Peche, who joined the Wiener Werkstätte much later than Wimmer, borrowed from Rococo forms in his coffee service (page 215) he executed in 1920–22. Yet the torsions, stiff forms and elongated lines nevertheless betray an artistic manner all his own, although one that was hardly capable of evolution.

The present. The political confusions before and during the Second World War inhibited many of the efforts to evolve a definite stylistic expression. In Denmark, the firm of Georg Jensens Sölvsmedie A/S in Copenhagen tried to promote the arts and crafts immediately after the war by employing proven and outstanding designers. The founder of the firm, Georg Jensen, who began by producing faience, had opened a jewellery and silverware shop in Copenhagen in 1904. At that time his name already stood for distinguished modest forms, often based on the products of old Scandinavian crafts. The Swedish artist-craftsman Sigvard Bernadotte, son of King Gustav Adolf VI, was a partner of Georg Jensen's firm in Copenhagen from 1934. He designed the iced-water jug (plate 218) in 1952, drawing from the traditions of the firm. The jug rises vertically from a heart-shaped base, becoming more slender towards the top. The wood-cased handle matches this plain form very well. Bernadotte had conceived the vessel as an independent plastic form, and deliberately exploited the effects of the precious metal. The time of doubt about the purpose, meaning and necessity of ornament is wholly forgotten now. The casserole designed by Henning Koppel (page 221) was also executed by Georg Jensen's Sölvsmedie in Copenhagen. The aims Van de Velde had set himself have been consistently carried out here. The function and form of the vessel are an indissoluble unity.

In England, the Worshipful Company of Goldsmiths was particularly concerned with promoting good craftsmanship. It tried to gain support for this by lectures, exhibitions and prizes. They bought the tea service designed by Robert Welch in 1962 (page 217) as an example of a good, artistically well-defined functional form. The triangular water jug by Gerald Whiles (page 219) also fulfills these demands. The semi-circular handle of the vessel is attached at the elegant, drawn-up point of the vessel, and is matched by the large spout. The handle and spout are so clearly related to one another that they predetermine the angle of pouring.

The altar cross by Graham Sutherland (page 220) comes from an entirely different world. It throws light on the importance gold and silver work still has for altar implements in the twentieth century. Such implements have at all times combined a 'cult' purpose with a high degree of artistic excellence. Sutherland is one of the most important contemporary English painters; his pictures hang on the walls of major exhibitions and decorate the walls of museums. Typical of Sutherland's style is the tendency towards imaginative, organic forms reminiscent of Surrealism. It is not chance that Sutherland should also have chosen to design this silver altar cross, for he began his art studies in 1921 at Goldsmith's College School of Art in London. Here he probably also developed the desire to express his artistic aims in precious metal. The body of Christ is cast in gold and nailed to the cross. Both body and cross hover before a curved plate that opens up like the calyx of a flower. The generous lines of the detail in the panel behind the cross also express the Passion. A fourfold repetition of the motif of the three nails surrounds the central image.

These examples of silverware from the twentieth century are intended to show that good, functional utility forms were the point of departure and artistic aim of the silversmiths from the beginning of the century. They continued on the lines of the concepts evolved round the turn of the century. Yet there is clearly no 'timeless and plain' form. There is always room for play with form and material. Today as always, artistic quality is the only criterion in the arts and crafts.

Outlines of types of table plate

Like all created works, table plate is subject to changes of style. Chronological and national styles and the powers of the individual determine its form, and so it has its place in the general course of stylistic developments. The fact that a Napoleonic cup looks different from a Late Gothic one is due to differing artistic concepts. Table plate is also a utility article, tied from the start to a purpose which predetermines its form to a certain extent. The purpose and use of table plate derive from our eating and drinking habits. Here too, various changes have occured through the ages. Foreign foods and drinks introduced into Europe provoked new types of vessel, while others died out. The increasing demands of a refined society, which reached a peak of culture and elegance in the eighteenth century, included table manners. The varieties of table plate never increased to such an extent as at that time. Much of what was created in the late seventeenth and in the eighteenth century is still in common use today, even if in a changed form.

Although we know of some Antique table plate, its development is not continuous until the later fifteenth century. We can only presume that the Late and Early Middle Ages set the festive table with silver vessels; so few, sporadic individual pieces have survived that we cannot draw any definite conclusions. The history of the development of certain types of vessels does not start until about 1500. It comes to an end with the beginnings of historicism.

Beakers and related forms

The beaker is one of the oldest and most used vessels. The basic principle is a round base and conical, widening walls, which were soon decorated. This simple shape has survived throughout history. Antiquity already furnished the beaker with handles to facilitate the grip, and thus created the preliminary form of the cup. But although the basic beaker form was preserved, it experienced many variants from the Late Middle Ages on. It could appear with or without its circular stand or foot-ring, with or without lid, with rounded or concave walls. Placed on a higher pedestal it is related to the goblet. The sixteenth century produced the so-called 'nesting' beaker, whose shape enabled sets of six or more similar beakers, usually with low foot, to be stacked one inside the other like a tower, and which is closed by a lid. The beaker occurs extremely frequently and became popular in the seventeenth century. The most usual form is the squat ball-footed beaker with pronounced relief decoration; it is generally lidded and often attains the size of a tankard. In the course of the eighteenth century, the silver beaker became more rare, to be replaced by the glass beaker. The nineteenth century made the silver beaker into a traditional christening gift.

Mug: A small drinking vessel with a single handle and no cover. The form of the body always followed the style of the contemporary tankard, since they were the popular expression of the more inaccessible and costly covered-top vessel.

The Tankard

Perhaps of German or Scandinavian origin, the tankard is a type of drinking vessel consisting of a cylindrical drum with hinged cover, having a thumb piece and a large scrolled handle. Its use was confined, in Europe, to the area north of the Alps. In England and the American colonies the tankard came into use at the end of the sixteenth century and was immensely popular in the seventeenth and eighteenth centuries. It was used for drinking beer and light wine, which was enjoyed in great quantities and at all times of the day. Tankards ranged in size from approximately a pint to over two quarts.

Pots and jugs

Pots and jugs were pouring vessels for drinks and water. The early form is the bottle-shaped jug found in Antiquity and in the Near Orient, with a strongly retracted foot, bulging body and high, slender lidded neck (page 29). It was in use until c. 1700, and became the model for the pear-shaped coffee pot common in the eighteenth century. Besides this we also find the more slender, taller form of jug with triangular opening in the sixteenth and seventeenth century, rather like a tankard. Towards the end of the seventeenth century it is sometimes equipped with a tubular spout, although it still does not serve as coffee pot. We also find the ewer together with a large, flat basin, the 'lavoir' (see pages 124 and 125), which was a coverless pouring vessel for washing the hands, necessary before the introduction of the fork, and above all during the princely ceremony of the lever. From around the mid-seventeenth century it took the form, derived from the beaker, of open jug with high foot, and walls drawn out into a triangular spout; this was a preliminary form of the helmet jug with its high baluster and walls, which was popular throughout the eighteenth century (cf. ill. p. 165). We find the same form of ewer and basin serving as baptismal implements, just as the lidded jug was used as a Protestant mass vessel. In the eighteenth century, when the indulgence of tea and coffee had become a social necessity, the lidded jug was mainly used at table as a hot-water jug, for preparing and diluting drinks, or in its smaller form as a cream or milk jug.

Tea and coffee plate

Porringer. In England, a two-handled bowl, usually with a cover, popular chiefly in the seventeenth century but made through the eighteenth century. Synonymous with caudle cups and posset pots (in England). Small varieties are sometimes called cupping or bleeding bowls. In the American colonies, a porringer was a shallow bowl with a horizontal pierced handle (with a few exceptions). Porringers were made as strictly utilitarian vessels for any "wet" food, in contradistinction to the caudle cup or the posset pot, which, in the colonies, were regarded as objects for use on special occasions.

Although these beverages had been known previously, the regular supply of tea and coffee to Europe did not begin until the 1660s. From then on these stimulants became increasingly popular, particularly in Holland and England. The same applies to chocolate, which had penetrated to the North via Spain or the West Indies somewhat earlier. But although their popularity spread quickly, new forms of vessel for their preparation were not evolved until the end of the century; they were fully developed in the first decades of the eighteenth century.

The form of the teapot has remained basically the same in spite of variants until the present time. It was modelled on the ceramic ware imported from Japan and China together with the tea. A squat, broad rather than tall shape proved most convenient for the preparation of the brew, for the tea would not draw so well in a high pot. As tea leaves settle, the spout is usually set rather low. We never find a triangular spout. Because silver is a good conductor of heat and becomes very hot, the handle is almost always wooden, or more rarely ivory. If it is silver, it is isolated by the introduction of little plaques of ivory at the points where it is attached.

In England, matching tea services were not made before 1725. Complete matching sets were occasionally made during the mid-eighteenth century but are rare before 1790.

The form of the can largely coincides with that of the teapot. Its collapsible handle arched over the whole body of the vessel. It stood on a *rechaud* (small wick burner) and served for keeping the water at boiling point for making fresh tea at a moment's notice (see page 160). We may presume, however, that tea was occasionally prepared in the kettle.

Unlike tea, there was no model for the coffee pot, even in its land of origin. So at first existing types of jug, which were mainly used as pouring vessels for wine during the seventeenth century, were used. In the early eighteenth century we find the slender pear-shaped form, reminiscent of the old bottle-shaped jug, and it soon became the prototype for the coffee pot. We find few variants before the end of the century (slender ovoid form, fluted cylinder).

The chocolate pot has the same form as the coffee pot. It can only be distinguished by the round opening in the cover, which can be closed by a sliding panel, for the introduction of the whisk for making the drink frothy. This habit taken over from the New World (the Conquistadores reported that Montezuma sipped chocolate from a great golden cup), and it survived until the end of the eighteenth century. Although the chocolate pot often has a straight handle set at right angles of the spout, this is not a characteristic feature. It usually occurs on pots resting on three small feet to facilitate placing them on the *rechaud*. Although in the case of chocolate it was particularly important to keep the drink warm, the straight handle and little feet also occur, although more rarely, on coffee pots. The preparation of tea or coffee at table included, although not as a general rule, the tea or coffee percolator, which has survived in Russia under the name '*samovar*' until the present day. A large, precious vessel, it offered every opportunity for rich decoration, which is another reason why it was not found on every table. The large, free-standing urn-, pear- or egg-shaped kettle has one or several spouts that can be closed by taps; it is always connected with a burner.

Inevitably one or more tea caddies stood on the tea table as containers for the brown or green tea leaves. Usually they are bottle-shaped or angular, rising vertically with a short, narrow neck. Later they often take the form of smooth, angular boxes with hinged lids. While cups and plates were always ceramic, the silver tea and coffee set were completed by a cream or milk jug, which could take the open form of helmet jug or be pear-shaped. The sugar caster usually looks like a small tureen. Towards the end of the eighteenth century it often has dainty perforations and is inset with dark blue glass.

Table services

The sixteenth century chiefly evolved ceremonial drinking vessels, while the food vessels consisted of less precious materials, even at noble tables. But the following century brought an increasing refinement and enrichment of table plate, which reached its peak in the eighteenth century. The drinking vessel, by contrast, is now glass. However numerous and varied the vessels and forms became, the plates and dishes, bowls and tureens were predominately silver.

The familiar form of plate, with round, depressed centre and broad rim (the 'flange') was used throughout the Middle Ages as a paten, but did not occur as secular plate until the sixteenth century. It has survived throughout the centuries, and the decoration is usually restricted to the flange. The numerous dishes necessary for serving the food, often equipped with a dish cover to keep it warm, are based on this flat, round form, although they also occur as ovals from the seventeenth century on. At the beginning of the eighteenth century, the broad flange shrank to a profiled rim surrounding the plates and dishes in scallops and buckles. The standing dish, known in the Middle Ages in the form of the salver, is occasionally a flat dish now. As a tray, the dish is sometimes furnished with two handles.

Trencher salt. Small individual containers for salt, taking their name from the trencher or plate by which they were placed.

Tureens and bowls

Tureen is an English word adapted from the French *terrine*, a pottery pot used to hold soup or stews and other semi-liquid foods. The vessel type came into use after 1700. Its basic form is a bulging oval with arched lid and two handles; it stands on a foot-ring or low feet. Its large, compact shape, the varied curves of its contours and the variety of sculptural decorative detail assured it an important place on the table. Even before the time of the Empire, when it usually gave up the oval shape in favour of a more rigid circle and was equipped with a retracted foot, we often find it standing on a separately made, gradated pedestal, which raises it even higher. Its predecessor may have been the '*écuelle*', the covered dish or bowl. It was known since the fifteenth century in the form of a round, moderately deep dish with two handles and a slightly domed cover. Often both the bowl and the cover are equipped with small feet, so that the cover can be taken off and turned upside down to be used as a plate (see page 132, below). This particular type continued from the sixteenth until well into the eighteenth century.

Then we find the emergence of a smaller, round or oval covered dish, whose form and shape scarcely differ from that of the tureen, and which often forms part of the same set.

Among the many additional types of table plate in the eighteenth century we must also note the 'saucière' or sauce tureen. It retained its boat shape until the end of the century, upon which we occasionally find covered, handled bowls. At first it served as a pouring vessel, with the pouring lip drawn out on one side and the handle on the other. Later, when a ladle was added, it still retained this form. Gradually a second pouring lip began to replace the handle as a support for the sauce ladle.

Condiments were placed on the table for each diner in special containers. There were salt cellars, mustard pots, condiment boxes – usually in two compartments with hinged lids – and stands with glass bottles for oil and vinegar. Casters were usually made in sets of three pieces: a larger one for sugar and two smaller ones for black and Cayenne pepper. Their basic shape is a narrow, tall body with a steeply rising, dome-like pierced cover. Occasionally a mustard pot belonged to the set, usually with handles and non-perforated lid. We may also note the sprinkling spoon, whose perforated bowl allows one to sprinkle the condiment evenly over the food.

Table candlesticks

The candlestick also belonged to the festive table, although it did not only serve as table plate. As a source of light, it could be stood anywhere in the room. The seventeenth century seems to have preferred either single candlesticks or pairs, which were not necessarily a set part of the table decoration. The silver candlestick does not appear frequently until the last decades of the century. The many sets of candlesticks from the eighteenth century suggest that a single candlestick belonged to every set of table plate. The structure is always the same: a heavy foot and a tall, slender stem ending in a socket for the candle, with a grease pan. From the mid-eighteenth century, multi-branched – usually triple-branched – candelabra or *girandoles* become more frequent, set on the central axis of the table. Often the three-branched upper part was made separately and could be fixed to the joint of the socket of a single candlestick to form a *girandole*.

Knives, forks and spoons

The spoon is the oldest eating tool. Worked in silver, it already appears in Roman Antiquity and survived throughout the Middle Ages until the present time. Its basic form, a bowl-shaped lip attached to a stem, has remained the same. The only changes were in the form of the lip, which could be round or oval, and in the length of the stem.

Although the knife is also one of the oldest implements known to man, it was not used at table until relatively late. Greek and Roman Antiquity did not use it, and throughout the Middle Ages the food was cut up by the carver *(tranchier)* beforehand. From the fifteenth century on, we find the table knife, which the guest usually brought with him in a sheath, together with his own small carving knife. The pointed blade was intended for spearing pieces of meat, if the diner did not wish to use his fingers. Since the blade was usually steel, because this cut best, the silver decoration was restricted to the 'haft', the handle. Only on smaller knives, such as dessert, fruit or fish knives, do we find a silver blade.

The fork is also a very old kitchen and carving implement, but it is only found recently as a current table implement. Antique Rome used a small fork and Byzantium seems to have used it more often for elegant tables. Thence it came to Venice in about 1000, where it was in use for a time. We find it on occasion in the Middle Ages, but it was still not generally adopted in the sixteenth century. It had something of the reputation of a 'tool of the devil'. The only type that became more popular was the small fork for sticky sweetmeats and fruit from Italy. Sometimes we also find the combined spoon and fork, a fork to whose prongs one could attach a removable bowl by means of strap joints. Previously there were only two-pronged forks; but at the end of the sixteenth century we find three prongs in Italy, and in France the four-pronged fork occurs in the seventeenth century. Towards the end of the seventeenth century it finally became part of a set, together with spoons and knives. From then on it became indispensable at table.

Row 1: Burgundy (?) c. 1450, England 1480, Basel (?) late fifteenth century, France late fifteenth century, England c. 1500; row 2: Basel 1531 (the angels' heads and engraving added in the seventeenth century), Schaffhausen c. 1500, Denmark mid-sixteenth century, Strasbourg 1560–7, London 1579; row 3: Holland early seventeenth century, Paris 1620–21, Holland c. 1640, Denmark 1641, Paris (?) c. 1645, Nuremberg mid-seventeenth century

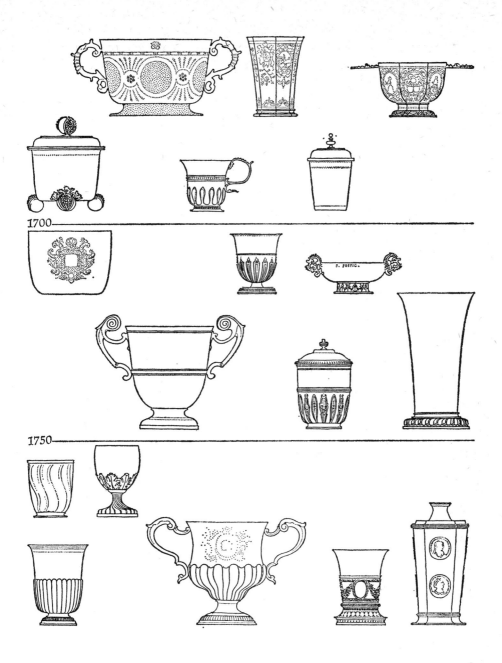

row 4: London 1654, Hamburg c. 1660, Sneek (Holland) c. 1675, Copenhagen 1688, Edinburgh 1691, Nuremberg c. 1700; row 5: London 1708, France first half of eighteenth century, Morlaix (France) c. 1725–30, Dublin 1734–5, France c. 1740, Amsterdam 1745; row 6: Augsburg 1749–51, Dublin 1770, Versailles 1775–80, Dublin 1785, Strasbourg 1789–98, Vienna 1803

Row 1: Germany c. 1540, London 1585, Kitzingen late sixteenth century; row 2: Essen or Baltikum, early seventeenth century, England 1619, Lübeck c. 1650; row 3: Augsburg c. 1670, London 1675, England 1699

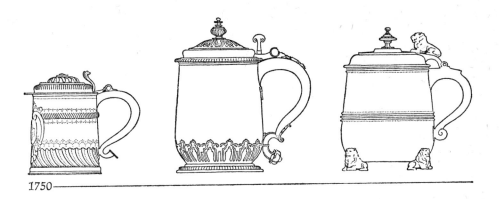

1750

row 4: London 1701–02, London 1703, England 1713; row 5: Augsburg 1761–3, Amsterdam 1770, London 1784

Row 1: England 1567, Lübeck *c.* 1570, London 1592; row 2: Paris first half of seventeenth century, Nuremberg *c.* 1650, Utrecht 1652; row 3: Utrecht 1654, London 1685, London 1699;

1750

row 4: Dijon 1700–01, Augsburg 1736–7, Paris 1736–7; row 5: Paris 1757, Birmingham 1774, England 1790

1700

1725

Row 1: London (?) c. 1685, Paris 1699–1700, France c. 1700, Groningen c. 1700; row 2: Randers (Denmark) 1700–10, London 1718–19, London 1719–20, Bordeaux 1724–5; row 3: Paris 1729–30, Edinburgh 1733, Dunkirk c. 1735, Bordeaux 1739–41;

row 4: Lille 1752 (?), Augsburg 1769–71, Nymegen 1767–70, Meddleburg 1770; row 5: London 1785, Paris 1794–1809, Paris 1794–1809, Sheffield late eighteenth century; row 6: London 1802–03, London 1814–15, Cassel (master's design) 1816, London 1827–8

1730

Row 1: London 1681–2, London 1711, London 1730; row 2: London 1736, Rome 1734–44, The Hague 1759;

1790

row 3: Sheffield 1760–70, Maastricht 1779, Paris 1785–6; row 4: Stuttgart early nineteenth century, Rome 1759–99, Würzburg *c.* 1810

Row 1: Edinburgh *c.* 1685, London early eighteenth century, Haarlem 1708, Halle 1716, Leeuwarden 1716; row 2: Haarlem 1735, London 1735–6, Paris 1743–4, Heide *c.* 1750, London 1759–60; row 3: Paris 1769–70, London 1773, London 1778–9, Maastricht 1781, York 1784–5

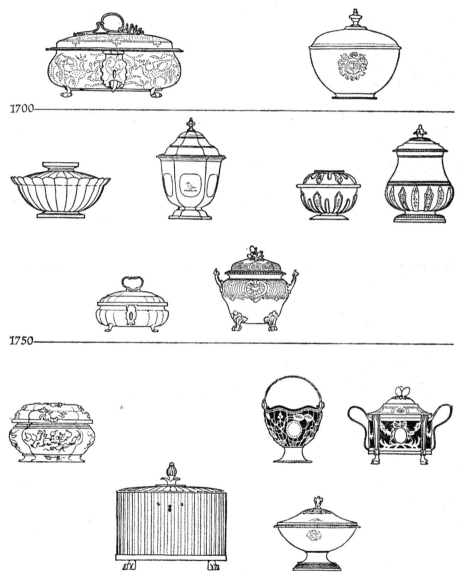

Row 1: London 1683–4, England 1691; row 2: England 1704, Dublin 1714, England 1728, Avignon (?) c. 1740, Danzig 1740, Paris 1748–9; row 3: Augsburg 1767–9, England 1773, Lyon 1775–81, Stockholm 1798–9, Paris 1794–1809

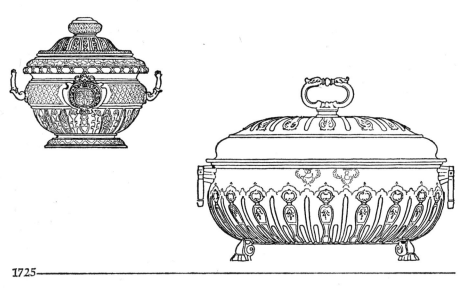

1725

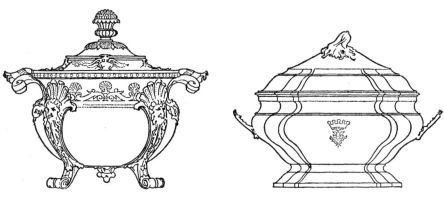

Row 1: Paris 1714–15, London c. 1726; row 2: Paris 1726–7, Copenhagen 1737;

1775

row 3: Augsburg 1751–3, Strasbourg 1757; row 4: London 1771, Stockholm 1798

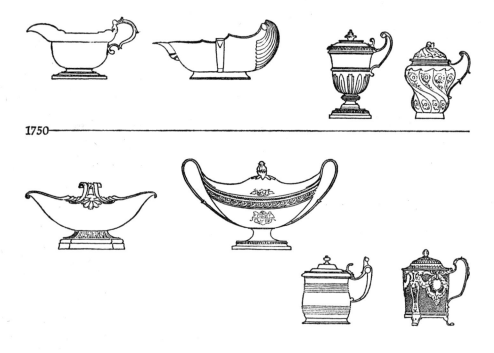

1750

Row 1: London 1732, Aachen mid-eighteenth century, Paris 1717–22, Thouars (France) 1745–7; row 2: Senlis 1769–71, London 1787, Paris 1758–9, Paris 1778–9

1700

1750

Row 1: Montpellier 1694–5, Delft 1696, London 1699, France c. 1700; row 2: London 1701, Toulouse first half of eighteenth century, Paris 1707–08, London 1716; row 3: Maastricht 1771, The Hague 1789, Amsterdam 1796

Table candlesticks

1650

Row 1: Amsterdam 1633, Paris 1636–7, Amsterdam 1642; row 2: Delft 1652, Amsterdam 1667, London 1675–6, Cassel *c.* 1685, Montpellier 1695–6;

1750

row 3: London 1720–1, Paris 1738–9, Paris 1744–5, Paris 1747–8; row 4: Paris 1767–8, Amsterdam 1770, Dresden or Leipzig *c.* 1770, German *c.* 1780, Augsburg 1800

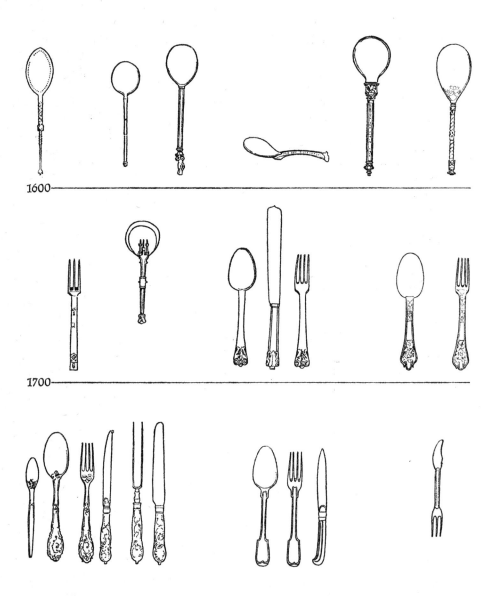

Row 1: Scotland late twelfth century; Scotland *c.* 1330, Leipzig third quarter of sixteenth century, Ingolstadt 1573, Breslau (?) late sixteenth century, South German (?) *c.* 1600; row 2: Paris first half of seventeenth century, Groningen 1663, Paris 1677, Paris 1683–4; row 3: probably south German mid-eighteenth century, Paris 1769–70, Paris 1778–9

Technique, history of the Guilds and hall-marks

Technique. Silver and gold are minerals. Neither is found in its pure form, but always associated with other metals – gold usually with silver, silver usually with other impure minerals. So they must be smelted and refined. In its pure form, gold is very stable, oxygen resistent and acid resistent, although extremely ductile. One gramme of gold can be drawn out into a wire two kilometres long, or rolled out into sheets up to 1/12,000 millimetres thin. Silver is less soft, and therefore more brittle to work with. Although it also resists oxygen, it can combine with sulphur to produce tarnishing in a thin, blackish layer on the surface. In their pure state gold and silver are too soft to be made into utensils so they are hardened by the addition of other metals. The goldsmith always alloyed the metal himself.

Most of what we know of the techniques of the old gold- and silversmiths comes from Theophilus Presbyter's *Schedula diversarum artium*, dating from c. 1100. Presumably the author is identical with the goldsmith-monk Roger von Helmarshausen. This handbook describes all the practices in detail, together with the tools and the most convenient site and equipment for the workshop. More than four and a half centuries later, in 1568, it is followed by Benvenuto Cellini's *Trattato dell'oreficeria*. This treatise shows that the goldsmiths' methods of works had scarcely changed. In fact most of the techniques were already fully developed and in use in Antiquity. So there has been no real technical evolution.

The most important processes have always been forging and embossing. First the heated metal is beaten into plate on the anvil with the planishing hammer, and then streched with a smaller hammer. Thanks to its malleability, the plate can be hammered into a hollow form. Reliefs and sculptural ornament are raised from underneath to produce the basic forms. The finer details on the surface are executed after the embossing with a chasing hammer or punches. Apart from embossing, hammering silver plate over a matrix or patrix (depressed or raised form) has also been known since early times; it was principally used for ornaments in continuous patterns. The smaller parts of the vessels, such as handles, spouts, lid knops, feet, small figures and various ornaments, were cast. This required a model, a two-part negative form into which the molten metal is poured. This is solid casting. The complicated method of hollow casting round a wax shape modelled around a clay core *(à cire perdue)* was used less for silver than for large-format bronze casting. The individual parts were usually mounted by means of soldering, riveting, joining or hinging. Finally the finished piece is cleaned by immersion in a boiling solution of sulphuric or tartaric acid and polished with jeweller's rouge, animal's claw or boar's tooth. Gilding was done by fire-gilding. In this process the gold is melted and mixed with mercury in a crucible, and the resulting creamy mass is applied in an even layer on the silver; the mercury is evaporated by heat and the film of gold fuses to the silver. Since mercury vapours are poisonous, more recent goldsmiths have only used the process of electrolyzed gilding discovered by Brugnatelli in 1805.

The goldsmith used a great number of decorative techniques. The most important are niello, enamel and – besides the art of setting precious stones – filigree. The latter, as its name implies (filum = thread, granum = corn) consists of twisted wires soldered into the ground and ending in little spheres. It can be worked *à jour* too, although this technique is more rare. Niello (from nigellus = blackish) is a fused mass of silver, lead, sulphur and borax, which can be melted into the design made on the silver with the graver or scorper and is then polished. The nineteenth-century pieces known as 'Thula' silver are also niello works. Enamel is a glass flux coloured with metallic oxides. They are melted on to a metal sheet at a temperature of 700–800°. The sheet is prepared for enamelling by soldering on thin cellular walls or wires, or by indentations (bosses, reliefs); the design on the metal is an essential artistic component of the process. Often a metalwork is entirely enamelled. Opaque and translucent enamel are two main types. The different techniques of enamelling reflect the different style and periods in precious metalwork.

History of guilds and hall-marks. In the early Middle Ages the monasteries and abbeys were the centres of all artistic creation. Besides workshops for handicrafts, they also housed the goldsmiths who belonged to the monastic order. They were the basis of the great achievements of Carolingian and Ottonian art; we need only recall Reichenau, Fulda and Hildesheim under Bishop Bernward. The large landowners also had their own craftsmen who settled at their residences. These were vassals who had to do socage. There was a lesser number of free, travelling craftsmen, who occasionally worked for the monasteries and Courts.

After about 1000, when the towns began to experience an economic flowering thanks to the imperial market privileges, they attracted the craftsmen. The slogan 'town air means freedom' provoked them to escape from their liege masters to seek freedom in the towns. This is when the guilds appeared, in the form of economic interest associations, whose main duties were to supervise the quality of the work and regulate trade by excluding free competition. But their economic efforts could only become fully effective if the guild was made into a compulsory organization, to which each craftsman within the walls of the city had to belong and whose laws he had to obey. Gradually, although not in all the crafts, this led to the so-called 'sworn in' crafts, in which the master of the guild was pledged by oath to the town council. After violent and prolonged disputes in the fourteenth and fifteenth centuries, the guilds were finally given political rights. In Italy they had already taken part in political life since the thirteenth century. The earliest guild of goldsmiths was that of Paris, of 1202, a fraternal association of masters. The first statutes of the 'corps d'orfèvres' date from 1260. Similar corporations soon formed in other towns too. Their patron saint was St Eloi (Eligius), who is said to have lived from 590–660. He had trained in Limoges in the workshop of Abbo and achieved such skill that his master recommended him to the treasure of King Clotair II in Paris. The king commissioned him to create a golden throne and supplied him with the material. But to his surprise Eloi used the gold to make not one, but two thrones. This honesty brought him the king's trust and Clotair made him his mint master and 'tesaurarius'. He retained this office under King Dagobert I too. It seems that no works of gold by his hand survive, but there are coins that name him as mint master. In 632 Eloi founded the monastery of Solignac near Limoges. When the king died in 639, he decided to devote himself to religion, was ordained and became Bishop of Noyon in 641. The first of the Paris fraternities of goldsmiths already referred to St Eloi, and henceforth he was celebrated as the patron saint of goldsmiths every first day of December.

The tasks of the guild included seeing to the training of new blood, which was subjected to specific regulations and allowed no exceptions. The guild of goldsmiths was one of the most distinguished, and in its choice of apprentices it took great care not to damage its reputation. Not everybody could learn the craft; a number of trades were excluded, in particular the 'dishonest' trades such as vagrants, knackers and quacks. A condition of entry was legitimate birth. On beginning his apprenticeship, the boy would be some fourteen years old, and had to train for three or four years. During this period he lived in the master's house and the latter's wife had to care for him as though he were one of her own. The apprenticeship was hard and the daily demands great. Usually the boy had to pay his master a teaching fee. After his 'release' at the end of his apprenticeship, the journeyman began to travel; this was obligatory in most countries for anyone who wanted to become a master. The period as journeyman lasted some five years. Often it was extended by a long period of waiting at the place where he wanted to acquire the right to live and work as master and citizen. Sons of goldsmiths were absolved from the period of waiting, and journeymen who married the daughter or widow of a master could immediately become masters. But in many towns, as in Nuremberg, a journeyman who had married before taking his master's examination could never become a master. To qualify he had to execute his 'master-piece' without any help, under the eyes of the master; its form was usually prescribed by the guild. In Nuremberg in the sixteenth century, the journeyman had to make en enamelled ring, a cut signet and an agate cup. After 1571, models were even made for the aspiring masters to copy. Three such model cups have survived in the Germanisches Nationalmuseum in Nuremberg and in the Victoria and Albert Museum in London. They are ascribed to Wenzel Jamnitzer. Unlike all the other contemporary work, they bear no master's mark or assay mark and are not gilt. This shows that the master's examination required skill but no artistic inspiration.

The most important task of the guild was to supervise the quality of the gold and silver work, on which its reputation and its well being depended. A carefully worked out system of controls ensured the equal quality of the materials. Since gold and silver are too soft in their pure form for making utensils, other metals are added to harden them. Gold is alloyed with copper and silver, silver usually with copper, i.e., with non-precious metals. The higher the proportion of copper, the less precious the resulting silver work will be. But the customer can neither recognize nor control these proportions. Without a guarantee he would have to depend blindly on the goldsmith's assurance that the work really had the degree of fine silver for which he was paying. The guild took over this guarantee. The strictness with which it controlled the degree of fine silver protected the buyer from cheating; for the guild itself, this guarantee was essential for the preservation of its high reputation.

A definite system had to be created in order to fix and judge the degree of fineness. In Germany the *Mark* was the most current unit of weight in earlier times. The Cologne *Mark*, whose weight was 233.86 grammes, was the most used. It became the measuring unit, but was different for gold and silver; the subdivisions were:

1 *Mark* gold into 24 carats, the carat into 12 grains

1 *Mark* silver into 16 *Lots*, the *Lot* into 18 grains

This is to say that fine gold (gold without any alloy) is 24 carat gold. But if the degree of alloy is 2 carats, it is called 22 carat gold: so the *Mark* of gold consists of 22 carats fine gold and 2 carats of alloy, whether this alloy be copper, silver or both. Fine silver is 16 *Lot*. For 14 *Lot* silver, the *Mark* of silver consists of 14 *Lot* fine silver and 2 *Lot* of alloy.

Although even 9 carat gold was worked, the usual alloy was 18 carat gold. The ideal fineness for works of art was 22 carat. We know that Cellini considerd a lower gold content too hard and too difficult to solder, while 23 carat gold was too soft. The fineness of silver could sink to 6 to 8 *Lot*, but this was only for making buttons, shoe buckles and similar fashionable articles. The most current alloys since the sixteenth century are 13.14 or even 12 *Lot*. 15 *Lot* silver has always existed, but was most current in the Middle Ages.

There were two methods of establishing the fineness of the silver. The 'streak' test was already known to the Greeks and Romans and is also found in the Early Middle Ages. If one brushes a streak of silver on the black, usually cut, unpolished touchstone, it will leave a streak of a certain colour. In fine silver it is light yellow, and the addition of copper will render it redder. So the colour of the streak gives the *Lot*. In order to make the comparison, a 'touch needle' was often used, that is to say, a series of small silver rods on a metal ring or plate corresponding to the *Lot* scale, either 1 *Lot* to 1 *Lot*, or 1/2 *Lot* to 1/2 *Lot*. So if an alloy is expected to be 13 *Lot*, the colour the streak must coincide with is that of the 13 *Lot* needle.

Since gold is alloyed with copper and with silver in various proportions, so many gradations of tone are possible on the streak that they give no idea of the fineness. But if nitric acid is put on the streak, its reaction to this acid will determine the fineness of the gold.

The second method, the cupellation method, is not so easy, but more precise. A small portion of silver is taken for trial and weighed. Then lead is added and it is melted in a small crucible, the cupel, during which time the copper separates from the silver and fuses with the lead; the litharge thus produced trickles into the cupel, and the silver can be taken out and weighed again. The difference between the two results shows the amount of copper that was added. This method allows one to determine the fineness of gold to 1/8 of a grain, silver to 1/4 grain, while the 'streak' test only shows differences of 1/2 carat (6 grains), or 1/4 *Lot* (4 1/2 grains). Yet the 'streak' test has been used throughout history because it is more convenient, and because its lack of precision was not always important. In any case one had to allow the gold-smiths a certain leeway in their alloys.

These tests were undertaken by assay masters of the guild, elected for a certain time. They were done on every silver work designed for trade, in order to test the fineness of the silver and to guarantee it for the customer. The assay masters would visit the masters' workshops at regular intervals, or even unexpectedly, and scratch off a small portion of silver with the graving needle from each piece of silver in the workshop for the cupellation test. This test produces a zig-zag scratch, which can be seen on countless silver works. A single portion of silver was, however, never sufficient for melting down. It was only by repeated scratching that enough silver was collected in the boxes of the assay masters for a test. If the fineness corresponded to the regulation laid down by the guild, the assay master marked the completed work with a stamp, the assay mark (Bz). Then the master added his own mark, the master's mark. These marks are the guarantees of the fineness. The penalties for breaking the rule were high, for instance if a piece was sold that had not been assayed.

Although marking was not a regular custom until after the sixteenth century, the guilds tried very early on to regulate the alloy by legislation and to guarantee it by stamps. Our earliest examples are on coins, whose impressed image guarantees the weight and fineness. The Roman stamps on gold and silver bars followed the principles of the coiner's mark. But completed works of gold never seem to have been stamped in Rome. Byzantine works, by contrast, have a stamp, usually consisting of five individual marks. They have not yet been fully identified. In the West, the first surviving record is a regulation issued by Philip the Bold in 1275 which required a city mark. In Germany (Erfurt), marking goes back to at least 1289. The first order for a simulataneous city mark and master's mark occurs in Montpellier in 1355; both were also demanded in Strasbourg in 1366. These early marking regulations were evidently not observed consistently, for no marked works have survived in Germany in spite of the number of original works. No doubt we may assume that the mark either consisted of the master's mark or of the city mark, and later of both. This rule was to apply in Germany until the mid-nineteenth century. Not until 1886 did an imperial law establish uniform regulations for the whole empire; at the same time we find the new division of the degree of fineness taken over and measured in thousandth parts in France. It still applies today.

For us these assay and master's marks are more than marks of guarantee, for they give us a chance to localize works and to attribute them to different masters. The assay mark, which usually consists of the city arms or one of its heraldic motifs, often varied according to date, as in the case of Augsburg. This often makes it possible to date a work precisely, as does the date letter used in some towns. The master's mark usually consists of his monogram, but figurative marks and house marks also occur. These master's marks can often only be identified and ascribed by laborious detail work in archives.

Marking customs varied from country to country and domain to domain. In Flanders, under Maxmilian, a uniform regulation concerning the date letter was issued in 1484. In 1501 Archduke Philip the Fair issued a goldsmiths' statute for Holland, Zeeland and Friesia; in 1502, for Antwerp. In 1517 a new regulation appeared, presumably embracing the entire Burgundian land; and in Brussels, on 13 April 1551, Emperor Charles V issued a goldsmiths' order for the Netherlands. In 1614 a regulation issued by Archduke Albrecht and Isabella demanded a second assay mark for every town in the Habsburg Netherlands. For the time being, the northern provinces (Holland), who had meanwhile gained independence, remained bound by Charles V's regulations. In 1661 the crowned provincial lion was added as a provincial mark of a superior degree of fineness. The order is now as follows: large plate with a superior fineness has to be punched with the master's mark, city arms, date letter and provincial lion; smaller pieces of the same superior fineness require at least the master's and the province's mark. Smaller pieces of a lower fineness could dispense with the date letter until 1733 (Rosenberg). This list of regulations and marks clearly shows the complexity of the system.

Of the more important marks, we shall discusss those from England, the American colonies and France. In England hall-marks, (more commonly termed "marks"), are found on all silver and silver-gilt plate that passed through the Assay office at Goldsmith's Hall in London. Provincial assay towns had their own individual town marks. In addition, English pieces of silver for export, wherever made, were often not fully marked. The subject of English silver marks is complex. It is necessary to study *all* the marks when trying to arrive at the date and the provenance of any individual piece. Handy pocket guides to English silver marks are readily available at most dealers in antique silver and Sheffield plate.

Each piece or seperate part of a piece of English silver should have at least four marks. (1) *The Hall or Assay Office Mark.* The *Leopard's Head, the* mark of London, was introduced in 1300. The Leopard's head was crowned, beginning in 1478; the crown being dropped in 1821 (2) *Maker's Mark* introduced in 1363. (3) *Annual Date Letter.* The letter is changed in sequence annually (in London pieces on May 29th), and in addition both letter and shield enclosing it are varied in size, shape and type to denote the difference in date in each cycle. The London assay office uses an alphabet of twenty letters, omitting 'J' and five letters from 'V' to 'Z'. (4) *Sterling Quality Mark.* The 'Sterling' mark is the Lion Passant (an heraldic lion walking past the spectator). Variations in the form of the lion, leopard and date letters should be very carefully observed since on four occasions this system has been altered as follows:

(a) silver made to the *Britannia standard,* compulsory from 1697 to 1719, and optional ever since. Britannia silver had a maker's mark and a date letter. The individual town mark and the sterling mark were dropped and replaced by two others – (1) the *Lion's Head Erased* (an heraldic lion's head in profile, jagged at the neck (2) the figure of a seated Britannia. (2) During the years 1784 to 1890, a special tax of sixpence an ounce on silver was receipted by a punch of the *Sovereign's Head* in profile in an oval (George III, George IV, William IV, and Victoria (up to 1890 when the tax was dropped). (3) Purely *voluntary* additions added a fifth mark which might be added from 1933–36 for the Silver Jubilee of George V, with a double profile of King George and Queen Mary. Also, *voluntary,* for the coronation of Queen Elizabeth II, followed by the date letters of 1952–1954.

In America, the colonies and later. In 17th century America, the craftsman's final step in the completion of a piece of silver was to strike his "mark" on his work, thus declaring not only its quality but his personal guarantee of its worth, in the absence of any legal assay office. In the American colonies silversmiths followed the English practice of stamping the first initials of the craftsman's name and surname, or, in some cases as a rebus (i. e. a rabbit, for John Coney). This was used chiefly for easy identification in case of lost or stolen silver. Early in the second quarter of the 18th century, the silversmith often used his full surname, preceded by his initial in a reserve or rectangle. The place of manufacture was commonly added on early 19th century silver from Philadelphia and New York, where craftsmen, influenced by the marks on imported English silver, also indulged in the use of pseudo hall-marks. The quality of the metal followed the English standard of sterling. Not until 1814 was any law enacted for state regulation and an assay office set up. The use of the word *Sterling* applied to marks in America, or elsewhere, is not commonly found until after 1860.

The decree issued by Philip the Bold of France in 1275, which demanded a city mark and a master's mark, applied to the whole of France. It scarcely changed for three centuries. But in 1577, Henry II decided to introduce a new control mark for the 'droit de remède' which he demanded for fiscal purposes, and in 1579 he appointed tax farmers who exacted fees for their charge marks. But the goldsmiths successfully opposed this government action. In 1631 Louis XIII again tried to introduce the decree, but it only survived for two years. This charge mark, called 'droit de marque sur l'or et l'argent', did not take effect until 1672, with the taxing of the whole kingdom; it remained valid until 1781. However, the border areas which were incorporated into France from the time of Louis XIII, the 'provinces réputées étrangères relativement à la régie', were excluded from the statute: Béarn, Alsace, Roussillon, Flanders and Hennegau, Franche-Comté and Lorraine.

At first the charge mark only consisted of a receipt mark. In 1681 it was joined by the discharge mark. So the marks were now as follows:

1. As soon as the preliminary work was completed, usually before it was mounted, the maker put his master's mark on each individual part – 'poinçon á contre saing', later called 'poinçon particulier de maître'.

2. In this state the work was laid before the official tax farmer in the 'bureau de la régie', where it was made liable for tax by the 'poinçon de charge'.

3. The master then presented his work to the guild, the 'bureau de maison commune', where it was tested by the assay master and punched with the city mark and usually the date letter.

4. Now at last the piece can be completed. Before being sold, it is given the discharge mark ('poinçon de décharge') in the same 'bureau de régie', which means that the tax has been paid to the tax-farmer (Rosenberg).

Each work has therefore four marks. Since the assay and discharge marks also varied according to fineness and size (large, small, and very small works), and the punches varied according to tax-farmer and region (généralités), the number of different marks extends into the thousands. After the charge mark was abolished in 1791, there came a period of very arbitrary marking. A new system was not introduced until 1797. Then the assay was done not by the guilds but the state, under the name 'garantie'. The fineness is denoted by the 'poinçon de titre', and the payment of tax by the 'poinçon de garantie'. The Paris marks differed from those of the Départements.

These basic principles of marking no doubt make it clear why we cannot give a complete list of marks. The inventories of marks according to towns and countries are already very extensive, but we have still not nearly discovered all the material. The following tables of marks (after Rosenberg and others) are intended to illustrate the main forms and variations.

Aachen
1: sixteenth century; 2: from 16 April 1573, c. 1624 and later; 3: c. 1808; 4: second half of nineteenth century

Aarhus (Jutland)

Aberdeen (Scotland)
1: seventeenth to eighteenth century; 2: eighteenth century

Altona
The oldest assay mark occurs on a piece dated 1702.
1: 1703; 2: 1761; 3: 1782; 4: mid-nineteenth century

Amsterdam
Separate mark with date letter since 1503.
1: c. 1566; 2: c. 1606; 3: c. 1694; 4/5: mid-eighteenth century

master's marks 6: Thomas Bogaert (* probably in Utrecht in 1597, Amsterdam c. 1625, d. 1652–3); 7: Johannes Bogaert, son of 6 (* 1626, d. 1677 or shortly before); 8: Joannes Lutma the Younger, son of 8 (* 1624, d. 1685)

Antwerp
separate mark with date letter from the early seventeenth century.
1: 1539–40; 2: 1616–07; 3: 1641–2; 4: 1738–9; 5: c. 1767

Augsburg
Marking since 1529. The change of assay mark corresponds to the change of assay master. With date letter since 1735.
1: 1567–85?; 2: 1586, 1591 and probably also later; 3: c. 1600; 4: 1610–25; 5: 1630 to 1645; 6: 1648–51?; 7: 1655–60; 8: 1674 to 1680; 9: 1685–1700?; 10: 1695 or earlier – 1705;

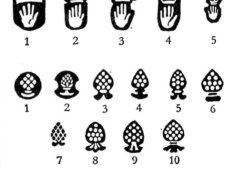

11: 1712–13; 12: 1716–20?; 13: 1723 to 1735; 14: 1743–5; 15: 1771–3, 16:1795 to 1797

11. 12 13 14 15 16

master's marks:
some members of the Biller family:
17: Johann Baptist B. (m. 1638, d. 1683); 18/19: probably Johann Ludwig B. II (* 1692, d. 1746); 20/21: probably Albrecht B. (* 1663, d. 1720); 22: perhaps Johann Jacob B. I (m. 1714, d. 1723)

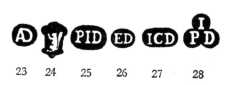

17 18 19 20 21 22

some members of the Drentwett family:
23: probably Abraham D. (mentioned 1649, d. 1666); 24: perhaps Christoph D. II (m. 1667, d. 1706); 25: probably Philipp Jacob D. (m. 1669, d. 1712); 26: perhaps Emanuel D. (* 1679, d. 1753 or 1755); 27: Johann Christoph D. (master 1718, d. 1763); 28: Philipp Jakob D. VI (master 1718, d. 1754); several other members of the family until the late eighteenth century

23 24 25 26 27 28

some members of the Gelb family:
29: perhaps Melchior G. (master c. 1617, d. 1654); 30/31: perhaps Matthäus G. (m. 1627, d. 1671); 32: probably Melchior G. (m. 1672, d. 1707); 33/34: probably also members of the family

29 30 31 32 33 34 35

35: probably Johannes Lencker (* 1573, d. 1637); 36: perhaps Heinrich Mannlich (* c. 1625, master in Troppau 1649, in Augsburg since 1651, d. 1698); 37: probably Johann Heinrich Mannlich (* 1660, d. 1718); 38–41: Johann Andreas Thelot (* 1655, d. 1734); many of his works signed in full

36 37 38 39 40 41

America
master's marks:

1: Mark of John Coney, used after about 1705. Coney, a Boston craftsman, was born in 1688, died in 1722

1

2: One of the marks of Jacob Hurd, of Boston (1702–1758)

2

3: The mark of Paul Revere (called "the patriot" to distinguish him from his father). 1735–1807

3

4: John McMullin, of Philadelphia (active c. 1791–1794). Pseudo-marks (eagle and star supplementing his name)

4

Bamberg

1: fifteenth-sixteenth century; 2: 1626; 3: 1639; 4: mid-eighteenth century; 5: late eigthteenth century

Barcelona

1: fourteenth-fifteenth century /?; 2: sixteenth century; 3: sixteenth (and seventeenth?) century

Basel

1/2: mid-seventeenth century; 3/4: seventeenth century; 5–7: eighteenth century

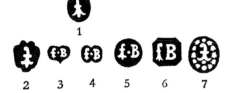

Bergen (Norway)
(Norway)

Probably date letter, (year number), month mark and assay mark separate since the late eighteenth century.

1: 1784; 2: 1820

Berlin

With letters in the assay mark since 1747

1/2: assay mark for 13 and 14 *Lot* silver (15 *Lot* shown by the figure 15) since 21 May 1735; 3: 12 *Lot* silver (without number!), first half of eighteenth century; 4: 1776

master's marks:

5: Daniel Männlich the Elder (* 1625 Olbersdorf nr. Troppau, 1650 Berlin, court goldsmith, d. 1701); 7: Christian Lieberkühn (1733, mentioned as court goldsmith 1738, d. after 1764)

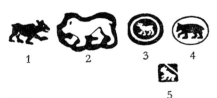

Bern

Self marking, *i. e.*, each master stamps the hall-mark himself. Work is in *14 Lot* since 1509, 13 *Lot* since 1726.

1–3: sixteenth century; 4: *c.* 1690; 5: *c.* 1800

Birmingham
since 1773

Bologna
eighteenth century

Bolsward (Friesia)
1725

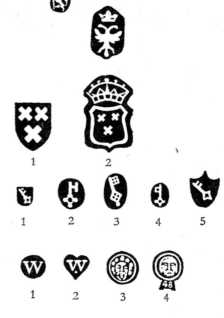

Breda (north Brabant, Netherlands)
1: fifteenth-sixteenth century; 2: sixteenth-
seventeenth century

1   2

Bremen
1: seventeenth century; 2: *c.* 1690; 3: seven-
teenth-eighteenth? century?; 4: *c.* 1720; 5:
nineteenth century

1   2   3   4   5

Breslau
Marking since 1539. Separate mark with date
letter since the early eighteenth century
1: 1553 to early seventeenth century; 2:
secondhalf of seventeenth century to after
1721: in 1677, 12 and 13 *Lot* silver was also
permitted besides the former 14 *Lot*. This
inferior silver was stamped by a new mark,
the head of St John. 3: in nineteen different
variations from the late seventeenth century
to 1842; 4: since 1843

1   2   3   4

Bruges
Separate mark with date letter
1: early sixteenth century; 2: *c.* 1613, perhaps
1622; 3: 1769

1   2

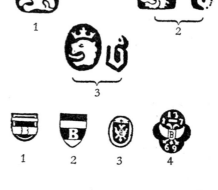

3

Brünn
1/2: to 1646; 3: 1683; 4: 1769

1   2   3   4

Brunswick
Probably separate mark with date letter
introduced late seventeenth century
1: seventeenth century; 2: *c.* 1695–1700; 2:
c. 1750; 4: 1790–1800

1   2   3   4

Brussels
Separate date letter
From *c.* 1513 the earlier assay marks were joined by the head of St. Michael as an additional mark. 1: early sixteenth century; 2: 1553; 3: *c.* 1660; 4. 1750 to *c.* 1760; 5: the rose occasionally appears with the lion and the head of St Michael, but usually replaces the latter. It disappears after 1660, to reappear in smaller format a century later; 6: since *c.* 1760

Budapest
Separate letter mark: year or assay mark.
1: seventeenth/eighteenth century; 2: eighteenth century; 3/4: eighteenth/nineteenth century

Chester (England)
1: with variants, seventeenth century and from 1780 to the present; 2: 1701–79

Chur (Switzerland)
1–3: sixteenth to seventeenth century

Colmar (Alsace)
sixteenth to seventeenth century

Cologne
With the *Lot* number (12, 13) since the first half of the eighteenth century.
1/2: sixteenth century; 3/4: sixteenth to seventeenth century; 5: second half of seventeenth century; 6: first half of eighteenth century; 7: mid-eighteenth century; 8: late eighteenth century

Constance
The great variety of assay marks suggest that the master who made the work stamped it himself. In this case the control of the fineness cannot be very precise.
1: *c.* 1557; 2–4: sixteenth to seventeenth century; 5–7: early seventeenth century; 8: late seventeenth century; 9–11: eighteenth century; 12: nineteenth century

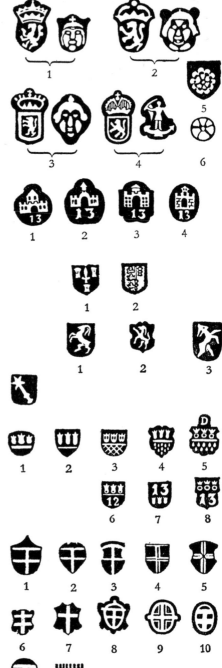

Copenhagen

Hall-marks were used before 1491, and after this year master's marks were also used. The assay mark with the three towers of the city arms since 1608. From 1685 all works of 5 *Lot* and more had to be tested for their fineness (13½ *Lot*) by the state (not guild) assay master and stamped with his own mark. In addition as special month mark (Zodiac sign) was introduced. So later works all have four different marks. From the outset, Copenhagen became the model for the whole of Denmark in matters concering the goldsmiths. 1: sixteenth century; 2: 1608; 3: 1645; 4: 1725; 5: 1769; 6: 1851

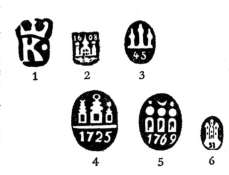

Danzig

One of the earliest recorded regulations on marking in Germany by the town council of Marienburg (representing Thorn, Elbing and Danzig) in 1395. Assay marks were only stamped occasionally, not regularly until 1621. In 1730, 13 *Lot* silver was required together with a special mark with the name of the assay master.
1: seventeenth century; 2: second half of seventeenth century; 3: seventeenth of eighteenth century; 4: seventeenth and early eighteenth century

Delft
1807–10

Dorpat (Estonia)
Marking since 1594
1: seventeenth century; 2: eighteenth century

Dresden

Special mark with date letter since 1702.
1: sixteenth to seventeenth century; from 1701–02 a new mark was introduced: The Saxon words with the D and the fineness (12–15 *Lot*). 2: mid-eighteenth century; 3–5: third thrid of eighteenth century; 6/7: nineteenth century

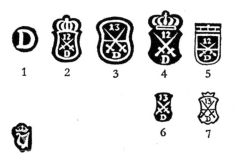

Dublin
in varying forms between the seventeenth and nineteenth century

Düsseldorf
Separate date letter since 1707.
1: seventeenth century; 2/3: seventeenth to eighteenth century; in 1707 a ruling that only 12 *Lot* silver could be worked. Later marks from the eighteenth century show, however, that 13 *Lot* silver was also used. 4–6: eighteenth century

1   2   3   4   5   6

Edinburgh
In varying forms from the sixteenth to seventeenth century

Eger (Bohemia)
1: seventeenth to eighteenth century; 2: eighteenth century

1   2

Einsiedeln (Switzerland)
1: seventeenth to eighteenth century; 2: eighteenth century

1   2

Elbing (west Prussia)
Early marks as in Danzig.
1: 1647 to late seventeenth century; 2: 1698–1705; 3: 1705; 4: 1742; 5: 1792–7, perhaps 1777–1811

1   2   3   4   5

Emden
With date letter since 1601
1: sixteenth century; 2. 1612; 3: 1645; 4: 1820

1   2   3   4

Erfurt
1: sixteenth century; 2: first half of seventeenth century; 3: second half of seventeenth century; 4: first half of eighteenth century; 5: second half of eighteenth century

1   2   3   4   5

Essen
seventeenth century

Ferrara
seventeenth century?

Florence
1: sixteenth century?; 2: seventeenth to eighteenth century; 3. eighteenth century

1   2   3

Frankfurt a.M.
Eagle mark since 1512
1: *c.* 1560: 2: sixteenth to seventeenth century; 3: seventeenth century; 4: early eighteenth century; 5/6: mid-eighteenth century; 7: late eighteenth century

1   2   3   4   5

6   7

268

Frankfurt a.d.O.
1: seventeenth to eighteenth century; 2: 1772

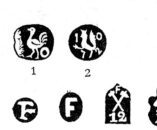

Freiberg i.S.
1: late sixteenth and early seventeenth century; 2: 1668; 3: eighteenth century; 4: mid-eighteenth century; 5: eighteenth to nineteenth century

Freiburg i.Br.
1: 1466; 2: c. 1528; 3: 1609; 4/5: seventeenth to eighteenth century

Freiburg (Switzerland)
1: c. 1630; 2: c. 1710; 3: c. 1750

Fürth
1: sixteenth century; 2 eighteenth century; 3: nineteenth century

Geneva
1/2: eighteenth century

Ghent
1: c. 1482; 2: second half of sixteenth century; 3: c. 1660; 4. c. 1722

Genoa
1: sixteenth century?; 2. seventeenth to eighteenth century; 3: late eighteenth century

Glasgow
In varying forms from the seventeenth century to the present day, a rectangular arms since 1781

(Swabian) Gmünd
Special mark with fineness in the eighteenth and nineteenth century.
1: in varying sizes from the sixteenth to early eighteenth century; 2: in varying sizes and slighly altered picture from c. 1720 to c. 1788; 3: c. 1762–86; 4: in varying arms early to mid-nineteenth century

Görlitz
1: sixteenth century; 2: seventeenth century; 3/4: eighteenth century

Göteborg
Special date letter since the late seventeenth
century; date alphabet as for Stockholm since
1759.
First half of eighteenth century, and earlier
and later in similar form

Goslar
until 1782, then an eagle with a 12 (fineness)
below

Gotha
1: seventeenth century; 2: c. 1688; 3: c. 1701
(doubtful whether Gotha)

1   2   3

Gouda (southern Holland)
sixteenth century

Graz
1: 1678; 2: 1732; 3: 1764, exceptionally with
the panther's head

1   2   3

The Hague
Special mark with date letter

Haarlem (northern Holland)
1: c. 1700; 2/3: eighteenth century

1   2   3

Halberstadt
1: mid-seventeenth century; 2: 1967; 3/4:
early eighteenth century; 5/6: mid-eighteenth
century

1   2   3   4   5

6

(Swabian) Hall
1: second half of sixteenth century; 2/3:
seventeenth century; 4: eighteenth century

1   2   3   4

Halle a.d.S.
Special mark with date letter and fineness
mark in eighteenth century.
1: sixteenth century; 2/3: seventeenth century; 4/5: seventeenth to eighteenth century

1   2   3   4   5

Hamburg

Marking since the late sixteenth century; date letter in the assay mark since *c.* mid-seventeenth century.
1: late sixteenth century; 2: sixteenth to seventeenth century; 3/4: early seventeenth century; 5–7: mid-seventeenth century; 8/9: late seventeenth century; 10: early eighteenth century; 11: late eighteenth century; 12: nineteenth century

master's marks:
13: Jakob Mores the Elder (master 1579, guild master 1599–1604, d. between 1610 and 1612); 14: Jakob Mores the Younger (* 1580, d. 1649); 15: Dietrich thor Moye (master 1633, d. 1652)

Hanau

From 1685, particularly since the early eighteenth century, Parisian Huguenot jewellers and engravers who had emigrated raised the standards of the jewelry factories, and in particular since the foundation of the academy of drawing in the second half of the eighteenth century
1: *c.* 1600; 2: sixteenth to seventeenth century; 3: seventeenth to eighteenth century (Alt-Hanau); 4: eighteenth century (Alt-Hanau); 5: mid-eighteenth century (Neu-Hanau)

Hannover

old town:
assay mark with date letter during the seventeenth century (earliest traces in 1637), but sometimes without the latter. With fineness (12–15 *Lot*) since the mid-eighteenth century. Separate letter mark of the assay master since late eighteenth century
1: 1640; 2: 1663; 3: early eighteenth century; 4: mid-eighteenth century
new town:
also possible with fineness mark. From 1725, separate date letter of the assay master.
5: seventeenth to eighteenth century; 6: 1726
court goldsmiths:
7/8: eighteenth century

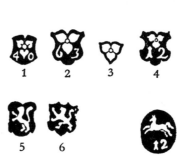

Heidelberg

1: seventeenth to eighteenth century; 2: eighteenth century; 3: eighteenth to nineteenth century

Heilbronn

1: mid-seventeenth century; 2: early eighteenth century

Herzogenbosch (Netherlands)
seventeenth century

Hildesheim
1: sixteenth century; 2: seventeenth century

1   2

Ingolstadt
1: fifteenth century; 2: fifteenth to sixteenth century; 3: seventeenth century; 4: eighteenth century

1   2   3   4

Innsbruck
seventeenth to eighteenth century

Karlsruhe
Formerly probably coat of arms with diagonal beam; difficult to identify since can be mistaken for other assay marks. With a crown from 1806
1/2 after 1806

1   2

Kaschow (Czechoslovakia)
1: sixteenth century; 2. seventeenth to eighteenth century

1   2

Kassel
Assay mark not before 1652. Date letter in the assay mark since in the course of the eighteenth century
1: seventeenth century; 2: seventeenth to eighteenth century; 3: eighteenth to nineteenth century

1   2   3

Kazan (Russia)
1763 and 1797

Kecskemet (Hungaria)
seventeenth century

Kiel
1: fifteenth century; 2/3: seventeenth century; 4/5: eighteenth century; 6: nineteenth century

1   2   3   4   5   6

Kiev
1: c. 1794; 2/3: nineteenth century

1   2   3

Klausenburg (Rumania)
1: sixteenth to seventeenth century; 2: 1833

1   2

Koblenz
1: seventeenth century (?); 2: eighteenth century

Königsberg (east Prussia)
Separate mark with date letter since the later seventeenth century
1: 1684–1703; 2: 1714 and later; 3: 1784–6; 4: 1788–1800

Köpnig (Sweden)
mid-seventeenth century

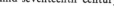

Krakow
1: 1807–09; 2/3: 1809–35

Kristianstad (Sweden)
1: seventeenth to eighteenth century; 2: eighteenth to nineteenth century

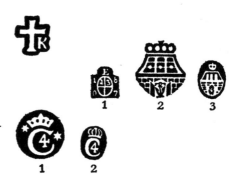

Landshut
1: sixteenth century; 2: 1723; 3: mid-eighteenth century; 4: late eighteenth century

Lausanne
eighteenth century

Leeuwarden (Holland)
seventeenth to eighteenth century

Leiden (Holland)
seventeenth century

Leipzig
Separate date letter since the sixteenth century
1: sixteenth century; 2/3: seventeenth century, perhaps also early eighteenth century; 4/5: eighteenth century; 6: late eighteenth century

Lemberg
1694

Leningrad (St. Petersburg)

Léon (Spain)
1: 1732

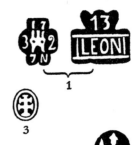

1

Leutschau (Czechoslovakia)
1: 1664; 2/3: seventeenth century

1   2   3

Lidköping (Sweden)
early eighteenth century

Liège
Archbishopric until 1794, that did not belong
to the Burgundian (later Habsburg) Netherlands and laid down its own regulations.
Apart from the assay mark, the arms of the
respective bishop prince were punched, in addition to the date letter (a new letter on each
change of bishop prince).
1: 1650–88, supplementary mark with the
arms of the bishop prince Maximilian Heinrich of Bavaria, 1650–88; 2: 1693 with the
Sedisvakanz mark (St Lambert); for sedisvakanz (satisfaction), the date letter A is
used; 3: 1772–84, supplementary mark with
the arms of the bishop prince Franz Carl
van Velbruck

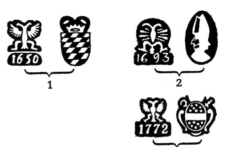

1   2

3

Liegnitz (Silesia)
with separate date letter in the eighteenth
century 1: early seventeenth century; 2: late
seventeenth century

1   2

Lincoln
c. 1624, 1640–50

Linköping (Sweden)
late eighteenth century

Lisbon
1: 1688; 2: seventeenth to eighteenth century;
3/4: eighteenth century

1   2   3   4

London
(for stamping system cf. p. 259)

Leopard's head
1: to c. 1470; 2: 1470–1515; 3: 1558–92, as
before and until 1680; 4: 1681–9, as before
till 1697; 5: 1719–40; 6: 1756–1821; 7: 1822–
36; 8: 1836–96; 9: 1896–1916; 10: since 1916

Lion passant
11: 1544–50; 12: 1550–58; 13: 1558–1679;
14: 1679–97 and 1719–39; 15: 1739–56; 16:
1756–1822; 17/18: 1822–96; 19: 1896–1916;
20: since 1916

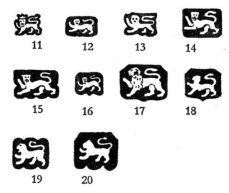

Britannia
21: 1697–1716; 22: 1716–17; 23: 1731–3; 24:
1863–4; 25: 1902

Lion's head erased
26: 1710–11; 27: 1717–18; 28: 1725–31; 29:
1726–7; 30: 1863–4
Duty marks:
31: head of King George III (1760–1820),
used 1784–6; 32: head of the same king, used
1786–1820; 33: head of King George IV
(1820–30), used 1820–30; 34: head of King
William IV (1830–37), used 1830–37; 35.
head of Queen Victoria (1837–89/90), used
1837–89/90

Master's marks:
36–8: Paul de Lamerie (earliest known work
dating from 1711–12, d. 1751); to 1732 in use
until 1732; 38: used since 1739; 39: Charles
Kandler (master 1727); 40: the second mark
used by Frederick Kandler (master 1735,

mentioned until 1760) since 1739; his first mark like that of Charles Kandler (cf. 39). (Perhaps the two goldsmiths were related to the Meissen porcelain modeller J. J. Kaendler). 41: Paul Storr (1771–1844)

 39   40   41

Lion
With special date letter
1: late fifteenth century; 2: *c.* 1500; 3: *c.* 1650; 4: 1772–3

 1   2   3   4

Lübeck
Mark with the city arms and master's mark since 1463
1: 1501; 2. sixteenth to seventeenth century; 3/4: eighteenth century

 1   2   3   4

Lucca (Italy)
seventeenth century

Lund (Sweden)
eighteenth century

Lüneburg
Mark with city arms and master's mark since 1463. Self marking in the sixteenth century *i. e.,* each master marked the city arms himself; hence the differences in the marks at this time.
1: fifteenth to sixteenth century; 2/3: first half of sixteenth century: 4–6: second half of sixteenth century; 7: *c:* 1650; 8: probably early nineteenth century introduced. Additional letter mark also introduced at this time by the alderman

 1   2   3   4

 5   6   7   8

Lucerne
1: sixteenth century; 2: 1891

 1   2

Maastricht
1: late eighteenth century; 2: with date letter, late eighteenth century

 1   2

Madrid
eighteenth century

Magdeburg
1: 1622; 2: 1666; 3: early eighteenth century

 1   2   3

Mainz
1: sixteenth century; 2: seventeenth century;
3: early eighteenth century; 4: 1761; 5: nineteenth century

Malmö (Sweden)
In varying forms from the seventeenth to
nineteenth century

Mannheim
Separate assay mark in the form of a letter
1: 1717; 2: 1727; 3: 1737–66

Mantua
seventeenth century

Marienburg (west Prussia)
assay mark only known since seventeenth
century
1: seventeenth century; 2: seventeenth to
eighteenth century; 3: nineteenth century

Marseille
1: 1760; 2: 1780

Mecheln (Belgium)
Separate date letter
1: 1513–37; 2: 1790; 3: 1791

Middelburg (Netherlands)
1726

Milan
A raised dragon in the seventeenth and eighteenth century devouring a man.
1/2: mark of the guarantee office 1810

Modena (Italy)
seventeenth century

Mons (Bergen, Belgium)
1: late fifteenth century; 2: seventeenth century; 3: 1766; 4. supplementary mark of
1608–93 (of varying size and shape) with the
initials of Archduke Albrecht and his wife
Elizabeth (Isabella of Sapin), the two regents
of the Netherlands 1598–1621. Also retained
in later times

Moscow

Marking silver began in Russia under the Peter the Great in 1700. The first marks had the monogram of the master and the date number. Under Anna Ivanovna 1720–40 (or earlier), a double eagle was used. Under Elizabeth Petrovna 1741–62 the city arms began to be used, while the fineness was marked in numbers. This applied to the whole of Russia.
1: 1734–41; 2: 1751; 3: 1778; 4: 1780; 5: 1790 to 1801

 1
 2
 3
 4
 5

Montpellier (Herault, France)
1: fourteenth and early fifteenth century; 2: c: 1750 with date letters

 1
 2

Munich

Assaying was already done in the fourteenth century. In the fifteenth century the assay mark was a monk's head with cowl and lappets, in sixteenth the century without cowl, from the second half of the seventeenth century the 'Munich Kindl'. From 1740 the date numbers were marked.
1: Fifteenth to sixteenth century; 2: sixteenth to seventeenth century; 3/4: second half of seventeenth century; 5: early eighteenth century; 6: 1773

 1
 2
 3
 4
 5
 6

Münster (Westphalia)
1/2: sixteenth century; 3/4: seventeenth century

 1
 2
 3
 4

Namur
1: 1505; 2: 1520; 3: 1682

 1
2
3

Nancy

Did not become part of France until 1766, and therefore has a new charge stamp. Stamping differs from that in France in that until 1789 the city arms and master's mark were combined. master's mark of Nicolas Poirot with city arms of thistle, 1709

Narva (Estonia)
1: seventeenth century; 2: eighteenth century

 1
2

Naumburg a.d.S.
Separate date letter since 1700
1: seventeenth century; 2/3: eighteenth century

 1
 2
3

Naples
1: c. 1400; 2: sixteenth century; 3: seventeenth century; 4: 1720

Neisse (Silesia)
1: 1610–14; 2: c. 1700; 3: 1742

Neuchatel (Switzerland)
1/2: seventeenth to eighteenth century; for gold and silver 1820–66

Newcastle
With different variants from 1672

Nivelles (Belgium)
mid-seventeenth century

Norwich
1: with different variants from 1565–1697, also 2: with different variants from 1581–1697

Nuremberg
Assay marks already required in the fourteenth century; the earliest recorded in c. 1400. Master's marks were demanded in 1541. From 1766, separate letter mark of the assay master.
1: late fifteenth century; 2: (1541?) 1550–1600; 3: (1541?) 1550–1650; 4: 1600–1700; 5: 1700 to 1750; 6: earlier assay mark nineteenth century; 7: later assay mark nineteenth century

master's marks:
The Jamnitzer family: 8 Wenzel Jamnitzer (* Vienna 1508, master at Nuremberg 1534, appointed to the grand council 1556, captain 1564, councillor 1573, d. 1585); 9: Albrecht Jamnitzer, brother of Wenzel (citizen 1544, master 1550, d. 1555); 10: Hans Jamnitzer, eldest son of Wenzel (* c. 1538, master 1561, appointed to the grand council 1596, d. 1603); 11: Abraham Jamnitzer, younger son of Wenzel (* 1555, master 1579, d. c. 1600); 12: Bartel Jamnitzer, son of Albrecht (* c. 1548, master 1575, d. 1596); 13: Christoph Jamnister, son of Hans (* 1563, master 1592, appointed to the Grand council 1607, sworn in 1613, d. 1618);
14: Hans Lencker the Elder (master 1550, d. 1585); 15: Elias Lencker (master 1562, previously seven years in France, d. 1591); 16:

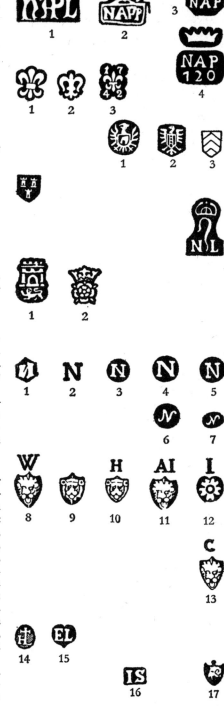

279

Jonas Silber (trained under Wenzel Jamnitzer, master 1572, two years in Heidelberg from 1578, two years in Danzig as coin cutter in 1587); 17: Hans Petzolt (* 1551, master 1578, d. 1633)

Nyköping (Sweden)
1: eighteenth century (after 1730); 2: early nineteenth century

Odense (Denmark)
1: 1625, 1763; 2: late (?) eighteenth century

Offenburg (Baden)
1515

Olmütz (Mähren)
1: 1593, 1599; 2. seventeenth century; 3: 1755; 4: 1769–76

Orleans
sixteenth (?) to eighteenth (?) century

Oslo (formerly Christiana)
assay mark of old Oslo till 1624, when the town was burned, was the crowned O. Assay of the rebuilt town under the name Christiania in 1624 was a crowned C with the date figure, here eighteenth century

Osnabrück
1: c. 1697–1709; 2: 1716

Paderborn
1: seventeenth century; 2: eighteenth century

Palermo
seventeenth century

Paris
for the marking system cf. p. 260–1
Marking was current since the thirteenth century, in 1461 a varying date letter was in roduced with henceforth also served as assay mark. In 1782 the date letter finally disappeared, to ber and the assay mark is joined by a P, changing yearly, with the two last figures of the year.
1: c. 1330; 2: fifteenth century (Paris ?, 1462 ?); 3: 1675–6; 4: 1764–5; 5: 1773–4; 6: 1784; 7: 1786; 8: 1787; 9: 1789

tax farmer's marks:
Charge and discharge marks. The charge mark always consists of a crowned A.
10: Pierre Perrine 1698–1703 (?); 11: Maitre Charles Cordier 1721–6; 12/13: Jean Baptiste Fouache 1774–7; 12: large silver works; 13: gold and small silver works
guarantee marks 1798–1809
14: large works of silver and gold; 15: medium-sized works of silver and gold; 16: small works of silver

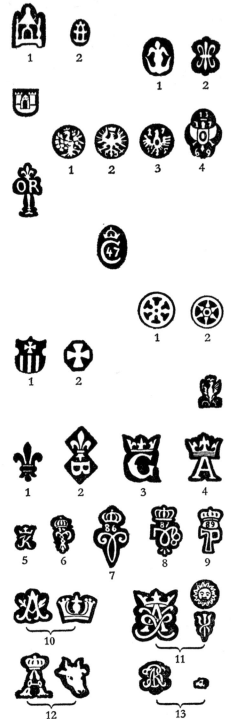

Fineness mark 1798–1809
17: 950⁰/₀₀; 18: 800⁰/₀₀
guarantee marks
19: large works; 20: medium-sized works;
21: small works
fineness marks 1809–19
22: 950⁰/₀₀; 23: 800⁰/₀₀
guarantee marks 1819–38
24: larger works; 25: medium-sized works;
26: small works
fineness marks 1819–30
27: 950⁰/₀₀; 28: 800⁰/₀₀. Since 1838 the Paris
guarantee and fineness marks correspond to
those of the Départements, except for small
works which still have a separate mark (29)

master's marks:
30: Thomas Germain, orfèvre du roi (* 1673,
at first painter, in Rome in 1688, becomes a
goldsmith there in 1691, 1720 in Paris, d.
1748); 31: Francois Thomas Germain, son of
Thomas, sculpteur et orfèvre du roi aux
galleries du Louvre (* 1726, master 1748, d.
1791); 32: Jacques Roëttiers, orfèvre du roi
(* 1717, master 1733, d. 1784); 33: Robert
Joseph Auguste, orfèvre du roi, pupil of
F. T. Germain (* 1725, d. 1805); 34: Jean
Baptiste Claude Odiot, worked for Napoleon
(b. 1763, Master 1785, retired after 1823, d.
1850); 35: Martin Guillaume Biennais, worked for Napoleon (still alive in 1832)

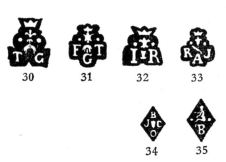

Parma (Italy)
seventeenth century

Passau
1: 1567; 2: seventeenth to eighteenth century;
3: nineteenth century

Pforzheim
1: assay mark and 2: fineness mark eighteenth
to nineteenth century

Posen
The assay mark does not seem to have been
applied regularly, since many pieces are only
marked with the master's mark. 1/2: seventeenth to eighteenth century

Potsdam
Separate fineness mark
1/2: eighteenth century

Prague
1: sixteenth century.
From the second half of the seventeenth century the individual parts of the town have
different assay marks.
2/3: Prague-Kleinseite 1673
From 1776 a common assay mark again.
4: 1795

Pressburg
Separate date letter
1: perhaps Pressburg sixteenth century; 2:
1841

Rapperswil (Switzerland)
1/2: sixteenth to seventeenth century; 3:
eighteenth century

Regensburg
1: sixteenth to seventeenth century; 2. seventeenth century; 3/4: eighteenth century

Reval
Special date letter
1: mid-sixteenth century; 2: c. 1690; 3: mid-
eighteenth century; 4/5: 1780

Riga
Special date letter of the assay marker since
the mid-eighteenth century
1: sixteenth century; 2: sixteenth to seventeenth century; 3: eighteenth century

Rome
1: seventeenth century; 2/3: late seventeenth
century; 4: seventeenth to eighteenth century; 5: eighteenth to nineteenth century

Rostock
1: 1593; 2: first half of seventeenth century

Rotterdam
Special date letters
1/2: eighteenth century

Salzburg
1: sixteenth century; 2: 1638; 3/4: seventeenth to eighteenth century

Santiago (Spain)
City arms recorded since 1400 mark sixteenth century. In the eighteenth century, various other forms of assay mark

Saragossa (Spain)
1: fourteenth to fifteenth century; 2: sixteenth century

Schaffhausen
1: sixteenth century; 2: seventeenth to eighteenth century; 3: eighteenth century

Sheffield
With different variants from 1773

Sitten (Switzerland)
1: sixteenth century; 2: seventeenth century; 3: eighteenth century

Soest
c. 1730

Soissons (Aisne)
First half of eighteenth century

Speyer
1: fifteenth to sixteenth century; 2/3: sixteenth century; 4: seventeenth century

Stettin
eighteenth century

Stockholm
City arms mark since 1596. First the city crown; from 1689 the head of St Eric: from the front until the early eighteenth century, from the profile to the right in c. 1720–40, profile to the left from c. 1730, at first beside the one turned to the right; 1: sixteenth to seventeenth century; 2: first half of seventeenth century; 3: 1650; 4: 1674; 5: late seventeenth century; 6: 1707; 7: 1745
Special date letter since 1689

St. Omer (Pas-de-Calais)
c. 1560 and later

St. Petersburg (cf. also Moscow)
1/2: c. 1730–40; 3: c. 1740–50; 4: c. 1820–80

Stralsund
1/2: seventeenth century

Strasbourg
Master's mark introduced in c. 1363, assay mark earlier.
After its inclusion into France in 1681, it remained untouched by the French system (like the whole of Alsace). No charge mark. However, besides the current 13 *Lot* silver, the Paris fineness of 11 denier 12 grains = 15$\frac{1}{3}$ *Lot* became current. These pieces were designated with a mark accordingly. Special date letters since 1752.
1: from c. 1472, in similar form until 1534; 2: 1534–67; 3/4: after 1567, before 1616; 5: 1656; 6: 1725; 7: 13 *Lot* silver c. 1750, with variants until the Revolution; 8: with French fineness c. 1690; 9: *ibid.*, variants still found in 1773

Stuttgart
1: late sixteenth century; 2: late seventeenth century; 2: eighteenth century; 4: nineteenth century

Thorn
cf. Danzig. The assay mark was introduced in the early seventeenth century, if not in the sixteenth century
1–3: seventeenth century; 4: eighteenth century

Tilsit
1: eighteenth century; 2: nineteenth century

Toledo
1: eighteenth century; 2: nineteenth century

Tondern (Denmark)
1/2: seventeenth century; 3: seventeenth to eighteenth century

Tongern (Belgium)
1/2: assay mark with supplementary mark c. 1759

Torgau
sixteenth to seventeenth century

Toulouse
1/2: assay mark with date letter *c.* 1735

Tournai
Special date letter
1: *c.* 1528 if not much later; 2: sixteenth to seventeenth century; 3: 1627; 4/5: *c.* 1766 and 1781

Trieste
1/2: eighteenth century

Troppau (Bohemia)
1: sixteenth to seventeenth century; 2: 1674; 3: 1759

Tübingen
1: seventeenth century; 2/3: eighteenth century

Turin
1: seventeenth century; 2/3: eighteenth century

Überlingen (Baden)
1: late sixteenth century; 2: sixteenth to seventeenth century; 3: seventeenth century; 4: eighteenth century

Ulm
1: sixteenth century; 2/3: seventeenth century; 4–6: seventeenth to eighteenth century; 7–9: eighteenth century

Uppsala
1: eighteenth century; 2: in different size and form during the seventeenth to nineteenth centuries

Utrecht
Special date letters
1: *c.* 1614; 2: *c.* 1710; 3/4: eighteenth century

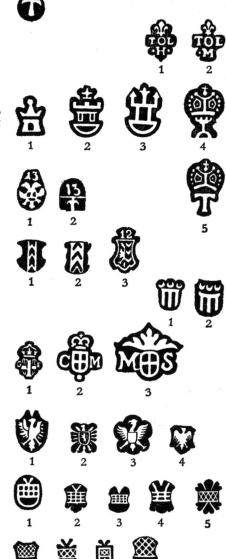

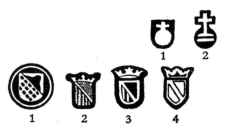

Venice
1: seventeenth to eighteenth century; 2: sixteenth to eighteenth century

1   2

Vienna
1: 1524; 2: 14 *Lot* silver, late sixteenth century to 1674; 3: 13 *Lot* silver 1699, with small variations until 1736; 4: 13 *Lot* silver 1737, with small variations until 1806; 5: 15 *Lot* silver 1737; since 1807, state mark with the official mark A of the chief punching office in Vienna; 6: official mark for 13 *Lot* silver 1807; 7: official mark for 15 *Lot* silver with varying date figure from 1819–66

1   2   3   4

5   6   7

Villingen
1: fifteenth to sixteenth century; 2: eighteenth century

1   2

Vladimir (Russia)
1763

Vologda (Russia)
eighteenth to nineteenth century

Warsaw
1: seventeenth to eighteenth century; 2: mid-nineteenth century

1   2

Weilheim (Bavaria)
1: seventeenth to eighteenth century; 2: eighteenth century

1   2

Weimar
1: early seventeenth century; 2: late seventeenth century

1   2

Wiborg (Finland)
eighteenth century

Wilna
sixteenth to seventeenth century

Winterthur
eighteenth century

Wismar
master's mark introduced 1439, assay mark 1463
1: late sixteenth century; 2: *c.* 1730–48; 3: nineteenth century

1   2   3

Wittenberg
mid-seventeenth century

Wolfenbüttel
1: 1668; 2: seventeenth century; 3: seventeenth to eighteenth century

1   2   3

Worms
1: sixteenth to seventeenth century; 2/3: seventeenth to eighteenth century

1   2   3

Würzburg
1: early eighteenth century; 2–4: eighteenth century; 5: early nineteenth century

1   2   3   4   5

York
1: with variants from 1562 to 1700; 2: with variants from 1700 to 1857 (and later?)

1   2

Ypres (Belgium)
Special date letter
1: c. 1525; 2/3: second half of seventeenth century; 4: late seventeenth century; 5: 1701–13; 6: supplementary mark 1750

1   2   3   4

5   6

Zittau
1: 1710; 2: 1731; 3: c. 1750

1   2   3

Znaim
With varying date number from 1769

Zofingen (Mähren)
eighteenth century

Zug (Switzerland)
1: 1584; 2: 1620; 3: seventeenth century; 4: eighteenth century

1   2   3   4

Zürich
Self marking since 1544
1: 1545; 2: before 1563; 3: 1638; 4/5: seventeenth to eighteenth century; 6: 1779

1   2   3   4   5   6

Zweibrücken
eighteenth century

Zwickau
1: sixteenth to seventeenth century; 2: seventeenth century

1   2

Zwolle (Netherlande)
Special date letters
1: seventeenth century; 2: *c.* 1721; 3: *c.* 1726 and later

1   2   3

Glossary of important technical terms

Agley: a cup whose bowl or body is formed in the shape of the harebell. One of the pieces the Nuremberg goldsmith had to execute for his master's examination, then also in other German towns. The basic form evolved in Gothic times recalls that the harebell was the symbol of Christ

amphora: Greek, two-handled, bulging vessel, used in Greece as a container for wine or oil

antependium: latin, gold or silver, usually the relieved covering of the altar frontal; also precious drapery for the same purpose

arabesque: ornament of foliage work, whose basic vegetal form was extended by figurative and architectural decoration. The arabesque, which has been particularly beloved since the Renaissance, derives from Hellenistic art

Assay: in silver, the test made to prove that the metal was of required quality

Beading: a border ornament composed of small half rounds resembling pearls or beads. Its repetitious, formal character was extremely popular in late eighteenth century English and American silver.

Britannia standard 1697–1719: enforced a fineness of 958 parts pure, in place of the old sterling 925 parts pure. Compulsory till 1719 and optional thereafter. Distinguished by a punch of the figure of a seated Britannia.

bright-cut engraving: sharp cut decoration in which metal is removed by bevelled cutting giving a faceted sparkle. Much used in England and America in the last years of the eighteenth century.

Buffet (Ital. buffeto, Fr. buffet): originally meant dresser, sideboard, cupboard, until in the seventeenth and eighteenth centuries it came to be very popular as a multi-part ceremonial structure for porcelain and silver plate in court circles

Cameo: precious or semi-precious stone with a picture in high relief

cartilage work: an ornament that appeared towards the beginning of the seventeenth century, formed of gnarled forms usually interspersed with fantastic beings

cast: pieces formed in a mold

caster: a cylindrical vessel with a pierced cover made singly or in sets of three, for sugar, pepper and other spices. In England and America casters were popular from about 1676. Frames for casters date from the early eighteenth century and often included oil and vinegar bottles

caudle: in seventeenth century England and America a popular drink made of thin oatmeal gruel, wine or ale, sugar and spice. Hence caudle cup, as a specialized silver form

chasing: A form of decoration produced by chisels and hammers as distinct from the cutting away process of an engraving tool. Chasing may be (1) embossed or repousse, in high relief, in which domed designs are made by punching the metal out from the back of the ware and (2) flat chasing, or surface chasing where designs are produced in very low relief

champlevé enamel: Fr., flat troughs are cut out of a strong metal panel, usually copper, into which the frit is melted; the surface is ground flush. For copper, translucent enamel is preferred

chinoiserie: European decoration very freely interpreted after oriental designs found in porcelains, textiles and lacquer.

ciborium: Lat., consecrated receptacle for the host, usually gold or silver

cloisonné enamel: enamelling by melting the frit into fields defined by wire soldered to the surface; derived from the Orient and much used in the Early Middle Ages

cut-card work: Pieces of silver sheet cut into patterns, usually of foliage or strapwork and soldered to the surface of objects such as cups, bowls, coffee-pots and tankards. Cut-card work not only produced ornament in relief, but added strength. In England, this process was popular about 1660 and was particularly used by Huguenot refugees. The same was true in the American colonies in centers such as New York where Huguenot immigrants formed a large percentage of the population

concetto: ital., the sketch (concept) on which the work of art is based

diptych: Greek, two-part panel

electroplating: a layer of pure silver applied to a base metal core, usually copper, by electrolysis. A technique commercialized in England in the 1840's by the Elkington Brothers

émail des peintres: Fr., the metal, usually copper, is covered with a layer of mono-coloured enamel, on which different colours of glass flux can be fused. It is often heightened in gold

embossing: see chasing

enamel painting: painting with pure metallic oxides on a white enamel ground applied on the metal ground, then fused on

enamel sculpture: (Fr., *émail en ronde bosse*) usually a figure or ornament cast or embossed in gold, which is covered with a molten layer of opaque or translucent enamel to form colourful enamel modelling

engraving: Decoration made by cutting into the surface of the metal using a tool called a graver. In England and America it was especially popular from the early eighteenth century onward for inscribing coats of arms and commemerative legends

épergne: a table centerpiece of elaborate design (from the French *épergner,* to save, (sparing the trouble of passing dishes at table). Épergnes became fashionable in England in the 1730's. In the American colonies they were advertised in Boston in 1757. In form, épergnes were originally elaborate, rococo fanciful *tours de force* of silversmithing, in which innumerable baskets and dishes for fruit or sweetmeats were suspended from branches. In the Adam period épergnes were characteristically composed of classical forms executed in pierced silver and wire work.

etching: surface decoration in which the pattern is eaten into the metal by using acid. During the Victorian period used on

silver to replace the time-consuming process of engraving.

filigree: lat., decoration of works of gold and silver by soldering thin wires of gold or silver on to the ground

finial: turret-like spire on a flying buttress

Gadrooning: a border device composed of stamped or cast convex curves, set vertically or slanting, slightly spiraled, to left or right. Gadrooning was very typical of late seventeenth century silver ornament in England and the American colonies, but even though a baroque device it was in continuous use during the eighteenth century

gem: lat., stone or semi-precious stone incised or engraved in depth with a pictorial image. The engraved gem is also called intaglio

glyptik: Gk., the art of cutting stone, cf. also gem and cameo

granulation: little grains of gold imposed, usually in dense rows, on works of gold and silver as decoration

grotesque: decoration of foliage work, with architectural elements, fruit, animals and fabulous beings. The grotesque derives from the paintings in Antique Roman grottoes, which the early sixteenth century adopted from Italian art and which then became widespread

guéridon: Fr., small high table serving as a candlestick stand

Kredenz (salver): (Ital. credenza), originally a piece of furniture for preparing dishes, later a round dish on a high stand for sweetmeats and fruit

Maiestas domini: lat., Christ enthroned in majesty on the circle of the world

moresque: an abstract surface ornament developed in the Near East consisting of lines and schematized foliage and flowers. A much-loved ornamental motif since the Renaissance

monstrance: Lat., originally a receptacle in a glass or rock crystal container for exposing relics (also ostensory). Since the fourteenth century it has been a liturgical display vessel for the host *nautilus cup:* a nautilus shell set in gold, *i. e.* a turbo snail mounted as a drinking vessel

niello: (Lat., *nigellus*, black): the incised design on a metal plaque, usually silver, is filled with a black fusible alloy of silver, copper, sulphur and lead, and then polished

nodus: Lat., the knop of a chalice

opus interrasile: Lat., usually metal open-work, in which ornaments are cut out of a metal panel

palliotto: Ital., gold or silver high altar panelling

paten: the flat dish for the host belonging with the Communion chalice

pax: lat., the small tablet, usually in ivory, bronze or precious metal, depicting religious scenes, which was handed to the priest and later to the entire congregation at Mass to be kissed

Pluvial fastening: large clasp on the sleeveless shoulder cloak of the Catholic priest
pyx: Gk., cylindrical box for the host, formerly made of boxwood, later also of ivory and silver

Reeding: a border molding composed of contiguous parallel convex members, stylized from long reed leaves as used in classical architecture

reliquary: receptacle for the relics of saints

rocaille: the basic ornamental principle of Rococo, evolved from the auricular style

rhyton: Gk., drinking horn in the form of

an animal scrollwork: sixteenth-century ornament of flat bands with furled ends

service: Fr., the set of table ware, including individual pieces such as plates, knives, forks and spoons, salt cellar, beakers, bowls, tureens, vases and candlesticks – usually of uniform design

Sheffield Plate, also commonly called Sheffield: a method invented about 1743 by Thomas Bolsover of Sheffield, England, of fusing a silver coat to a core of copper by heating and rolling. By 1763, widely used for making wares in imitation of silver at a saving of considerable cost.

silver relief enamel (émail translucide de basse taille) Fr.: The design is cut into the silver picture zone as a flat relief and covered with translucent enamel. The incised design is thus heightened by the colourful, glowing enamel

Sterling: in English silver the quality of .925 pure silver in an alloy, usually with copper, of .075 base metal

tiara: the tall papal crown, richly decorated and usually of gold

toreutic: Gk., the art of chasing, embossing, hammering, punching and casting in metal

trefoil: in medieval measures this was three three-quarter circles inscribed into a circle to form a clover leaf

wire enamel: wires are soldered on to the metal surface (gold or silver) to form the outlines of the ornamental decoration. The molten enamel is sunk between the wires

Bibliography

Accascina, M. L'oreficeria italiana. Florence 1934
Andersson, A.: *Silberne Abendmahlsgeräte in Schweden aus dem 14. Jahrhundert.* Stockholm 1956
Appuhn, H.: *Das Lüneburger Ratssilber.* Exhibition catalogue. Lüneburg 1956
Augsburger Barock. Exhibition catalogue. Augsburg 1968
Ausgewählte Werke. Kunstgewerbemuseum Schloß Charlottenburg. Catalogue of the Kunstgewerbemuseum Berlin, Vol. 1, Berlin 1963

Babelon, J.: *L'Orfèvrerie française.* Paris 1946
Bassermann-Jordan, E. and W. W. Schmidt: *Der Bamberger Domschatz.* Munich 1914
Bayerische Frömmigkeit, 1400 Jahre Christliches Bayern. Exhibition catalogue. Munich 1960
Berliner, R.: *Ornamentale Vorlegeblätter des 15. bis 18. Jahrhunderts.* 2 vols. Leipzig 1925–26
Beuque, E.: *Dictionnaire des poinçons officiels français et étrangers, anciens et modernes de leur création à nos jours.* Paris 1962–64
Beuque, E. and M. Frapsauce: *Dictionnaire des poinçons de maîtres-orfèvres français du 14e siècle à 1838.* Paris 1964
Blum, A.: *Les nielles du Quattrocento. Musée du Louvre. Cabinet d'estampes Edmond de Rothschild.* Paris 1950
Böhm, E.: *Hans Petzolt, ein deutscher Goldschmied.* Munich 1939
Bosen, G. and Chr. A. Bøje: *Old Danish Silver.* Copenhagen 1949
Bouilhet, H.: *L'Orfèvrerie française aux XVIIIe et XIXe siècles.* 3 vols., Paris 1908–12
Brault, S. and Y. Bottineau: *L'Orfèvrerie française du XVIIIe siècle.* Paris 1959.
Braun, E. W.: *Die Silberkammer eines Reichsfürsten. Das Lobkowitzsche Inventar.* Leipzig 1923
Braun, E. W.: 'Über einige Nürnberger Goldschmiedezeichnungen aus der ersten Hälfte des 16. Jahrhunderts.' From *Germanisches Nationalmuseum Nürnberg, 94. Jahresbericht,* 1949, pp. 9 ff.
Braun, J.: *Das christliche Altargerät.* Munich 1932
Braun, J.: *Die Reliquiare des christlichen Kultes und ihre Entstehung.* Freiburg 1940
Braun-Feldweg, W.: *Metall – Werkformen und Arbeitsweisen.* Ravensburg 1950
Brunner, H.: *Altes Tafelsilber.* Munich 1964
Buddensieg, T.: 'Die Basler Altartafel Heinrich II.' From *Wallraf-Richartz-Jahrbuch* 1957, pp. 133 ff.
Bulgari, C. G.: *Argentieri gemmari e orafi d'Italia.* 2 vols. Rome 1958
Bunt, C. G. E.: *The Goldsmiths of Italy.* London 1926
Bunt, C. G. E.: 'Die silberne Altarfront des Baptisteriums in Florenz'. From *Pantheon* 1930, pp. 221 ff.
Burckhardt, J.: *The Civilization of the Renaissance in Italy.* English edition pub. by Phaidon, London 1944
Burckhardt, R. F.: *Der Baseler Münsterschatz.* Basle 1933
Burger, W.: *Abendländische Schmelzarbeiten.* Berlin 1930

Carré, L.: *Les poinçons de l'orfevrerie française du 14e siècle jusqu'au début du 19e siècle.* Paris 1940
Catalogus van Goud en Zilverwerken. Rijksmuseum Amsterdam 1952, 2nd ed.
Cellini, Benvenuto: *Due Trattati: uno intorno alle otto principali Arti dell'oreficeria, l'altro in materia dell'Arte della Scultura.* Florenz 1568. German edition pub. by J. Brinckmann, Leipzig 1867
Cellini: *Life of Benvenuto Cellini written by himself.* English edition pub. by Phaidon, London 1949
Creutz, M.: *Kunstgeschichte der edlen Metalle. Geschichte der Metallkunst* Vol. 2. Stuttgart 1909
Czihak, E. v.: *Die Edelschmiedekunst früherer Zeiten in Preußen.* 2 vols., Düsseldorf 1903 and 1908

Delieb, E.: *The Great Silver Manufactory,* London 1971
Delieb, E.: *Silver Boxes,* London 1968
Dernandt, K. E.: 'Der spätmittelalterliche Silberschatz des hessischen Fürstenhauses.' From *Hessenland,* Vol. 50, 1939, pp. 21 ff.
Drach, C. A. v.: *Ältere Silberarbeiten in den Kgl. Sammlungen zu Kassel.* Marburg 1888
Dennis, F.: *Three Centuries of French Domestic Silver.* New York 1960

Elbern, V. H.: *Das erste Jahrtausend. Kultur und Kunst im werdenden Abendland an Rhein und Ruhr.* Düsseldorf 1962
Evans, J.: *A History of Jewellery 1100–1870.* London 1951

Falke, O. v.: 'Die Neugotik im Kunstgewerbe der Spätrenaissance.' From *Jahrbuch der Preu-ßischen Kunstsammlungen*, Vol. 40, 1919, pp. 76

Falke, O. v., R. Schmidt and G. Swarzenski: *Der Welfenschatz*. Frankfurt am Main 1930

Filimonoff, G.: *Beschreibung der Moskauer Rüstkammer*. 4 vols., Moscow 1884–93 (Russian)

Fillitz, H.: *Die Insignien und Kleinodien des Heiligen Römischen Reiches*. Vienna/Munich 1954

Fillitz, H.: *Die Schatzkammer in Wien*. Vienna/Munich 1964

Finlay, J.: *Scottish Gold and Silver Work*. London 1956

Foelkersam, A. de: *Inventaire de l'Argenterie conservée dans les Garde-Meubles des Palais Impériaux*. St. Petersburg 1907 (Russian)

Forssmann, E.: *Anders Zorns Silversamling*. Stockholm 1955

Frankenburger, M.: *Die Alt-Münchener Goldschmiede und ihre Kunst*. Munich 1912

Frankenburger, M.: *Die Silberkammer der Münchener Residenz*. Munich 1923

Frederiks, J. W.: *Dutch Silver*. 4 vols., The Hague 1952–61

Friedenthal, A.: *Die Goldschmiede Revals*. Lübeck 1931

Fritz, J. M.: *Gestochene Bilder. Gravierungen auf deutschen Goldschmiedearbeiten der Spät-gotik*. Cologne 1966

Gehrig, U.: *Hildesheimer Silberfund. Bilderhefte der Staatlichen Museen Preußischer Kultur-besitz, H. 4*. Berlin 1967

Geschichte des Kunstgewerbes aller Zeiten und Völker. Pub. by H. Th. Bossert. 6 vols., Berlin 1928–35

Goldschmiedekunst des 18. Jahrhunderts in Augsburg und München. Exhibition catalogue. Munich 1952

Griesebach, A.: *Carl Friedrich Schinkel*. Leipzig 1924

Gündel, Chr.: *Die Goldschmiedekunst in Breslau*. Berlin 1940

Guth-Dreyfus, K.: *Transluzides Email in der ersten Hälfte des 14. Jahrhunderts am Ober-, Mittel- und Niederrhein*. Basle 1954

Grandjean, S.: *L'Orfèvrerie du XIXe siècle en Europe*. Paris 1962

Grimme, E. G.: *Aachener Goldschmiedekunst im Mittelalter*. Cologne 1957

Gans, M. H. and Th. M. Duyvené de Wit-Klinkhamer: *Dutch Silver*. London 1961

Grevenor, H. and Th. B. Kielland: *Guldsmedskunstverket i Osla og Kristiania*. Oslo 1924

Hackenbroch, Y.: *English and other Silver in the Irwin Untermyer Collection*. London 1963

Haeberle, A.: *Die Goldschmiede in Ulm*. Ulm 1934

Hahnloser, H. R. (pub.): *Il Tesoro di San Marco. La Pala d'oro*. Florence 1965

Hallo, R.: *Die Kasseler Goldschmiede. Gold-Silber-Eisen*. Pub. by the Hessisches Landes-museum in Kassel 1929

Halm, Ph. M. and R. Berliner: *Das Hallesche Heiltum*. Berlin 1931

Haseloff, G.: *Der Tassilokelch*. Munich 1951

Hayward, J. F.: *Huguenot Silver in England 1688–1727*. London 1959

Hayward, J. F.: 'The Mannerist Goldsmiths.' From *The Connoisseur*, 1962 ff., issues 601, 614, 615, 628–30, 637, 640, 652, 659–62, 665, 675, 677

Havard, H.: *Histoire de l'Orfèvrerie française*. Paris 1896

Hernmarck, C.: *Svensk Silver 1580–1800 i Nationalmusei Samlingar*. Stockholm 1951

(Woeckel, G. and) E. Herzog: 'Ignaz Günthers Frühwerk in Koprivná (Geppersdorf)/CSSR, II.' From *Pantheon XXIV* 1966

Hildesia Sacra. Exhibition catalogue. Hanover 1962

Hintze, E. and K. Massner: *Goldschmiedearbeiten Schlesiens*. Breslau 1911

Holzhausen, W.: 'Studien zum Schatz des Lorenzo Magnifico.' From *Mitteilungen des Kunst-historischen Instituts Florenz*, III, 1919–31, pp. 104 ff.

Holzhausen, W.: *Prachtgefäße, Geschmeide, Kabinettstücke. Die Goldschmiedekunst der deutschen Städte: Dresden*. Tübingen 1966

Honour, H.: *Goldsmiths and Silversmiths*, London 1971

Hughes, G.: *Modern Silver throughout the World 1880–1967*. London 1967

Hüseler, K.: *Hamburger Silber 1600–1800*. Darmstadt n.d. (1955)

Ilg, A.: *Theophilus Presbyter, Schedula diversarum artium*. Vienna 1874

Jackson, C. J.: *English Goldsmiths and their Marks*. London 1964. 2nd ed.
Jantzen, H.: *Ottonische Kunst*. Hamburg 1959, 2nd. ed.
Jessen, P.: *Der Ornamentstich. Geschichte der Vorlagen des Kunsthandwerks seit dem Mittelalter*. Berlin 1920
Justi, C.: 'Die Goldschmiedefamilie der Arphe.' From *Miscellaneen aus drei Jahrhunderten spanischen Kunstlebens*, vol. I, Berlin 1908, pp. 269 ff.

Kaellstroem, O. and C. Hernmarck: *Svenskt Silversmede 1520–1850*. Stockholm n.d.
Karcher, R.: *Das deutsche Goldschmiedehandwerk bis ins 15. Jahrhundert*. Leipzig 1911
Kesting, A. M.: *Anton Eisenhoit, ein westfälischer Kupferstecher und Goldschmied*. Münster 1964
Kielland, T. B.: *Norsk guldsmedskunst i middelalderen*. Oslo 1927
Klein, W.: *Geschichte des Gmünder Goldschmiedegewerbes*. Stuttgart 1920
Kohlhaussen, H.: *Geschichte des deutschen Kunsthandwerks*. Munich 1955
Kohlhaussen, H.: *Nürnberger Goldschmiedekunst des Mittelalters und der Dürerzeit 1240 bis 1540*. Berlin 1968
Kris, E. and O. v. Falke: 'Beiträge zu den Werken von Christoph und Hans Jamnitzer.' From *Jahrbuch der Preußischen Kunstsammlungen*, Vol. 47, 1926, pp. 185 ff.
Kris, E.: *Meister und Meisterwerke der Steinschneidekunst in der Italienischen Renaissance*. 2 vols., Vienna 1929
Kris, E.: 'Der Stil "rustique". Die Verwendung des Naturabgusses bei Wenzel Jamnitzer und Bernard Palissy.' From *Jahrbuch der Kunsthistorischen Sammlungen in Wien*, New Series, Vol. 1, 1926, pp. 137 ff.
Kris, E.: *Goldschmiedearbeiten des Mittelalters, der Renaissance und des Barock. Publikationen aus den kunsthistorischen Sammlungen in Wien*. Vienna 1932
Kunsthandwerk um 1900. Jugendstil – art nouveau – modern style – nieuwe kunst. Hessisches Landesmuseum Darmstadt 1965

La Baume, P.: *Römisches Kunstgewerbe zwischen Christi Geburt und 400*. Brunswick 1964
Le Corbeiller, C.: *European und American Snuff Boxes 1730–1830*. London 1966
Leitermann, H.: *Deutsche Goldschmiedekunst*. Stuttgart 1953
Lessing, J.: *Gold und Silber. Kunstgewerbemuseum Berlin*. Berlin 1907, 2nd ed.
Link, E. M.: *Hugo von Oignies*. Dissertation. Freiburg 1964
Lotz, W.: *Gold und Silber. Deutsche Goldschmiedearbeiten der Gegenwart*. Berlin 1926
Lübecker Silber 1480–1800. Exhibition catalogue. Lübeck 1965

Mahn, H.: *Lorenz und Georg Strauch. Beiträge zur Kunstgeschichte Nürnbergs im 16. und 17. Jahrhundert*. Reutlingen 1927
Marquet de Vasselot, J.-J.: *Catalogue sommaire de l'Orfèvrerie, de l'Emaillerie et des Gemmes*. Musée National du Louvre. Paris 1914
Medding-Alp, E.: *Rheinische Goldschmiedekunst in ottonischer Zeit*. Coblenz n. d. (1952)
Meinz, M.: *Schönes Silber*. Munich 1964
Meinz, M.: *Darstellungen auf Silbergerät. Die Jagd in der Kunst*. Hamburg/Berlin 1965
Meinz, M.: *Altes Tafelgerät. Sammlung Udo u. Mania Bey*. Exhibition catalogue. Hamburg 1966
Menzhausen, J.: *Das Grüne Gewölbe*. Leipzig 1968
Metall im Kunsthandwerk. Exhibition catalogue. Kunstgewerbemuseum Berlin Schloß Köpenick. Berlin 1967
Morassi, A.: *Antica Oreficeria italiana*. Milan 1936
Morazzoni, G.: *Argenterie Genovesi*. Milan 1955
Moskau – Die Staatliche Rüstkammer des Moskauer Kreml. Moscow 1958 (Russian)
Mostra del Barocco Piemontese. Exhibition catalogue. Turin 1963

Nederlands Zilver 1815–1960. Exhibition catalogue. The Hague 1961
Nocq, H., P. Alfassa and J. Guérin: *Orfèvrerie civile française du XVIe au début du XIXe siècle*. Paris 1927–30

Oman, C.: *English Church Plate 597–1830*. London 1957
Oman, C.: *The English Silver in the Kremlin 1557–1663*. London 1961
Oman, C.: *English Domestic Silver*. London 1965, 6th ed.
Oman, C.: *English Silversmiths' Work*. Victoria and Albert Museum London 1965

Paris – *Catalogue de l'Orfèvrerie du XVIIe, du XVIIIe et du XIXe siècle*. Musée du Louvre et Musée de Cluny. Paris 1958
Paris – *Les Trésors des Églises de France*. Exhibition catalogue. Paris 1965
Paris – *L'Europe Gothique. XIIe–XIVe siècles*. Exhibition catalogue. Paris 1968
Pazaurek, G. E.: *Alte Goldschmiedearbeiten aus schwäbischen Kirchenschätzen*. Leipzig 1912
Pechstein, K.: 'Jamnitzer-Studien.' From *Jahrbuch der Berliner Museen*, Vol. 8, 1966, pp. 237 ff.
Perpeet-Frech, L.: *Die gotischen Monstranzen im Rheinland*. Düsseldorf 1964
Phillips, P. A. S.: *Paul de Lamerie. His Life and Work*. London 1935
Phillips, P. A. S.: *Paul de Lamerie, Citizen and Goldsmith of London*. London 1968

Rathke-Köhl, S.: *Geschichte des Augsburger Goldschmiedegewerbes vom Ende des 17. bis zum Ende des 18. Jahrhunderts*. Augsburg 1964
Redslob, E.: *Deutsche Goldschmiedeplastik*. Munich 1922
Rohde, A. and U. Stöver (compilers): *Goldschmiedekunst in Königsberg*. Stuttgart 1959
Rittmeyer, D. F.: *Hans Jakob Läublin, Goldschmied in Schaffhausen 1664–1730*. Schaffhausen 1959
Röhrig, F.: *Der Verduner Altar*. Vienna/Munich 1955
Rosenberg, M.: *Geschichte der Goldschmiedekunst auf technischer Grundlage. Niello. Zellenschmelz. Granulation*. 4 vols., Frankfurt 1910–25
Rosenberg, M.: *Jamnitzer*. Frankfurt am Main 1920
Rosenberg, M.: *Der Goldschmiede Merkzeichen*. 4 vols., Berlin 1922–28, 3rd. ed.
Rossacher, K.: *Der Schatz des Erzstiftes Salzburg*. Salzburg 1966
Rossi, F.: *Italienische Goldschmiedekunst*. Munich 1956
Rowe, R.: *Adam Silver*. London 1965

Salzburgs alte Schatzkammer. Exhibition catalogue. Salzburg 1967
Sandrart, Joachim von: *Teutsche Academie der edlen Bau- Bild und Mahlerey Künste ...*, 2 parts, Nuremberg 1675 and 1679 (new ed. by R. A. Peltzer, Munich 1925)
Scheffler, W.: Die Meisterstücke der Berliner Goldschmiede von 1766 bis 1836. From *Zeitschrift des Vereins für die Geschichte Berlins*, New Series, Year LIX, 1942
Scheffler, W.: *Goldschmiede Niedersachsens*. 2 vols., Berlin 1965
Scheidig, W.: *Bauhaus Weimar 1919–24. Werkstattarbeiten*. Munich 1966
Schlosser, J. v.: *Die Kunst- und Wunderkammern der Spätrenaissance*. Leipzig 1908
Schlosser, J. v.: *Leben und Meinungen des florentinischen Bildners Lorenzo Ghiberti*. Basle 1941
Schnitzler, H.: *Rheinische Schatzkammer*. 2 vols., Düsseldorf 1959
Schönberger, A.: 'Die "Weltallschale" Kaiser Rudolfs II.' From *Studien zur Geschichte der europäischen Plastik. Festschrift Th. Müller*. Munich 1965, pp. 253 ff.
Schröder, A.: *Leipziger Goldschmiede aus fünf Jahrhunderten (1350–1850)*. Leipzig 1935
Schwahn, Chr.: *Die Metalle, ihre Legierungen und Lote*. Halle 1949, 3rd ed.

Seidel, P.: *Der Gold- und Silberschatz der Hohenzollern im königlichen Schlosse zu Berlin*. Berlin 1895
Sponsel, J. L.: *Das Grüne Gewölbe zu Dresden*. 4 vols., Leipzig 1925–32
Steingräber, E.: *Alter Schmuck*. Munich 1956
Steingräber, E.: 'Email'. From *Reallexikon zur deutschen Kunstgeschichte*, Vol. 5, Stuttgart 1959, cols. 1 ff.
Steingräber, E.: *Der Goldschmied. Vom alten Handwerk der Gold- und Silberarbeiter*. Munich 1966
Steingräber, E. (pub.): *Schatzkammern Europas. Weltliche Schatzkammern*. Munich 1968

Stierling, H.: *Goldschmiedezeichen von Altona bis Tondern*. Neumünster 1955
Stohlmann, F.: *Gli smalti del Museo Vaticano*. Vatican 1939
Strong, D. E.: *Greek and Roman Gold and Silver Plate*. London 1966
Swarzenski, G.: 'Aus dem Umkreis Heinrichs des Löwen.' From *Städel-Jahrbuch VII*, 1932
Swarzenski, H.: *Monuments of Romanesque Art. The Art of Church Treasures in North-West Europe*. Chicago 1954

Thoma, H.: *Kronen und Kleinodien*. Munich 1955
Thoma, H. and H. Brunner: *Schatzkammer der Residenz München. Katalog*. Munich 1964, 2nd ed.

Upmark, G.: *Guld- och Silversmeder i Sverige 1520–1850*. Stockholm 1943

Voet, E.: *Merken van Amsterdamsche Goud- en Zilversmeden*. The Hague 1912
Voet, E.: *Haarlemsche Goud- en Zilversmeden en hunne merken*. Haarlem 1928
Voet, E. and R. Visscher: *Merken van Friesche Goud- en Zilversmeden*. The Hague 1932
Voet, E. and H. E. v. Gelder: *Merken van Haagsche Goud- en Zilversmeden*. The Hague 1941
Voet, E.: *Nederlandse Goud- en Zilversmeden 1445–1951*. The Hague 1951

Wardle, P.: *Victorian Silver and Silver Plate*. London 1964
Warncke, J.: *Die Edelschmiedekunst in Lübeck und ihre Meister*. Lübeck 1927
Watzdorf, E. v.: *Johann Melchior Dinglinger. Der Goldschmied des deutschen Barock*. 2 vols., Berlin 1962
Weber, P.: *Der Domschatz zu Trier*. Augsburg 1928
Weiß, A.: *Das Handwerk der Goldschmiede zu Augsburg bis zum Jahre 1681*. Leipzig 1897
Weihrauch, H. R.: 'Italienische Bronzen als Vorbilder deutscher Goldschmiedekunst.' From *Studien zur Geschichte der europäischen Plastik. Festschrift Th. Müller*. Munich 1965, pp. 263 ff.
Weisgerber, A.: *Studien zu Nikolaus von Verdun und der rheinischen Goldschmiedekunst im 12. Jahrhundert*. Bonn 1940
Weiss, A.: *Das Handwerk der Goldschmiede zu Augsburg bis zum Jahre 1681*. Leipzig 1897
Werke um 1900. Kataloge des Kunstgewerbemuseums Berlin, Vol. 2. Compiled by W. Scheffler. Berlin 1966
Werner, A.: *Augsburger Goldschmiede 1343–1803*. Augsburg 1913
Wien – *Die Wiener Werkstätte. Modernes Kunsthandwerk von 1903–1932*. Exhibition catalogue. Wien 1967
Witte, F.: *Die liturgischen Geräte der Sammlung Schnütgen*. Berlin 1913

Sources of illustrations   *The numbers refer to pages*

Fratelli Alinari, Florence 81, 82, 83, 88, 119 right
Amsterdam, Rijksmuseum 124, 127, 130, 131, 133
Antikvarisk-topografiska Arkivet, Stockholm 143
Baltimore, Walters Art Gallery 94
Basle, Historisches Museum 63, 70, 71 right, 77
Berlin, Staatl. Museen Preußischer Kulturbesitz, Antikenmuseum 25
Berlin, Staatl. Museen Preußischer Kulturbesitz, Kunstgewerbemuseum (Photos Elsa Postel) 61, 79, 91 right, 93, 176, 205, 210, 213
Berlin, Kunstgewerbemuseum Schloß Köpenick 86, 145
Birmingham, Assay Office 183 above

Vienna, Kunsthistorisches Museum 28, 71 above, 91 left, 92, 118, 126, 128
Vienna, Museum für angewandte Kunst 188, 206, 218, 219
Zürich, Kunstgewerbemuseum 214 above, 215, 216, 220 above
Zürich, Schweizerisches Landesmuseum 80
Exhibition catalogue 'Bayerische Frömmigkeit', Munich 174, 175 right and left

Text illustrations:
38 from: E. Paoletti, *Il Fiore di Venezia*, Vol. II, Venice 1839
107 from: C. Just, *Miscellaneen aus drei Jahrhunderten spanischen Kunstlebens*, Vol. 1, Berlin 1908
154 Erlangen, Universitätsbibliothek
162 from: 100 Planches de Jean Bérain, Paris n. d.

Index of Artists and Craftsmen

WATFORD PUBLIC LIBRARY